Date Due

APR 1 2 2011			
MAY - 2 2011			

BRODART   Cat. No. 23 233   Printed in U.S.A

Global diasporas

Series Editor: Robin Cohen

The assumption that minorities and migrants will demonstrate an exclusive loyalty to the nation-state is now questionable. Scholars of nationalism, international migration and ethnic relations need new conceptual maps and fresh case studies to understand the growth of complex transnational identities. The old idea of "diaspora" may provide this framework. Though often conceived in terms of a catastrophic dispersion, widening the notion of diaspora to include trade, imperial, labour and cultural diasporas can provide a more nuanced understanding of the often positive relationships between migrants' homelands and their places of work and settlement.

This book forms part of an ambitious and interlinked series of volumes trying to capture the new relationships between home and abroad. Historians, political scientists and sociologists from a number of countries have collaborated on this forward-looking project. Two introductory books will provide the defining, comparative and synoptic aspects of diasporas, while over fifteen further titles are planned. These will look both at traditionally recognized diasporas and those newer claimants who are in the process of defining their collective experiences and aspirations in terms of a diasporic identity. A comprehensive bibliography and study guide will conclude the series.

Also in this series

New diasporas: the mass exodus, dispersal and regrouping of migrant communities. Nicholas van Hear
The Chinese diaspora. Chan Kwok Bun
The Greek diaspora: from Odyssey to EU. George Stubos

Global diasporas

An introduction

Robin Cohen
University of Warwick

University of Washington Press
Seattle

© Robin Cohen, 1997

First published in 1997 by UCL Press

UCL Press Limited
1 Gunpowder Square
London EC4A 3DE
UK

The name of University College London (UCL) is a registered
trade mark used by UCL Press with the consent of the owner.

Published simultaneously in the United States of America
by the University of Washington Press, P.O. Box 50096, Seattle,
WA 98145-5096

Library of Congress Cataloging-in-Publication Data
Cohen, Robin, 1944 -
  Global diasporas : an introduction / Robin Cohen.
   p.   cm. -- (Global diasporas : 1)
  Includes bibliographical references and index.
  ISBN 0-295-97619-5 (cloth). -- ISBN 0-295-97620-9 (pbk.)
   1. Emigration and immigration--History. I. Title. II. Series.
JV6021.C64 1997
325.2 -- dc21   96-51988
                                                                  CIP

Typeset in Palatino.
Printed and bound in Great Britain.

Contents

Acknowledgements   vii
List of tables   viii
Introduction   ix

1 Classical notions of diaspora: transcending the Jewish tradition   **1**
"Babylon" as the site of oppression   3
"Babylon" as the site of creativity   4
The Jewish diaspora and Christianity   6
The Jewish diaspora and Islam   10
Ashkenazi fates   15
Inferences from the Jewish diasporic tradition   21
Conclusion   25

2 Victim diasporas: Africans and Armenians   **31**
Origins of the African diaspora   33
The African diaspora: homeland and return   36
Other aspects of the African diaspora   40
The creation of the Armenian diaspora   42
After the massacres: Armenians at home and abroad   46
Soviet Armenia and after   52
Conclusion   54

3 Labour and imperial diasporas: Indians and British   **57**
A new system of slavery?   59
The songs of Ramayana and political outcomes   62
Imperial diasporas   66

The settlement of the British empire   67
The end of the dominion diaspora   74
Conclusion   78

4 Trade diasporas: Chinese and Lebanese   83
   The making of the Chinese diaspora   85
   The Chinese as minorities   89
   The great Lebanese emigration   94
   The Lebanese diaspora: butterflies and caterpillars   98
   Conclusion: ethnic entrepreneurs and trade diasporas 101

5 Diasporas and their homelands: Sikhs and Zionists   105
   The origins of the Sikh diaspora   107
   Sikhs: the lure of homeland   110
   Can Israel be a "normal" state?   115
   Israel and the diaspora   118
   Conclusion   125

6 Cultural diasporas: the Caribbean case   127
   Postmodern views of diaspora   129
   Travelling cultures, travelling nations   134
   The Caribbean: migration and diaspora   137
   Caribbean peoples as a cultural diaspora   144
   Conclusion   151

7 Diasporas in the age of globalization   155
   Relevant aspects of globalization   157
   A world economy   158
   International migration   162
   Global cities   165
   Cosmopolitanism and localism   169
   Deterritorialized social identities   173
   Conclusion   175

8 Conclusion: diasporas, their types and their future   177
   Comparing diasporas   180
   Cognate phenomena   187
   Negative reactions to the growth of diasporas   192
   Final remarks   194

   Notes   197
   References   209
   Index   221

Acknowledgements

This book has been long in the making, indeed parts of it have only recently been dredged from the subterranean alcoves of my mind. As an international migrant myself and the child of two more, autobiography, family history and recollection have a way of subtly meshing with a systematic attempt to analyze the history and sociology of the world's diasporas. Be that as it may. Repressed cogitation needed a few Svengalis to allow it to see the light of day. I am indebted to the Economic and Social Research Council, who awarded me a Senior Research Fellowship to work on the Global Diasporas project. My publisher, Justin Vaughan, was patient and encouraging while his successor, Caroline Wintersgill, has been enthusiastic about the book and the wider series. Nick Van Hear has been a good lunch companion at Queen Elizabeth House, which has provided a friendly academic base in Oxford. Steve Vertovec has generously helped with ideas, references and photocopies. Selina Cohen and Sharon Molteno carefully read the manuscript for errors. Oxford University Computing Services have allowed me to piggy-back on their UNIX system to examine my Warwick University electronic mail. Through this means I have discovered other scholars in diaspora, migration and ethnic studies all over the world who have demonstrated that there may be some meaning to the notion of a "virtual community".

Robin Cohen
Warwick and Oxford

List of tables

1.1 Common features of a diaspora   26

2.1 Armenians worldwide   48

3.1 Indentured Indian workers and Indian population, 1980   60

4.1 Occupations of Chinese in Los Angeles
     and New York, 1980 (%)   93

4.2 Declared occupations at points of entry:
     Middle East arrivals in Argentina (% in brackets)   96

4.3 The Lebanese diaspora by country of residence, 1990   99

5.1 The Sikh diaspora, by country of residence   110

7.1 Global cities   166

8.1 The good gardener's guide to diasporas   178

Introduction

The word "diaspora" is derived from the Greek verb *speiro* (to sow) and the preposition *dia* (over). When applied to humans, the ancient Greeks thought of diaspora as migration and colonization. By contrast, for Jews, Africans, Palestinians and Armenians the expression acquired a more sinister and brutal meaning. Diaspora signified a collective trauma, a banishment, where one dreamed of home but lived in exile. Other peoples abroad who have also maintained strong collective identities have, in recent years, defined themselves as diasporas, though they were neither active agents of colonization nor passive victims of persecution.

The idea of a diaspora thus varies greatly. However, all diasporic communities settled outside their natal (or imagined natal) territories, acknowledge that "the old country" – a notion often buried deep in language, religion, custom or folklore – always has some claim on their loyalty and emotions. That claim may be strong or weak, or boldly or meekly articulated in a given circumstance or historical period, but a member's adherence to a diasporic community is demonstrated by an acceptance of an inescapable link with their past migration history and a sense of co-ethnicity with others of a similar background.

What implications does this phenomenon have for the international state system? By the end of the twentieth century it is likely that the membership of the United Nations will comprise about 200 states. However, the number of "nation-peoples" (groups evincing a "peoplehood" through the retention or expression of separate languages, customs, folkways and religions) is estimated at 2000, ten times the anticipated number of recognized nation-states. Such peoples are only imperfectly, and sometimes only violently, held within the confines of the existing nation-states – as the multiplicity of secessionist movements, civil wars and the fragmentation of the former Soviet Union and several of its allies testify.

Even within settled liberal democracies, the old assumption that immigrants would identify with their adopted country in terms of political loyalty, culture and language can no longer be taken for granted. To the immigrants of old are added millions of refugees and exiles whose movements are primarily dictated by circumstances in their home countries rather than by a desire to establish a new life. Often received with hostility and resentment by the indigenous population and the assimilated citizenry, there is little bonding in the new setting. The description or self-description of such groups as diasporas is now common and may indeed be functional – allowing a certain degree of social distance to displace a high degree of psychological alienation.

Though common, the notion of a diaspora is often used casually, in an untheorized or undertheorized way. In this introductory volume I have tried to give consideration to all the credible meanings of diaspora. Because of the need to be comprehensive there are, inevitably, some superficialities in the treatment of some diasporas and some topics. The typology I have proposed – victim, labour, trade, imperial and cultural diasporas – is more unambiguous than the history and development of diasporas suggest. Some groups take dual or multiple forms, others change their character over time. The qualifications and subtleties of the argument appear occasionally in the text and often in the notes.

The chapters are organized thematically, but in most one or two particular groups have been used as exemplary cases. Thus, when considering the most prevalent concept of disapora, the Jews have been selected to illustrate the argument. Africans and Armenians are shown to be analogous victim diasporas. The British have been represented as an imperial diaspora, the Indians as a labour diaspora, while the trading diasporas have been typified by the Chinese and Lebanese. Finally, the peoples of the Caribbean abroad are, I suggest, usefully characterized as a cultural diaspora.

It is important to emphasize at the outset that I am not suggesting a perfect match between a particular ethnic group and a specific type of diaspora. Quite the contrary. I am fully aware that the Jews were not only a victim diaspora, but also one that was periodically successful in trade and commerce and one also that now evinces a high level degree of cosmopolitanism appropriate to our global age. Likewise, the Chinese were indentured labourers (therefore a labour diaspora) as well as a successful trading diaspora. In the case of the Indians, exactly the reverse holds. While they are regarded as archetypes of a labour diaspora, they also have an important mercantile history.

There is, none the less, method in my apparent madness. Categorization and theory-building are empty exercises without examples. The cases I provide are prompts, models and guides. They demonstrate and illuminate and are not meant to preclude other diasporas sharing similar characteristics or to conceal the secondary aspects of any one diaspora. Drawing attention to all similarities throughout the text is both tedious and potentially confusing. Instead, I have relied on presenting unusual comparisons and juxtaposing implicative and arresting examples.

In brief, the plan of the book is as follows:

In Chapter 1 the diasporic experience of the Jews is considered, the people who provide the source for most characterizations of the diasporic condition. Many writers emphasize a diaspora's catastrophic origins, mass nature and disquieting effects. But must notions of diaspora remain confined to the victim tradition? And was the experience of the Jews in the diaspora so uniformly terrible? How do we transcend the Jewish tradition?

In Chapter 2 I take the opportunity to review the cases of victim groups with profiles not unlike that of the Jews. The horrific African slave trade, the potato famine in Ireland and the brutal treatment of the Armenians by the Turks also reinforced the catastrophic tradition of diaspora. State formation and displacement precipitated the Palestinian diaspora, ironically this time at the hands of the Jews in their reconstituted homeland. Again, is the diasporic experience benign in some respects, even for the victim diasporas?

In Chapter 3 the indenture of millions of Indians during the period of British colonialism is seen as creating a distinctive labour diaspora. By contrast, the expansion of the powerful nation-states, especially in Europe, led to the development of their own imperial diasporas abroad. Spanish, Portuguese, Dutch, German, French and British colonists fanned out to most parts of the world, the British being particularly successful in establishing overseas settlements.

The expression "trade diasporas" is used to describe networks of proactive merchants who transport, buy and sell their goods over long distances – a phenomenon that has been documented for a number of the world's regions. In Chapter 4, the Chinese traders in South East Asia, and the Lebanese in West Africa and the Americas, are discussed as prototypical cases of ethnic entrepreneurship that has been invigorated by the formation of diasporas.

The relationships between diasporas and their homelands provides a crucial political nexus. In Chapter 5 I contrast the case of a diaspora that has successfully created a national homeland (the Jews and Israel) with one that has not (the Sikhs and Khalistan). I raise the question of whether it is necessary or ethically defensible for diasporas to continue to insist on territorializing their identity, an issue I return to later in the book.

I swim (perhaps flounder would be more accurate) in the choppy seas of postmodernism in Chapter 6, trying to make sense of the idea of fragmented, postcolonial and "hybridized" identities and how these might relate to the case of the Caribbean. I find that there is a strong argument that the Caribbean peoples form a cultural diaspora, cemented as much by literature, political ideas, religious convictions, music and life-styles as by permanent migration.

Globalization has enhanced the practical, economic and affective roles of diasporas, showing them to be particularly adaptive forms of social organization. This has important implications for the conduct of commerce and industry and also changes the nature of certain cities, turning them into "global cities" or cosmopoli. These issues are considered in Chapter 7.

In my concluding chapter I return to the issue of comparing and theorizing diasporas. I do not pretend to have developed a grand overarching theory (which I judge to be impossible). However, I advance a number of taxonomic and typological claims, examine the extent to which diasporas present a threat to the nation-state and speculate about the future of global diasporas.

ONE

Classical notions of diaspora: transcending the Jewish tradition

By the waters of Babylon we sat down and wept: when we
  remembered thee, O Sion.
As for our harps we hangèd them up: upon the trees that
  are therein.
For they that led us away captive required of us then a
  song, and melody, in our heaviness:
Sing us one of the songs of Sion.

The loneliness and sadness of the diasporic experience of the Jews
is poignantly evoked in this psalm (reproduced here in the English
Book of Common Prayer version). Such evocations are common.
Indeed, until a few years ago most characterizations of diasporas
emphasized their catastrophic origins, their mass nature and their
disturbing effects. The idea that diaspora implied forcible dispersion was found in Deuteronomy (28: 58–68) with the addition of a
typically thunderous Old Testament warning to a people who had
forsaken the righteous paths and abandoned the old ways:

If you do not observe and fulfil all the law . . . the Lord will
scatter you among all peoples from one end of the earth to
the other. . . . Among these nations you will find no peace,
no rest for the sole of your foot. Then the Lord will give you
an unquiet mind, dim eyes and a failing appetite. Your life
will hang continually in suspense, fear will beset you night
and day, and you will find no security all your life long.

Every morning you will say "Would God it were evening!"
and every evening, "Would God it were morning!" for the
fear that lives in your heart.

So closely had diaspora become associated with this biblical use
that the origins of the word have virtually been lost. In fact, the
term is found in the Greek translation of the Bible and originates in
the verb "to sow" and the preposition "over".[1] For the Greeks, the
expression was used to describe the colonization of Asia Minor and
the Mediterranean in the Archaic period (800–600 BC). Although
there was some displacement of the ancient Greeks to Asia Minor
as a result of poverty, overpopulation and inter-state war, diaspora
essentially had a positive connotation. Expansion through plunder, military conquest, colonization and migration were the predominant features of the Greek diaspora.

The opposing notions of a victim diaspora and a diaspora of
active colonization were resolved by over 2000 years of special
pleading – based, to be sure, on many negative experiences –
on behalf of the first interpretation. However, Jewish diasporic
experiences were much more diverse and more complex than the
catastrophic tradition allows and, as I shall show, such an interpretation was imposed as well as internalized, advanced as well as
contested. One way or another, it is impossible to understand
notions of diaspora without first coming to grips with some central
aspects of the Jewish experience.

Even for those who find in the changed meanings of the contemporary concept a new and exciting way of understanding cultural
difference and identity politics, the classical origins and connota-
tions of the term have to be assimilated and understood before
they can be transcended. Thus, James Clifford (1994: 303) avers
that:

> We should be able to recognize the strong entailment of
> Jewish history on the language of diaspora without making
> that history a definitive model. Jewish (and Greek and
> Armenian) diasporas can be taken as non-normative start-
> ing points for a discourse that is travelling in new global
> conditions.

Similarly, while accepting Clifford's argument that the Jews should not be thought of as the normative model, Kirschenblatt-Gimblett (1994: 340) argues that in discussing issues of homelessness, placelessness and statelessness, "the Jew has served as the oncomouse of social theory". Finally, Jonathan Boyarin (1995: 5) holds that: "It is important to insist, not on the centrality of Jewish diaspora nor on its *logical priority* within comparative diaspora studies, yet still on the need to refer to, and better understand, Jewish diaspora history within the contemporary diasporic rubric".

How do we interrogate and seek to supersede the Jewish tradition of diaspora?

"Babylon" as the site of oppression

The destruction of Jerusalem and razing of the walls of its Temple in 586 BC created the central folk memory of the negative, victim diaspora tradition – in particular the experience of enslavement, exile and displacement. The Jewish leader of the time, Zedikiah, had vacillated for a decade, then impulsively sanctioned a rebellion against the powerful Mesopotamian empire. No mercy for his impudence was shown by the Babylonian king, Nebuchadnezzar. His soldiers forced Zedikiah to witness the execution of his sons; the Jewish leader was then blinded and dragged in chains to Babylon. Peasants were left behind in Judah to till the soil, but the key military, civic and religious personnel accompanied Zedikiah to captivity in Babylon (Goldberg & Raynor 1989: 46–8). Jews had been compelled to desert the land "promised" to them by God to Moses and thereafter, the tradition suggests, forever became dispersed.

Babylon subsequently became a codeword among Jews (and, as we shall see in Ch.2, Africans) for the afflictions, isolation and insecurity of living in a foreign place, set adrift, cut off from their roots and their sense of identity, oppressed by an alien ruling class. Since the Babylonian exile, "the homelessness of Jews has been a leitmotiv in Jewish literature, art, culture, and of course, prayer" (Ages 1973: 10). Jewish folklore and its strong oral tradition retold stories of the perceived, or actual, trauma of their historical experiences. The use of the word Babylon alone was enough to evoke a sense of captivity, exile, alienation and isolation. Collectively, Jews were seen as helpless chaff in the wind. At an individual level, diasporic Jews were depicted as pathological half-persons – destined never to realize themselves or to attain completeness, tranquillity or happiness so long as they were in exile.

"Babylon" as the site of creativity

Perhaps the obvious starting point to a revisionist view of Babylon is that the benefits of integration into a rich and diverse alien culture were evident both to many of the first group of Judaeans and to their immediate descendants. A substantial number adopted Babylonian names and customs; the group as a whole used the Babylonian calendar and embraced the language of Aramaic.

For those who wished to stay true to their roots, their enforced residence in Babylon provided an opportunity to construct and define their historical experience, to invent their tradition. Myth, folk-tales, oral history and legal records were combined into the embryonic Bible, while the earnest discussion groups at the homes of charismatic figures like Jeremiah and Ezekiel ("the prophets") turned into rudimentary synagogues.

It was, however, the stirring prophecies of a figure known as the second Isaiah (not his real name, but subsequent editors of the Bible perpetrated this error) that galvanized a return movement of the exiles. Isaiah hurled colourful imprecations at Babylon and the Babylonians:

> wild beasts of the desert shall lie there; and their houses
>   shall be full of doleful creatures; and owls shall dwell
>   there, and satyrs shall dance there.
> And the wild beasts of the islands shall cry in their deso-
>   late houses, and dragons in their pleasant palaces; and
>   her time is near to come, and her days shall not be
>   prolonged. (Isaiah 13: 21–2)

While denouncing Babylon, Isaiah hammered home the message that "the remnant of Israel" had to return to Jerusalem to rebuild the Temple. If they did so redemption (another great diasporic theme) would surely follow. Return some did, but the purpose of the journey was neither quite so heroic nor so spiritually pure as Isaiah suggested. Cyrus, the Persian king who had conquered Babylon, permitted and even encouraged the return of groups of Judaeans as a form of enlightened colonialism. "It suited him to have an enclave of beholden Jews in Palestine, close to the Egyptian border." (Goldberg & Raynor 1989: 53)

Moreover, the return was not a triumphant success. The restored Temple (completed in 515 BC) was a paltry affair; the priests were venal and the returnees rubbed raw with the Judaeans who had remained. It took a Persian-supported Babylonian priest, Ezra, to implement the law codified in Babylon (the Torah). His reforms led to a much greater ethnic particularism and religious fundamentalism. Although previously common, exogenous marriages were now frowned upon, while the highly prescribed purification rituals (including circumcision, atonement, and the stringent dietary laws) also date from Ezra's period. For the next five centuries the evolution of Judaism in Palestine was marked by apocalyptic dreamers, messianic claimants, zealots, revolutionaries and mystics. Crude attempts by the Greeks to Hellenize the country (a pig was sacrificed on an altar to Zeus set up in the Temple in 167 BC) then to Romanize it, served only to fan the flames of resistance and play into the hands of the fundamentalists.

By contrast, the Jewish communities in Alexandria, Antioch, Damascus, Asia Minor and Babylon became centres of civilization, culture and learning. The Exilarch (the head of the Babylonian Jews) held a position of honour among Jews and non-Jews alike, Jewish academies of learning flourished, while the centrepiece of theological exegesis, the Babylonian Talmud, comprising 2.5 million words, made the religious leaders, the Gaons, the cynosure of Jewish culture until the early eleventh century. Sassanian Persia had tolerated and encouraged a cultural *mélange* of several brands of Christianity, astrology, a Persian literary revival, Zoroastrianism, and Indian and Hellenistic thought. Judaism thrived in this hothouse through engagement, encounter, competition and the cut and thrust of religious and intellectual debate.

Therefore, although the word Babylon often connotes captivity and oppression, a rereading of the Babylonian period of exile can thus be shown to demonstrate the development of a new creative

energy in a challenging, pluralistic context outside the natal homeland. When the Romans destroyed the Second Temple in AD 70, it
was Babylon that remained as the nerve- and brain-centre for Jewish life and thought.

Beyond Babylon, there were flourishing Jewish communities all
over the Hellenic world. In Alexandria the Greek translation of the
Scriptures was completed (and the word diaspora put into general
use among the literate), while under the Egyptian Ptolemies, Jews
served as administrators and army officers. Despite occasional
outbursts of hostility, philo-Semitism was the normal experience
of the many Jewish communities scattered around the Graeco-
Roman world. By the fourth century BC there were already more
Jews living outside than inside the land of Israel (Ages 1973: 3–7).

The Jewish diaspora and Christianity

If we accept that there are positive early historical experiences to
record with respect to at least one of the most prominent victim
diasporas and that a number of the far-flung Jewish communities
were *not* forcibly dispersed, we are faced with an inevitable consequential question. How is it that the received wisdom in describing
the Jewish diaspora is generally so doleful? To explain this, we
need to return, if only briefly, to the opening of the Christian era.

Superficially, the crushing of the revolt of the Judaeans against
the Romans and the destruction of the Second Temple by the
Roman general Titus in AD 70 precisely confirmed the catastrophic
tradition. Once again, Jews had been unable to sustain a national
homeland and were scattered to the far corners of the world. However, numerically and experientially, the exodus of the Jews after
Titus's campaign was not that decisive an event. It was, none the
less, so construed by prominent Christian theologians, who were
anxious to demonstrate that God's punishment followed what
they regarded as the Jews' heinous crime in acting as accomplices
to deicide. The fact that the bulk of the Jewish diaspora long preceded the rise of Christianity, or the destruction of the Second Temple, was conveniently forgotten.

The image of the "wandering Jew" became part of a continuing
Christian myth, a myth often absorbed and perpetuated by Jews

themselves. Jews are forced to wander, so the dogma goes, because of their part in the killing of Christ. The Son of God is said personally (so to speak) to have condemned them to eternal restlessness (Hasan-Rokem and Dundes 1986). In this respect, orthodox Jewish and firebrand Christian theologians are curiously united. Both see the dispersion of the Jews as a suitable punishment for their sin, though the sins thought to be committed are different – disobeying the law in the first case, unforgivable deicide in the second. Beyond the idea of perpetual wandering, the extraordinary longevity of the Jewish people attracted a good deal of convoluted speculation and even backhanded compliments from certain historians, philosophers and Christian dogmatists. The seventeenth-century philosopher Pascal, for example, noted that of all the peoples of antiquity only the Jewish people remained intact. (The Parsees and other groups of Asian-origin would have some right, incidentally, to dispute this claim.) He considered the Jews' endurance to be divinely sanctioned. The suffering of the "carnal Jews" had to be patently visible to all in order to demonstrate the veracity of Christianity. The presence of Jews in the Christian world therefore acted as a form of living witness to the truth of biblical claims.

For many in European Christendom this living witness was like a ghastly parade of the "living dead". The American experience tended to the fabulation of individual Wandering Jews, such as this nineteenth century account appearing in a Mormon newspaper (cited Glantz 1986: 108):

> A sensation was created in William Street on Thursday morning by the appearance of a man on the pave with a long floating beard, and dressed in loose pantaloons, with a turban on his head . . . He represented himself as the veritable Wandering Jew. Nobody knows who he is or where he comes from. A learned Jewish rabbi was sent to converse with him, which they did in the Hebrew language, and the stranger was found to be perfect in his knowledge of that most difficult tongue. . . . The rabbi invited him to his house but, said the stranger, "nay I cannot stop. The Crucified One of the Calvary has pronounced the edict and I must not rest. I must move on – ever on."

These mysterious, eternal, wandering Jews were not only objects of curiosity. They were feared as much as they were despised. Jews had not only mulishly refused to acknowledge the Saviour, but also helped to crucify Him. (The "helped to" was discretionary in some circles.) This perception produced a complicated and contradictory set of Christian attitudes to the Jews. By being responsible for a god's death, they were condemned to eternal suffering. Why then did they endure and sometimes even prosper? Perhaps it would be a good Christian's duty to punish them for their unforgivable sin? By murdering a god, Jews had murdered life itself. Attempts on their own lives were therefore only to be expected. Equally, they could never be entirely innocent victims. Jewish people, some Christian theologians thought, could neither repent nor be reprieved. They were doomed, forever, to carry a "death taint stigma".

Despite the sinister tone of these muddled theological musings, until the eleventh century the level of discrimination against the Jews in the Roman world was quite modest. This was to change dramatically for the worse with the Crusaders, fired as they were by the desire for vengeance for the blood of Jesus. In the summer of 1096, as they were passing through European towns on their way to Jerusalem, they found it offensive to encounter peaceful, thriving Jewish quarters. Beginning at Rouen, they slaughtered or forcibly converted the majority of Jews in the Rhine valley, killing 1,000 in Mainz alone. When the Crusaders finally arrived in Jerusalem in 1099 they gathered all the Jews they could find into a convenient synagogue and burned them alive.

The Catholic hierarchy also remained wedded to its hostile position for centuries. As late as the turn of the century, Pius X (1903–14) told the Zionist Theodor Herzl that, so long as the Jews refused to convert, the Church would not recognize the Jewish people, nor would he sanction their remigration to their historic homeland (Ages 1973: 9). He warned that "If you come to Palestine and settle your people there, we shall have churches and priests ready to baptize all of you" (*Encyclopaedia Judaica* 1971, vol. 13: 571). At least, we can agree, baptism was a rather more agreeable prospect than being incinerated by Crusaders. After the foundation of the state of Israel in 1948, the Vatican conspicuously ignored its existence. An agreement to exchange diplomats was made only in 1995, nearly half a century after the *fait accompli*. The delegiti-mation of the Israeli state is a tradition continued by many Chris-tian pilgrims coming to visit the Holy Sites, who still insist on calling their destination "The Holy Land", thus desecularizing Israel and doggedly continuing the 2,000-year-old tradition of deterritorializing the Jews.

Other examples of Christian religious intolerance abound. Between 1290 and 1293 the Jewish communities in the Kingdom of Naples were almost entirely destroyed, Dominican monks having led a campaign for their forcible conversion. The fervour of reli-gious zealotry was also behind the most famous example of Catho-lic hostility towards the Jews – the Spanish Inquisition. It is, of course, important to remember that the Inquisition was directed against Muslims as well as Jews. After the Moorish conquest of Spain in AD 711, Jews and Moors had co-operated for seven centu-ries in helping to make southern Spain a centre of literacy and enlightenment. Thousands of *Marrano*s (Jews and Muslims who pretended to be Christians to avoid persecution) were denounced, tortured and put to the stake.[2] Unsurprisingly, for those who can hazard a guess about the psychology of such matters, the first, most vicious and most dreaded inquisitor-general, Torquemada, was himself of Jewish origin. In the summer of 1492, between 100,000 and 150,000 Jews fled Spain to the sound of "lively music" ordered by the rabbis.[3]

Fortunately for the Jews in the Protestant parts of Europe, unrelieved theological animosity was seen as being, to some degree, internally inconsistent. After all, Christ had preached for-giveness not punishment. Were not the disciples Jewish? And was not Christ, in his human aspect at least, also a Jew? Protestants in Amsterdam and Puritans in England were both more pragmatic and more open to these contrary religious positions. Amsterdam welcomed *Marrano* traders for the role they could play in enhanc-ing its budding mercantilist empire. In England, the Puritans were genuinely curious about the people of the Old Testament and one of their number, Sir Henry Finch, a lawyer active in James I's reign, advanced the bold theory that the Jews would all soon be con-verted and their dispersion would be at an end. Even more fanci-fully, he affirmed that a Jewish king would once again reside in Jerusalem and have dominion over all the peoples of the world.

This last idea rather alarmed James I, who promptly had Sir Henry arrested. The king none the less allowed the translation of the Hebrew scriptures (the famous King James Bible) to go ahead. The now popularly available Bible fed the convictions of those who found the fire and brimstone of the Old Testament much more to their liking than the milk and water of the New.

The breakthrough in England finally came in Oliver Cromwell's period. A rabbi friend of Rembrandt, Manasseh ben Israel, petitioned Cromwell to allow Jews to return. Amidst much hatred, all Jews in England had been expelled in 1290 in the reign of Edward I. Cromwell had to move slowly. Church dignitaries feared that the Jews would proselytize and warned that "Moloch-worship" would stalk the land. Merchants were alarmed at the thought of new competition. When Cromwell refused to accept his petition, ben Israel returned to Amsterdam to die broken-hearted. However, not long afterwards, a fortuitous legal decision in favour of a Portuguese Jewish merchant, who had had his property seized for being an illegal resident, gave legal force to the idea that Jews already living in England could not be treated differently from other residents. Twenty *Marrano* families "came out" (as we would say today) and established a synagogue and a Jewish cemetery. One of their number was admitted to the Royal Exchange without having to swear a Christian oath. In Amsterdam and London, Jews had finally gained a toehold in Protestant Europe (Wilson 1959: 168–9).

The Jewish diaspora and Islam

Anxious to dispel current images, there is a good deal of special pleading in the literature on behalf of the proposition that Jews were well treated in Islamic societies and accorded respect as "scripturaries", i.e. people of the Book. This attempt at a historical corrective is hardly surprising in view of what Said (1991: 26–7) calls

> the almost total absence of any cultural position [in the West] making it possible either to identify with or dispassionately to discuss the Arabs or Islam. . . . The web of racism, cultural stereotypes, political imperialism, dehu-

10

manizing ideology holding in the Arab or the Muslim is very strong indeed.

One cannot but feel some sympathy with this outburst of indignation.

Although anti-Muslim sentiments are general in many Western societies, there is no doubt that some Zionists, particularly from the USA, have perpetuated some of the wilder notions of an eternal war of hate between Jews and Muslims. Yet there were many occasions when the two communities shared a common fate. I have already mentioned that Jews and Moors were both victims to the zeal of the Inquisition and *Reconquista* in the case of fifteenth-century Spain. Many of the expelled Jews were to find refuge in Muslim Africa and the Middle East. What I omitted to say, as I was dealing earlier with Christian attitudes to Jews, was that, like the Jews, the Muslims of Jerusalem were also ruthlessly attacked by the Crusaders four centuries earlier, to the point that "not a single Muslim was left alive within the city walls" (Maalouf 1984: ii). At a more general level, one can make a good case that until the creation of an aggressive Zionist movement in the late nineteenth and twentieth centuries, Jews were generally well treated in Islamic societies.

None the less, it would be over-egging the historical custard to suggest that there were not tensions between Jews and Muslims right from the start. When Muhammad fled in AD 622 to Medina (a town extensively populated, some sources say founded, by Jewish date growers), it was only the Jews who resisted his message that he was a true prophet in the line of Moses and Abraham. As he won the allegiance of the local Arabs and Bedouin, he was strong enough to expel the Jews from Medina and force those at Khaybar into a tributary relationship. Bernard Lewis (1970: 40–1) maintains that expulsion was not their only fate: "As soon as the Arabs had attained unity through the agency of Muhammed they attacked and ultimately eliminated the Jews [of Medina]."

With the spectacular military success of the Muslim armies over the next century, the caliphs had to evolve a *modus vivendi* with the many religious minorities over whom they presided. Notable among these groups were the Jews and Christians, both groups being known as *dhimmi*, the subservient people. Under the Pact of

Omar (*c.* AD 800), the *dhimmi* were accorded religious autonomy, security of life and property and exemption from military service. In return, they had to show due deference to Muslims by not bearing arms, riding horses or building new synagogues, churches or houses grander than those of their Muslim neighbours (Goldberg & Raynor 1989: 92). In AD 850–4, Christians and Jews had to affix wooden images of devils to their houses, wear yellow garb and put yellow spots on the dress of their slaves. The word of a Jew or Christian could not be accepted against that of a Muslim (Hitti 1974: 533–4).

While not seeking to minimize these considerable formal restrictions, it is true that many Jews managed to evade their spirit and often attained considerable prestige and prosperity in Muslim societies. Hitti (1974: 356–7) quotes a contemporary traveller to Syria in AD 985 to the effect that "most of the money-changers and bankers were Jews". In Baghdad, the traveller continued, the Jews maintained "a good-sized colony", while the Exilarch

> seems to have lived in affluence and owned gardens, houses and rich plantations. On his way to any audience with the caliph he appeared dressed in embroidered silk, wore a white turban gleaming with gems and was accompanied by a retinue of horsemen. Ahead of him marched a herald calling out "Make way before our lord, the son of David".

Though recognizably separate, the Jews were heavily dominated by Muslim culture. The eminent scholar of the Jews of the Arab world, Goitein (1971: 407), concludes the second volume of his massive study of eleventh-century Mediterranean society by suggesting that, although communal life was left to their own initiative, "Christians and Jews shared with their Muslim compatriots their language, economy, and most of their social notions and habits". As for the Jews, they tended to write and speak Arabic (though Aramaic and Hebrew were never totally displaced). Freely made conversions to Islam were relatively common either for personal reasons or on grounds of conviction.

Perhaps the most extraordinary figure to emerge from this nesting of Jewish community life within an overarching Islamic culture was Moses Maimonides (1135–1204). He was born in Cordoba,

Spain, which fell to the fundamentalist Almohades in the summer of 1148. He and his family were forced into exile. They settled in Fez in 1160 (where there is some speculation that he converted to Islam), then left for Acre, Alexandria and Cairo. Along the way he became a veritable sponge for every fragment of knowledge about medicine, law, philosophy and religion. In Cairo, he was the court physician to the vizier appointed by Saladin, while simultaneously attaining the unquestioned spiritual leadership of the Jewish community. His vast output of theological exegesis included the definitive religious tract, *The recapitulation of the Law*, but he also contributed to general philosophy in his famous book, *Guide to the perplexed*.

The Almohades were eventually to snuff the life from this creative intersection of Judaism and Islam. The centre of Jewish intellectual and spiritual life gradually moved to the Ottoman empire, then to northern Europe. Before I turn to these experiences, I want to draw one key inference from the period up to the thirteenth century. The Jewish communities in Babylon, North Africa, Spain and the rest of the Mediterranean were *not* primarily defined by their attachment to a lost homeland in Judaea. Drawing on Goitein's work cited earlier, Clifford (1994: 305) describes the Jews of the Arab world in these terms:

> This sprawling social world was linked through cultural forms, kinship relations, business circuits, and travel trajectories as well as through loyalty to the religious centers of the diaspora (in Babylon, Palestine and Egypt). The attachment to specific cities (sometimes superseding ties of religion and ethnicity) characteristic of Goitein's medieval world casts doubt on any definition that would "center" the Jewish diaspora in a single land. Among Sephardim [even] after 1492, the longing for "home" could be focused on a city in Spain at the same time as the Holy Land.

The position of the Jews under the Ottomans (c. 1300–1918) did not vary a great deal from the earlier Muslim regimes. Jewish (and Christian) communities were accepted as scripturaries, who believed in God, the prophets and judgement, and who belonged to the same spiritual family as Muslims. From the time of the capture of Constantinople, the Great Rabbi received official investiture from the sultan and represented the Jews of the empire to the government (Hourani 1983: 30). Inside each community spiritual heads were responsible for legal matters, for collecting the poll tax and for maintaining law and order. Individual Jews often attained high office under the Ottomans. For example, there were Jewish bankers, finance ministers and advisers to the district governors of Baghdad, Basra, Damascus and Aleppo (Woolfson 1980: 86). Generally, trade in the Ottoman empire passed into the hands of oriental Christians and Jews. They often enjoyed consular protection and possessed knowledge of European languages and business methods. The Jews of Damascus, Aleppo and the coastal towns were able to build a trading network to Alexandria, Livorno, Trieste and Marseilles (Hourani 1983: 57).

Again, however, one must be careful not to exaggerate the well-being of the Jews under the Ottomans. They were kept firmly in their place. They governed themselves, but partly because the authorities regarded Muslim law as too sacred to be applied to them. Protection was often afforded to them, but largely because they were economically useful. They were "integrated to the body politic", but "did not fully belong to it" (Hourani 1991: 220). It was even regarded as "unsporting" to kill them, because they were so evidently inferior. (Although an offensive notion this was, at least, a bizarre form of guardianship.) Like others before it, the Ottoman empire began to lose control of its marginal lands, including Palestine – an outcome crucial to the fate of the Jewish diaspora. Instead of the established oriental Jews and those who came to study, pray or die, a new sort of Jew from eastern and central Europe began to arrive in Palestine. In defiance of the complex, multi-faceted, multi-located history of Jewish life in the diaspora, the new settlers were motivated by Western concepts of the unbreakable link between race, nation and territory. Despite the Ottoman government's opposition and the increasing alarm of the local Arab population, by 1914 Palestine's Jewish population was 85,000, 12 per cent of the total. Moreover, one quarter of them were settled by the Jewish National Fund on land that was deemed by the organization to be the inalienable property of the Jewish people (Hourani 1991: 288–9). The clash between those who advocated the territorialization of Jewish identity as a solution to "the Jewish problem" and those who held that a viable and enriching life in the diaspora was possible was to be played out with considerable fervour among the Ashkenazi Jews.

Ashkenazi fates

Who are the Ashkenazim? The conventional Jewish histories made the perfectly proper trisection between the Jews of the Iberian peninsula (the Sephardim), those of the Muslim Middle East, and the Ashkenazim of northern Europe.[4] They suggest that, in an attempt to pick up the pieces of the Roman empire, Charlemagne had encouraged the immigration of Jewish merchants because of their strong economic connections with the Mediterranean and the Middle East. From these pioneer merchants, such accounts continue, there evolved a community life, a distinctive language (Yiddish), and shared customs and religious traditions.

A far more controversial scenario is advanced by the heterodox political commentator, Arthur Koestler (1976). He describes how precisely at the period when Charlemagne was crowned Emperor of the West, the area between the Caucausus and the Volga was dominated by the Khazar empire. As Judaism had historically rarely been a proselytizing religion, it was surprising to discover that the ruling classes and much of the citizenry of Khazaria were recently converted Jews. When the empire was crushed by the Russians in AD985, the Khazars migrated north, retaining their Jewish faith. With little supporting evidence and a vast leap of historical imagination, Koestler claims that most of the Ashkenazim arose from this group of migrants. It followed that their descendants (in Europe, the Americas and South Africa) make up most of the world's Jews. He concedes readily enough that forcible miscegenation, two-way conversions and intermarriage complicate the picture, but essentially he sees the Turkic Khazars as a wholly different people from the Semitic Sephardim.[5] In his appendix, Koestler (1976: 223) says that it does not really matter whether the chromosomes of the world's Jews are of Khazar, Semitic, Roman or Spanish origin. What then is the point of his thesis? Though it was clearly exaggerated, his argument did undoubtedly provoke a challenge to conventional accounts of Jewish diasporic history. Is there, for example, a single Jewish people who were dispersed? Does the diaspora bond a distinctive *volkish* essence?[6] Is there a continuous claim for an ancient homeland that applies to all Jews? Is it not more accurate to consider the Jewish diaspora as ethnically and culturally diverse?

What then happened to the Khazar–Turkic–Ashkenazi part of the Jewish diaspora? Here, I shall have to cut a long story very short. I shall use the scholars' shorthand, the device of a case study, taking the Russian Pale in the first instance (as the home of most Ashkenazim and the source of the diaspora's biggest emigration between 1881 and 1914) and France in the second (as one site where the tensions between integration into the local citizenship and Zionism were sharply posed).

It is no great revelation to declare that the tsarist authorities did not get on well with their Jewish subjects. The Russian rulers had always been hostile to Jewish settlement (could this possibly date to their historic conflict with Khazaria?) while they inherited a large Jewish population by accident with the partition of Poland in the eighteenth century. The Jews did not want to be there and the Russian authorities did not know what to do with them. By the 1870s anti-Jewish sentiment was prevalent in official circles and among the Russian population at large. The pogroms of the spring of 1881 affected more than 100 Jewish communities, but far from condemning these outbreaks, the tsar used them as a cheap means to garner populist sentiment in favour of the monarchy. A set of special commissions was established to examine the "harm" caused by Jewish economic activity on the "main population". Jewish schools were shut down because, it was argued, the "main population" did not have sufficient schooling itself. Quotas were then established (1882) restricting the number of Jews who could enter the professions or higher education, while heavy fines were imposed on the families of those who did not report for military service.

The *rekrutchina* (draft) was indeed a fearsome prospect, as the tsar could demand no less than 25 years of military service. The attempts to evade the draft also split the Russian Jews by class. Jewish *knappers* (recruiters) rounded up draft dodgers, but wealthier families could usually bribe them to ignore their own children at the expense of the poorer families (Lindemann 1993: 132–3). The combination of draft evasion and fear of pogroms (over 600 were recorded from 1903 to 1906) propelled the major political response of the Jews of the Russian pale – emigration. In the first national census of the Russian empire in 1897, 5,189,401 Jews were recorded (Baron 1964: 76). Over half of this number emigrated. Some, in response to the earnest pleadings of the Zionist movement, found their way to Palestine and emerged as the creators of the state of Israel and the elite of its political parties, labour movement and social life. Most, however, headed west to other European countries or to the principal magnet, the USA.

Those who stayed in the Pale often sought to preserve community life and their rabbinical traditions. This turned out to be a poor option. The pogroms continued with increasing intensity under the tsars, while there was little respite under the Bolsheviks, who frequently denounced Jews as troublemakers or exploiters. Later, in the 1940s, those in the areas that were about to be overrun by the advancing Nazi armies found the local population enthusiastically butchering them before the Nazis arrived and in the certain knowledge that they would approve. A final option, taken by a significant number of intellectuals and workers, was to join the socialist and communist movements, either by assimilating directly to progressive Russian parties or by organizing separately in youth movements or in bodies like the Jewish Bund (which was affiliated to the Social Democratic Workers' Party). Jewish employers, tsarist officials and Zionists alike were angry and frustrated at the attractiveness of socialist internationalism to Jewish activists. The prominent Zionist Chaim Weizmann, for example, lamented that "The large part of the contemporary younger generation is anti-Zionist, not from a desire to assimilate, as in Western Europe, but through revolutionary conviction" (cited Lindemann 1993: 145).[7] The relationship between Zionists and the Jewish diaspora in the wake of the formation of the state of Israel is further discussed in Chapter 5.

The tutor to Nicholas II is said to have remarked that the "Jewish Question" in Russia would be solved by the conversion of one-third of the Jews, the emigration of another third and by the death of the remaining third. Play around with these proportions and allow that the "conversion" was to socialism rather than to the Russian Orthodox Church and one has a roughly accurate way of describing the fate of the Russian Jews.

Let me now turn to the second of my case studies, that of the Jews in France. Like their counterparts in Germany, Hungary and Austria, the Jews of France stood in marked contrast to the *Ostjuden* of the Russian Pale. They were more sophisticated, more liberal and more bourgeois. In Berlin, Budapest, Vienna and Paris, Jews had made notable contributions to the professions and to intellectual, literary and artistic life. Normally, their primary loyalties were to their countries of settlement rather than to their religion, even less to their ethnicity. In France, legal emancipation had fostered the belief that adherence to the Jewish religion was no barrier to full citizenship and integration into France.[8] However, as Muslims are currently discovering in France, the revolutionary civic tradition in France has compelling secular implications. As one nineteenth-century French politician bluntly put it: "To the Jews as Jews, nothing. To the Jews as citizens, everything."

French Jews who chose to ride both horses – Judaism plus emancipation – were from time to time confronted with significant crises of loyalty. The first major dilemma arose in the 1840s. At the beginning of that decade the Sharif Pasha of Syria had arrested a Jewish barber on the charge of ritual murder after the mysterious disappearance of an Italian friar and his servant. Confessions under duress, the arrest of Jewish children and mob violence followed. Because of the then heated European rivalries in the Middle East, the "Damascus Affair" commanded much attention. The French government got drawn into supporting the charges, the Austrian and British governments denounced them. French Jews were suddenly confronted with an impossible conundrum. To advance French international ambitions, the state that had emancipated them was prepared to countenance an anti-Semitic libel. After much shillyshallying, the initiative was seized by Adolphe Crémieux, a Jew and prominent French politician, who co-operated with eminent Jews in Great Britain and Austria (France's enemies) to secure the release of the prisoners in Damascus. The outcome was an apparent victory in humanitarian terms but, as Lindemann (1993: 35–93) shows, it was a Pyrrhic one. Thereafter, French patriots argued that love of their brethren would always be greater than the love of French Jews for France. Jews would always be Jews. Moreover, their increasing prominence in commerce and banking meant that wealthy and powerful Jews could act against the nation's interest. It was but a small step to convince fellow patriots that Jews were part of an omnipotent global conspiracy. Such a widely held perception was later to fuel nineteenth and twentieth-century anti-Semitism.

The Damascus Affair was followed by an equally momentous event, the Dreyfus Affair, when in 1894 a French Jewish army officer was falsely accused of spying for the Germans.[9] "The Affair", as it came to be known, led to a profound change of heart for Teodor Herzl, hitherto an assimilated, bourgeois, Viennese journalist, who had been sent to cover the Dreyfus trial and later became the key advocate of Zionism. More in sadness than in anger, he (cited Goldberg & Raynor 1989: 166) concluded:

Everywhere we Jews have tried honestly to assimilate into the nations around us, preserving only the religion of our fathers. We have not been permitted to. . . . We are a nation – the enemy has made us one without our desiring it. . . . We do have the strength to create a state and, moreover, a model state.

Faced with apparently inevitable outbursts of anti-Semitism, even in a country like France which proclaimed the revolutionary ideals of Liberty, Equality and Fraternity, it was all too easy for Zionist ideologues to promote the idea of creating a national homeland as an alternative to a doomed attempt at assimilation.[10] The partial acceptance of such an aspiration lent further support to the charges of dual loyalty, even if not to the more fanciful notions of an international conspiracy. The apparently persistent belief in France that Jews essentially remained an alien element was given dramatic affirmation in Vichy France where, half a century after the event, disturbing evidence emerged that collaboration with the Nazis to identify and round up Jews for the death camps was widespread (Marrus 1981).

If I try to summarize the fates of the Ashkenazi emigrants, I would start by insisting on the diversity of outcomes. Although there were often serious outbreaks of anti-Semitism in France, Britain or the USA from time to time, it would be unduly perverse to compare them in scale and intensity to the unremitting pogroms of the Russian empire or the stunning, virtually incomprehensible horror of the Holocaust in Nazi Germany and Nazi-occupied territories. Those parts of the diaspora in the more benign countries of settlement were often beneficiaries of tolerance and acceptance and, like the Jews of Babylon, profited from the stimulus of cosmopolitanism and pluralism. None the less, the Zionists have their strongest point in the argument that the outcome is essentially unpredictable, whatever appearances might suggest. It is virtually unimaginable to construct a scene of state-sponsored genocidal killers or mass anti-Semitism either in contemporary Britain or in the USA. Yet the obvious riposte is that German Jews of the 1930s could equally not believe this possibility and it was precisely their stubborn lack of prescience that contributed to the scale of their appalling fate. Although the French events of the 1940s were of a lesser magnitude, there was an equal incomprehension that a friendly neighbour, *boulangeur* or *restaurateur* could harbour such a reservoir of hatred that they happily identified Jews to the Nazi authorities.

The history of the Jewish diaspora is one not only of endurance and achievement but also of anxiety and distrust. However economically or professionally successful, however long settled in peaceful settings, it is difficult for many Jews in the diaspora not to "keep their guard up", to feel the weight of their history and the cold clammy fear that brings the demons in the night to remind them of their murdered ancestors. The sense of unease or difference that members of the diaspora feel in their countries of settlement often results in a felt need for protective cover in the bosom of the community or a tendency to identify closely with the imagined homeland and with co-ethnic communities in other countries. Bonds of language, religion, culture and a sense of a common history and perhaps a common fate impregnate such a transnational relationship and give to it an affective, intimate quality that formal citizenship or even long settlement frequently lack. Thence arises the Catch-22 of many Jewish communities. Their fear breeds an ingroup mentality. This is sensed by the peoples among whom they live, which in turn breeds distance, suspicion, hostility and, ultimately, anti-Semitism. The system is complete when manifestations of prejudice engender new sources of apprehension and further inclinations to clannishness and endogamy.

Inferences from the Jewish diasporic tradition

All scholars of diaspora recognize that the Jewish tradition is at the heart of any definition of the concept. Yet if it is necessary to take full account of this tradition, it is also necessary to transcend it – for at least two reasons. First, as I have been shown, the tradition is much more complex and diverse than many assume. The religious zealots in the tradition of Ezra and the prophets should not be allowed to appropriate the Babylonian and Sephardi experiences to their cause. Those experiences were distinguished by considerable intellectual and spiritual achievements which simply could not have happened in a narrow tribal society like that of ancient Judaea. The voluntarist component in the history of Jewish migration should also not be overlooked. Not all Jewish communities outside the natal homeland resulted from forcible dispersal.[11] Indeed, there is considerable evidence to suggest that the Jews are not a single people with a single origin and a single migration history. Again, it concedes too much to Zionist opinion to depict the diaspora as ultimately and inevitably doomed. The diasporic experience in all areas has been enriching and creative as well as enervating and fearful. Besides – a point that I shall address in Chapter 5 in more detail – it may be that the Jewish diaspora is well on the way to solving the issue of preserving a secure Jewish identity without having to embrace the destructive territorialism of the Zionists.

The second reason why we have to transcend the Jewish tradition is that the word diaspora is now being used, whether purists approve or not, in a variety of new, but interesting and suggestive contexts. To mount a defence of an orthodox definition of diaspora, which in any case has been shown to be dubious, is akin to commanding the waves no longer to break on the shore. As Safran (1991: 83) notes, diaspora is now deployed as "a metaphoric designation" to describe *different categories* of people – "expatriates, expellees, political refugees, alien residents, immigrants and ethnic and racial minorities *tout court*". Moreover, a point again made by Safran, the term now designates a vast array of *different peoples*. Safran lists Cubans and Mexicans in the USA, Pakistanis in Britain, Maghrebis in France, Turks in Germany, the Chinese in South East Asia, Greeks, Poles, Palestinians, blacks in North America and the

21

Caribbean, Indians and Armenians "in various countries", Corsicans in Marseilles and "even French-speaking Belgians living in communal enclaves in Wallonia".

In trying to draw generalized inferences from the Jewish tradition it is necessary both to draw critically from that tradition and to be sensitive to the inevitable dilutions, changes and expansions of the meaning of the term diaspora as it comes to be more widely applied. Looking at Safran's list in that light and even accepting that he probably means to be indicative rather than comprehensive, his inclusions inevitably invite refutation and argument. What has happened to the Ukrainians, the Irish, the Italians, the Russians, the Germans or the Kurds – all of whom might have at least as strong a claim to inclusion as some of the peoples he identifies? There are also many more ambiguous cases – the Japanese, the Gypsies, the Hungarians, the Croatians, the Serbs, the British, the Sikhs, Caribbean peoples, to name but some possibilities.[12]

Again, I would take issue with his expression "diaspora X in country Y". It is perhaps unnecessary that all diasporas are, such as the prophets in the Bible claimed of the Jews, "scattered to all lands", but I imagine most would agree that in order to qualify perhaps they should be dispersed to more than one. (Paradoxically, Safran himself makes this point elsewhere.) This makes Safran's listing of the Mexicans and (to a lesser extent) Cubans somewhat doubtful. This is less of a problem in some of the other diaspora destination examples he includes, for in some cases at least the dispersal is greater than he indicates. The Turks are now more widely dispersed in Europe than just in Germany, although we may need longer to establish whether they will become a diaspora. Equally, the overseas Chinese embrace many more destinations than South East Asia. However, I think that it will open a Pandora's box to include cases of minorities (like Flemish-speaking Belgians) living in ethnic enclaves inside a country or in nearby countries. Such circumstances often arise when borders are artificially drawn – as they were for Africa by the Congress of Berlin, or as in central and eastern Europe and the Balkans as a result of periodic shifts in the fortunes of empire or as a result of civil war. The stranded minority is not in my view (normally) a diaspora.

Whatever my immediate difficulties with Safran's argument, his subsequent list of the key characteristics of diasporas commands attention and emulation. He is properly relaxed in allowing no contemporary diaspora to fulfil all the definitional desiderata. However, he maintains (1991: 83–4) that the concept of a diaspora can be applied when members of an "expatriate minority community" share several of the following features:

- They, or their ancestors, have been dispersed from an original "centre" to two or more foreign regions;
- they retain a collective memory, vision or myth about their original homeland including its location, history and achievements;
- they believe they are not – and perhaps can never be – fully accepted in their host societies and so remain partly separate;
- their ancestral home is idealized and it is thought that, when conditions are favourable, either they, or their descendants should return;
- they believe all members of the diaspora should be committed to the maintenance or restoration of the original homeland and to its safety and prosperity; and
- they continue in various ways to relate to that homeland and their ethnocommunal consciousness and solidarity are in an important way defined by the existence of such a relationship.

Although this is a very useful list, four of the six features mentioned are concerned with the relationship of the diasporic group to its homeland. Although this aspect is clearly of crucial importance, there is some degree of repetition of the argument. I also believe that two features should be "tweaked", while four other features need to be added, mainly concerning the nature of the diasporic group in its countries of exile. I would amend the first stated feature by adding that dispersal from an original centre is often accompanied by the memory of a single traumatic event that provides the folk memory of the great historic injustice that binds the group together. I would adapt the penultimate characteristic to allow the case of not only the "maintenance or restoration" of a homeland, but also its very creation. This will cover the case of an "imagined homeland" that only resembles the original history and geography of the diaspora's natality in the remotest way. (In some cases – the Kurds or Sikhs come to mind – a homeland is clearly an *ex post facto* construction.)

Now to the additional features. The first is that we may wish to include in the category diaspora, groups that scatter for aggressive or voluntarist reasons. This is probably the most controversial departure from the Jewish diasporic tradition, but one that I think can be justified by reference to the case of the ancient Greeks (who, after all, coined the word) and to the duality, voluntary *and* compelled, of the Jews' own migration patterns. It also conforms to the use of the word to describe trading and commercial networks (the Lebanese, for example, have been so described), to those seeking work abroad and to imperial or colonial settlers. When dealing with trade, labour or imperial diasporas, it is still necessary to the notion of diaspora that they "creolize" or indigenize not at all or only in a very limited way and continue to retain their link, sometimes their dependence, on the "motherland".

Secondly, a point strongly emphasized by Marienstras (1989: 25), is that "time has to pass" before we can know that any community that has migrated "is really a diaspora". In other words, one does not announce the formation of the diaspora the moment the representatives of a people first get off the boat at Ellis Island (or wherever). Many members of a particular ethnic group may intend to and be able to merge into the crowd, lose their prior identity and achieve individualized forms of social mobility. (The changing of ethnically identifiable names by new immigrants signals this intention.) Other groups may intermarry with the locals and slowly disappear as a separable ethnic group. A strong tie to the past or a block to assimilation in the present and future must exist in order to permit a diasporic consciousness to emerge or be retained.

Thirdly, I would add that there must be more recognition of the positive virtues of retaining a diasporic identity than is implied in Safran's list. The tension between an ethnic, a national and a transnational identity is often a creative, enriching one. As I have shown in the instance of the Jews in Babylon, the Islamic world and in early modern Spain, there are many advances to record – in medicine, theology, art, music, philosophy, literature, science, industry and commerce. Although one must be careful to distinguish hagiography from history, it is difficult to discount the achievements of diasporic Jews in such diverse areas as Bombay, Baghdad or Vienna (Grunwald 1936, Israel 1971). One or two writers (for example, Zborowski et al. 1952) have even found the *shetls* (ghetto villages) of the Russian Pale to be a source of dewy-eyed authenticity and solidarity, although I must confess that I always found those folk-tales of wise Ashkenazi rabbis coming up with brilliant solutions to everyday problems both mawkish and unconvincing. Even if there is a degree of subterranean anxiety in the diaspora, it may be possible to argue that this is precisely what motivates the need for achievement. If life is too comfortable, Neusner (1985) convincingly argues, creativity may dry up. His apprehension is contradicted by one – admittedly crude – index of the continuing successes of Western diasporic Jews. I refer to the extraordinary number of Nobel prizes won in the arts, medicine and the sciences, a record, incidentally, in notable contrast to the mediocre performance of the Israeli Jews.[13] The final feature I would add to the Safran list is that members of a diaspora characteristically sense not only a collective identity in a place of settlement, nor again only a relationship with an imagined, putative or real homeland, but also a common identity with co-ethnic members in other countries. Sympathy with the maligned Jews in the "Damascas Affair" was, as I described above, what got the French Jews into such hot water. Bonds of language, religion, culture and a sense of a common fate impregnate such a transnational relationship and give to it an affective, intimate quality that formal citizenship or long settlement frequently lack. None the less, there is often a great deal of tension in the relationship between scattered co-ethnic communities. A bond of loyalty to the country of refuge/ settlement competes with ethnic solidarity, while there is frequently a considerable reluctance by those who have achieved national social mobility to accept too close a link with a despised or low-status ethnic group abroad, even if it happens to be their own.

Conclusion

At the risk of repeating myself, it is still probably worth consolidating what we have learned so far into a common set of propositions. However, before I present this, I want to emphasize again that conceptions of diaspora, even from the earliest times, are far more diverse than the commonly accepted catastrophic tradition. The original Greek word, signifying expansion and settler colonization, can loosely be compared to the later European (especially British, Portuguese and Spanish) settlements of the mercantile and colonial period. However, this meaning was "hijacked" to describe a forcible dispersal of a people and their subsequent unhappiness (or assumed unhappiness) in their countries of exile. Nowadays, with the increased use of the term to describe many kinds of migrants from diverse ethnic backgrounds, a more relaxed definition seems appropriate. Moreover, transnational bonds no longer have to be cemented by migration or by exclusive territorial claims. In the age of cyberspace, a diaspora can, to some degree, be held together or re-created through the mind, through cultural artefacts and through a shared imagination.

Some of these questions are addressed later in the book and a more complete synthesis of contemporary uses of diaspora is provided in Chapter 7. However, in the first instance, I need to produce a consolidated list of the "common features" of a diaspora, drawing on the classical tradition, on Safran's desiderata, my modifications to his list and on my own views (see Table 1.1).

Let me, by way of illustration, take just one of these features to see how it might work in practice – the idea of dispersal, following a traumatic event in the homeland, to two or more foreign destina-

Table 1.1 Common features of a diaspora.

1.	Dispersal from an original homeland, often traumatically, to two or more foreign regions;
2.	alternatively, the expansion from a homeland in search of work, in pursuit of trade or to further colonial ambitions;
3.	a collective memory and myth about the homeland, including its location, history and achievements;
4.	an idealization of the putative ancestral home and a collective commitment to its maintenance, restoration, safety and prosperity, even to its creation;
5.	the development of a return movement that gains collective approbation;
6.	a strong ethnic group conciousness sustained over a long time and based on a sense of distinctiveness, a common history and the belief in a common fate;
7.	a troubled relationship with host societies, suggesting a lack of acceptance at the least or the possibility that another calamity might befall the group;
8.	a sense of empathy and solidarity with co-ethnic members in other countries of settlement; and
9.	the possibility of a distinctive creative, enriching life in host countries with a tolerance for pluralism.

tions. Migration scholars often find it remarkably difficult to separate the compelling from the voluntary elements in the motivation to move.[14] However, when we talk of a trauma afflicting a group collectively, it is perhaps possible to isolate those events in which the suddenness, scale and intensity of exogenous factors unambiguously compel migration or flight. Being dragged off in manacles (as were the Jews to Babylon), being expelled, or being coerced to leave by force of arms appear qualitatively different phenomena from the general pressures of overpopulation, land hunger, poverty or an unsympathetic political regime.

In the Jewish case, the catastrophic origins of the diaspora have been unduly emphasized in folk memory – although I by no means wish to understate some of the calamities that afflicted the group in the diaspora. At least four other cases have had unambiguously grisly episodes in their history that led to their original or further dispersion:

- The horror and cruelty of the African slave trade has been exposed so many times that justifiably hyperbolic language begins to lose its force. Although many Africans are found in Asia and the Middle East, the forcible transhipment of ten million people across the Atlantic for mass slavery and coerced plantation labour in the Americas provided the defining and constituent elements of the African diaspora.

- Although the origins of the Armenian diaspora were in commerce and trade, the Armenians can be characterized as a victim diaspora following the massacres of the late nineteenth century and their forced displacement during 1915–16, when the Turks deported two-thirds of their number (1.75 million people) to Syria and Palestine. Many Armenians subsequently landed up in France and the USA. It is now widely accepted (though still implausibly disputed by Turkish sources) that a million Armenians were either killed or died of starvation during this mass displacement, the twentieth century's first major example of what has come to be known as "ethnic cleansing".

- The migration of the Irish over the period 1845 to 1852, following the famine, can be regarded as an analogous trauma. To be sure, there have been ups and downs by Irish historians of migration in seeking to assess just how salient the famine

27

was in propelling the vast and continuous transatlantic migrations of the nineteenth century. However, in her up-to-date, powerfully argued and scholarly account, Kinealy (1995) shows there was much more deliberation in the British response to the potato blight than has previously been adduced. She suggests that, far from *laissez-faire* attitudes governing policy, the British government had a hidden agenda of population control, the modernization of agriculture and land reform. This gives the Irish events a greater similarity to those that propelled the Jewish, African and Armenian diasporas.

- When Britain withdrew from Palestine on 14 May 1948, the Israeli army occupied the vacuum and the ethnically based state of Israel was proclaimed. First out of prudence, then out of panic, two-thirds of the Arab population of Palestine left their homes and became refugees, at first in neighbouring countries, then all over the Middle East and beyond. The Palestinian diaspora had been born and, ironically and tragically, the midwife was the homecoming of the Jewish diaspora.

The scarring historical event – Babylon for the Jews, slavery for the Africans, famine for the Irish, genocide for the Armenians and the formation of the state of Israel for the Palestinians – lends a particular colouring to these five diasporas. They are, above all, victim diasporas in their historical experience. This does not mean that they do not share several or all of the other nine characteristics I have placed in my consolidated list, merely that their victim origin is either self-affirmed or accepted by outside observers as determining their essential character.

By contrast, there may be compelling elements in the history of other diasporas, but these either may have involved less cruelty or may have had less impact on the natal society. For example, let me take the nineteenth-century system of indentured labour abroad, which affected many Indians, Japanese and Chinese. It does not minimize the oppressive aspects involved in this system of labour control to say that in some crucial respects they differed from those of the victim diasporas. In all three Asian cases, the numbers involved in indenture were a very small fraction of the total population, the migrants had the legal right to return and the recruitment process and work conditions were legally regulated, however badly.

The defining feature of the Indian indentured migrants was that they were recruited for their labour-power for use in the tropical plantations. They could therefore, with some justification be called a "labour diaspora" – even though there was a coercive element in their recruitment. In the example of the Chinese, at least as many traders as indentured labourers had begun to spill outside the Chinese mainland to the rest of South East Asia. Moreover, the merchants' long-term influence was far greater. It therefore seems more appropriate to describe the Chinese as primarily a "trade diaspora".

Through the use of a qualifying adjective (victim, labour, trade and imperial), I now have a simple means of typologizing various diasporas, not by ignoring what they share in common, but by highlighting their most important characteristics. In the next three chapters of this book I probe the nature of these "adjectival diasporas", using key examples. Thereafter, in Chapter 5, I am concerned with the politics of "homeland" and the quest for a state. In Chapter 6 I show how cultural diasporas have created bonds of the imagination without the normal features of (physical) migration and the territorialization of identity, while in Chapter 7 I examine how globalization has affected the creation of new diasporas and influenced their character. In the final chapter I compare the principal features of diasporas and look to their fate and future.

TWO

Victim diasporas:
Africans and Armenians

In Chapter 1 I identified the Jewish, Palestinian, Irish, African and Armenian diasporas as the principal ones that can be described with the preceding adjective of "victim". Although this is primarily a scholarly grouping, writers and political leaders representing these peoples reinforce this classification with their constant cross-references and comparisons to one another. Readers with literary leanings might, for example, remember one of the characters in James Joyce's famous novel *Ulysses* (1922) talking of the Irish peasants in the "black 1847" as being driven out "in hordes". "Twenty-thousand of them died in the coffin ships" (a description frequently used of the African slave ships). "But", his character continues, "those who came to the land of the free remember the land of bondage" (a clear reference to the way the biblical Jews conceived ancient Egypt).

It is perhaps not surprising that the Jews often provided the point of comparison for other victim diasporas. Africans abroad have long felt an affinity with the Jewish diaspora,[1] although it is thought that the expressions black diaspora or African diaspora were not used until the mid-1950s or 1960s. Tenuous support for the idea of an African diaspora was said to been found in the phrase "Ethiopia shall soon stretch out her hands unto God" (Psalms 68: 31), although this passage seems unusually elliptical, even by biblical standards. There are much more potent and obvious parallels between the Jewish and African historical experiences. Servitude, forced migration, exile and the development of a

31

return movement are all similarities noted by a number of writers of African descent in the Americas in the nineteenth century as well as by early West African nationalists (Shepperson 1993).

For Armenian commentators, the obvious point of comparison is between the Armenian massacres of 1915–22 and the Jewish Holocaust of the Second World War. In contrast to the massacres of earlier historical periods, Dekmejian (1991: 86) argues that these two events were characterized by "supranationalist ruling elites" who were bureaucratically organized and had the technological capacity and ideological imperative to carry out mass extermination. Although the level of technological sophistication is questionable in the Ottoman case, "the scale, speed, and efficiency of human destruction and its systematic implementation through impersonal bureaucratic rationality . . . [were] five characteristics [all] present in the Armenian and Jewish cases".

In this chapter, I propose to investigate these two victim diasporas, African and Armenian, looking both at how they compare with the earlier victim tradition and at how they conform to the list of common characteristics of all diasporas developed in Chapter 1. However, we must be aware of some obvious limitations to an assumption of similitude. For example, unlike the Africans, Ashkenazi Jews did not arrive in the New World as slaves. Nor were they that different phenotypically from the majority of immigrants to the Americas. This made it easier for them to be absorbed into, or accepted by, the white populations and thereby become less obvious targets of discrimination. As the rate of social mobility of US Jews accelerated so too did their tendencies to vote Republican, to abandon their old urban haunts and, with them, their progressive social and political attitudes. Those Jews who remained – either as landlords or small businesspeople, or as highly visible followers of religious sects – have recently been the target of furious hate campaigns by some militant black leaders.

Likewise, we have to remember the fundamental differences between the Armenian and Jewish diasporas. While the Holocaust occurred when the Jewish diaspora had already been in existence for over 2,000 years, the massacres of Armenians in the late nineteenth century and again during the First World War constituted the primary trauma events, which occasioned the creation of a significant diaspora for the first time. Dekmejian (1991: 94) makes a related point in a different way – whereas, he reminds us, the Armenians were an indigenous population, the European Jews of the Second World War were a minority. And, he adds, whereas the Nazis regarded the Jews as racially inferior, the Young Turks accused the Armenians of elitism. Again, while Nazi Germany was in an advanced stage of modernization, the Ottoman empire remained something of a feudal shambles, despite the Young Turks' aspirations to modernity.

Origins of the African diaspora

It is often argued of an oppressive social practice – be it the beheading of murderers, the circumcision of women or the burning of witches – that we have to understand the meaning of such practices to the local actors who were bound by their own time and circumstances. So we must. However, we must also guard against the opposite danger of accepting, under the guise of an actor-directed view of the word, the sort of cultural relativity that leaves the historian and social scientist in a pilotless moral vacuum. The apologia of a different time is, in any case, impossible to mount with respect to African slavery, as there is a wealth of evidence that those who conducted the trade were well aware that they offended *contemporary* standards. Take, for example, the account of one William Bosman, the chief agent of the Dutch West India Company at its main slave trading station in modern-day Ghana (cited Segal 1995: 28):

> When these Slaves come to Fida, they are put in Prison altogether, and when we treat concerning buying them, they are all brought out together in a large Plain; where by our Chiurgeons, whose Province it is, they are thoroughly examined, even to the smallest Member, and that naked too both Men and Women, without the least Distinction of Modesty. Those which are approved as good are set on one side; and the lame and faulty are set by as Invalides . . . the remainder are numbred, and it is entred who delivered them. In the mean while a burning iron, with the Arms or Name of the Companies, lyes in the Fire; with which ours

are marked on the Breast. . . . *I doubt not but this Trade seems very barbarous to you, but since it is followed by meer necessity it must go on*; but we yet take all possible care that they are not burned too hard, especially the Women, who are more tender than the Men (emphasis added).

For "necessity" read "profit". For the more considerate treatment meted out to women read "moral humbug". For the ship captains, merchants (European and African) and, above all, for the plantation owners in the New World, African slaves meant vast profits for a relatively modest outlay. And when there were plenty of slaves to be had, the cruelty was quite profligate. Some slaves were branded several times over – to prove ownership, to demonstrate that export duty had been paid, to show their vassalage to the king of the country concerned or, in a supreme act of double standards, to indicate that they had been baptized. In 1813, branding was replaced by a metal collar or bracelet, but it was restored five years later, this time with a silver branding iron and still with the evident intention of making clear that the slave was a commodity, not a person (Segal 1995: 31).

The transatlantic trade deposited Africans in the Caribbean, Mexico and Brazil – in each case to work on tropical plantations. Their suffering has been embellished on the consciousness of Europeans and Americans partly because of their own complicity in owning and exploiting slave labour, but also by the extraordinary success of New World Africans in conveying a sense of their plight through art, literature, music, dance and religious expression. However momentous and powerful the experience of the Atlantic diaspora, it is important not to overlook the commencement of Africa's experience of a slave trade and forced migration during the Islamic hegemony of the seventh and eighth centuries. As Hunwick (1993: 289) contends,

Beginning some eight centuries before the transatlantic slave trade, and not ending until several decades after the latter was halted, the movement of slaves across the Sahara, up the Nile Valley and the Red Sea, and across the Indian Ocean to the Persian Gulf and India, probably accounted for the uprooting of as many Africans from their societies as did the transatlantic trade.

George Shepperson (1993) also fires a useful warning shot across the bows in discussing the comparison of the Jewish and African diasporas. Arguing that the expression "African diaspora" has been one-sided and drawn only on the victim tradition, he counsels (p. 46):

> Some knowledge of Jewish history would help students of Africans abroad to realize that, in the expression "the African diaspora" *diaspora* is being used metaphorically. This would prevent it becoming an overrigid, ideologized concept, to the detriment of serious and imaginative research. Furthermore, knowledge of Jewish usage enables the appreciation of the voluntary as opposed to the involuntary element in the diaspora of the Jews.... Excessive concentration on the western rather than the eastern direction of the African diaspora may be responsible for the concealment of the voluntary element in the dispersal, even in the slave days.

These comments are pertinent, giving us a richer and more complex reading of the origins and destinations of the African diaspora. Africans ended up in Asia (see Harris 1971) and the Mediterranean, as well as in the Americas, and some of the non-American migrants were traders rather than slaves. But neither author cited would wish to minimize the element of compulsion and collective trauma that accompanied the creation of the transatlantic African diaspora. Where, clearly, we do need to draw a distinction between the African and some other diasporas, is in the prolonged timescale of African-Atlantic and Islamic slavery – the latter from the seventh to the nineteenth centuries. (Indeed the Anti-Slavery Society occasionally publicizes social practices in the Red Sea area and Sudan that suggest that the long-distance slave trade still continues.) Whereas the creation of the African diaspora was a prolonged affair, the Palestinians, Armenians and, more uncertainly, the Irish diaspora were propelled by a single set of events. Although the Jewish diaspora has also been assumed to have been galvanized by a single cataclysmic event, as we have seen in Chapter 1, the destructions of the two Temples were spaced widely apart and many early Jewish colonies were the result of trade and voluntary settlement, not forcible dispersal.

The African diaspora: homeland and return

Is there a collective myth about the African homeland, including its location, history and achievements? Is there a desire to return? In fact, the African diaspora in the New World generated a number of myths about its origins.[2] In Haiti, for example, Montilus (1993: 160–4) notes the presence of two contrasting myths. A "macho" man might have beaten his chest and boasted that he was *neg Ginin* (a black from Guinea). "Guinea" had come to symbolize the "mythical origin of valour and virtue". It referred to "a mythical place of origin that had became an ideal of resistance to slavery, its suffering, and its humiliation".[3] By contrast, a Haitian would be insulted to be called *neg Congo* (a black from the Congo). This designation was used to allude to Haitians who had been under Western influence, in particular Christianity, even in Africa. It was imputed that they were docile and used as house slaves – in contrast to the sturdy, solidaristic fieldhands. The pantheon of spirits was also divided in two. The Guinean spirits, *lwa Ginin*, were bold, strong, helpful and efficient, while the *lwa Congo* were uninterested in the destiny of the people. Their redeeming feature was that they were gentle and encouraged joyful dances expressing good humour and the desire for a happy life. After their lives in exile the dead would return to Guinea: their souls would transmigrate and they would return to their ancestors' shrine.

Other African "homelands" were constructed from the places where African returnees, or liberated or manumitted slaves, were conveyed by the European and American powers. Perhaps I could elaborate with a personal experience? I once worked on the remote island of St Helena in the south Atlantic – halfway between Angola and Brazil. In the period after 1807, when the British slave trade (as opposed to slavery, which went on far longer) had been abolished, Portuguese slavers had been intercepted on the high seas by the British navy. Their wretched human cargo had been deposited on a forsaken beach on the island, where a hospital had been established. As I paced alongside the ruins of the hospital, I was overpowered by a sense of the agonies of the many who had died there and, by contrast, felt the half flicker of hope of those who were told they would be taken from the island to Freetown (in Sierra Leone), one of the ports at which the recaptives were landed. Some recaptives actually made their way back from Sierra Leone to their original homes, but most stayed. Those that did found in Freetown – so named because of their presence – 400 Westernized Christianized returnees from England (plus a few from the USA, Canada and Jamaica) who had been sent to Sierra Leone under the sponsorship of British abolitionists. The groups congealed to become the core of an educated, Westernized bourgeoisie who reached elite positions in the church, in commerce and in government. In 1879, the son of a recaptive, Gurney Nicol, became the first African graduate of Cambridge University (Fyfe 1962). Returnees from Brazil created a similar Westernized bourgeoisie in Lagos and other port cities in West Africa where their substantial, if somewhat dilapidated, houses can still be observed (Boadi-Siaw 1993).

"Homeland" also was Liberia. Again the name signified the involvement of abolitionists, this time from the USA. The repatriates to Liberia were from the USA and many had already achieved a modest independent status in America. This meant they came back as settlers rather than impoverished returnees. The Americo-Liberians, as they were called, soon took on the appearance of colonists – refusing to learn the local languages, imposing American-style institutions, acquiring the airs of a social elite and ruthlessly monopolizing political power. In the 1930s a League of Nations investigation found that some Americo-Liberians, including a number holding political office, had reinstituted slavery – this time, however, with the boot on the other foot. In short, Liberia was quite a long way off from utopia. Nevertheless, the Liberian constitution committed the country "to provide a home for the dispersed and oppressed children of Africa" and for many black intellectuals and political leaders in the diaspora it remained an island of hope in a sea of racial discrimination and colonial domination.

Guinea, Freetown and Liberia were all versions of "homeland". But by far the most significant notions of the African homeland were imbricated in "Ethiopia" – the place, the symbol, the idea and the promise (Lemelle et al. 1994). Ethiopia was seen as the heartland of African civilization, indeed – a claim replicated in a number of self-images of different diasporas – the heartland of *all* civilization. A favourite quotation in demonstration of this belief was from the pre-Christian Greek historian, Diodorous Siculus, who wrote, "The Ethiopians conceived themselves to be of greater antiquity than any other nation, and it is probable that, born under the sun's path, its warmth may have ripened them sooner than other men. They supposed themselves to be the inventors of Worship, of festivals, of solemn assemblies, of sacrifice, and every religious practice." One typical African-American pamphlet, in the style of a Ripley's "Believe-It-Or-Not" story, claimed that "Ethiopia, that is Negroes, gave the world the first idea of right and wrong and this laid the basis of religion and all true culture and civilization" (both citations in Magubane 1987: 163).

Just as "Zion" and "Israel" were often imagined entities, for many New World Africans "Ethiopia" was more of a concept of "blackness" or "Africanity", only loosely connected with the country of Ethiopia itself.[4] None the less, the fictive community generated real enough social movements. For example, in the 1930s the precursor to Rastafarianism in Jamaica was "Ethiopianism". As Ken Post (1978: 172) notes, the movement made the connection with Jewish history and reinforced the negative version of their experiences in Babylon.

> Generally throughout Jamaican Ethiopianism, the sense of a Negro awakening combined with the feeling of being a scattered and oppressed, but nevertheless "chosen" people in a way which made it easy to identify "Babylon" – the white or near-white establishment. . . . It was thus a feature of Jamaican Ethiopianism as an ideology that it moved from a sense of being a chosen people to the identification of Babylon with the white enslaver, and thence to an interpretation of history which predicated the doom of the oppressor.

The spiritual and mystical forms of Ethiopianism were suddenly given a massive boost after the crowning of Ras (meaning "prince") Tafari as Emperor Haile Selassie of Ethiopia in November 1930. This led directly to the formation of the Rastafarian movement in Jamaica. Among the Jamaican Rastafarians, the cross-identification with the biblical Jews was complete. As Boot & Thomas (1976: 78) suggest:

> The Rastas take it from the Bible that they are the true Jews of the prophecy, buried alive in a hostile and godless white

society that couldn't care less about the black man down at the bottom of the heap. They never wanted to come here and they don't want to stay. So they take no part. They have disenfranchized themselves. . . . They have defected body and soul from Jamaican society into an outcast astral identity beyond the law.

The newly independent government of Jamaica, anxious at the large following that the movement was attracting, thought they would prick the balloon by inviting Haile Selassie on a state visit. Far from having the intended effect, seeing the sedate figure of the Emperor on the steps of an aircraft at Kingston airport propelled an even more fervent belief in Rastafarianism and in his divinity.

The attack on Ethiopia by the Italian Fascists in October 1935 had, however, brought the astral aspects of Ethiopianism down with a thump. Suddenly the very existence of this potent symbol of black pride and independence was imperilled. In the USA, feeling spilled over in East Harlem with African-Americans attacking their Italian neighbours. Joe Louis's boxing triumph over Primo Carnera was seen as a successful attack on the Fascists. Some 20,000 protesters, some bearing Ethiopian flags, marched in a rally to Madison Square. The spirit of the times was well captured by a Cleveland physician, Joe E. Thomas (cited Magubane 1987: 167), who urged that "every son and daughter of African descent should render assistance to their blood relatives in Ethiopia. We must not desert our Race in Africa. We must stand, 'One for all, All for one'." Despite this help from the diaspora, and only after a brave fight, Haile Selassie was forced to flee into exile in Britain. In its notorious period of appeasement before the Second World War, the British government at first capitulated to Italy's demands for recognition of its new-found empire, but finally swung to the Emperor's side, recognizing that it was impossible to accommodate the Axis powers. Its fear of mass revolt in the British colonies also pushed the British government to a more militant anti-Fascist stance. With the help of the British, but not forgetting the commendable heroism of the Ethiopian patriots, Haile Selassie was finally restored to his throne in 1941.[5]

Other aspects of the African diaspora

Despite the attempt to promote ancient Ethiopia as a major world civilization, one major hurdle for those promoting a positive idea of Africa was that for many African-Americans its image was singularly depressing. To many, "Africa" signified enslavement, poverty, denigration, exploitation, white superiority, the loss of language and the loss of self-respect. It is little wonder that the key basis of the appeal of populist leaders like the Jamaican-born Marcus Garvey was to the desperate need to escape this abasement and self-hatred and to express self-esteem and dignity. Richard Wright, although too sophisticated to sign up himself, was a perceptive observer of this early movement of black consciousness. To him (Wright 1944: 28), the Garveyites showed:

> a passionate rejection of America, for they sensed with a directness of which only the simple are capable that they had no chance to live a full human life in America. . . . The Garveyites had embraced a totally racialist outlook which endowed them with a dignity I had never seen before in Negroes. On the walls of their dingy flats were maps of Africa and India and Japan . : . the faces of coloured men and women from all parts of the world. . . . I gave no credence to the ideology of Garveyism; it was, rather, the emotional dynamics of its adherents that evoked my admiration.

Garveyism has normally been analyzed as a failed return movement. Certainly, the small colonies sent to Liberia and elsewhere on the continent were ill-fated. However, it is worth remembering that the name of Garvey's movement was the Universal Negro Improvement Association and its immense popularity was closely related to its promotion of self-pride and self-betterment. This could involve continuing to stay in the Americas, while idealizing the homeland and undertaking a commitment to its restoration, safety and prosperity. At the height of his influence, Garvey proclaimed himself provisional president of Africa, but he never visited the continent and died in obscurity in London after his movement was infiltrated, then discredited, by the American authorities. Garvey created a court of Ethiopia with dukes, duchesses and knights commander of the Distinguished Order of Ethiopia. By 1921, the organization claimed a membership of four million people, the largest following of African-Americans ever mustered, before or since. Like the prophet Isaiah, Garvey thundered, "No one knows when the hour of Africa's redemption cometh. It is in the wind. It is coming. One day, like a storm it will be here" (Ottley 1948: 235).

Another towering leader of the African diaspora was W. E. B. DuBois, whose writings perfectly expressed two desiderata of a diaspora – that there should be a sense of empathy and solidarity with co-ethnic members worldwide and that there should be a sense of distinctiveness, a common history and the belief in a common fate. What was it, DuBois (cited Magubane 1987: 149–50) asked himself, that tied him to Africa so strongly?

On this vast continent were born and lived a large proportion of my direct ancestors going back a thousand years or more. But one thing is sure and that is the fact that since the fifteenth century these ancestors of mine and their other descendants have had a common history, have suffered a common disaster and have one long memory. . . . But the physical bond is the least [tie] and [merely] the badge; the real essence of this kinship is its social heritage of slavery, the discrimination and insult; and this heritage binds together not simply the children of Africa but extends through yellow Asia and into the South Seas. It is this Unity that draws me to Africa.

DuBois became a central figure in the early Pan-African movement, a political commitment that also excited visionaries from the black Caribbean. The movement articulated a sense of a common fate, particularly in the New World, and a common purpose to build a powerful, united and wealthy Africa. One of the Caribbean leaders was the formidable Trinidadian Trotskyist C. L. R. James who, although more of an internationalist than an African nationalist, was none the less influential in African anti-colonial circles. He was joined by his influential fellow-Trinidadian, the communist George Padmore, who finally made his break with the

41

Comintern (the communist international movement) when it started issuing denunciatory statements about Liberia.[6] These and other Caribbean leaders were partly responsible for convening the watershed Manchester Conference of 1945, when the basic lines of struggle for African self-determination were articulated and agreed. Other manifestations of black solidarity on the part of New World Africans took a more cultural than political appearance. In the francophone Caribbean, Aimé Césaire made his spiritual journey in *Return to my native land* (1956). He was also an important influence on the Négritude movement and, more generally, had a continuing dialogue with Africans and the peoples of African descent in literary and political journals such as *Présence Africaine*.

Reference to the literary talents of a Caribbean writer and politician leads me to the final feature of the African diaspora on which I wish to comment – namely its extraordinary cultural achievements (see also Ch. 6). This is true of dance, literature, architecture, sculpture and art. Perhaps the most notable contribution, however, has been in the development of a musical tradition centred in the USA, but now with an appreciative following in most countries. The most inclusive and popular general designation of this musical tradition is "jazz", but within and alongside that catch-all word are spirituals, the blues (derived from the West African *griot* tradition), ragtime, gospel music and swing. Particular styles also developed – New Orleans, Chicago, bop, bebop, modern jazz, free jazz, and so on. And the music attained a mass following through its commercial derivatives like rhythm and blues, rock,[7] fusion music, pop and Motown (an abbreviation of Motortown, so named by African-Americans working in the Detroit car factories). Nor were other diasporic Africans musically out in the cold. To mention only the obvious, the diaspora in Brazil gave us samba, that in Trinidad the calypso and from Jamaica came ska and reggae – the last dominated by the Rastafarian Bob Marley and full of explicit diasporic themes (Segal 1995: 375–95; see also Oliver 1970, Collier 1978).

The creation of the Armenian diaspora

Armenians are a people to whom the appellation "diaspora" has often been applied both by themselves and by outsiders. They qualify on the criteria set out in Chapter 1 in a number of important ways. The Armenians, for example, share a common myth of origin, centred around the figure of Haik – the derivative word "Hay" is a name that Armenians apply to themselves (Kurkjian 1964: 49). While earlier research suggested that the "original" peoples of Armenia migrated from central Europe, newer theories suggest ethnogenesis arose in Asia Minor itself. Armenian writers claim that the places and peoples known as Armani, Hayasa, Biainili and Urartu all alluded to Armenia and Armenians. The heroic tradition, moreover, boasts that Urartus ("the land of Ararat") survived its rival nation Assyria by some 300 years.

Rather as Ethiopia was claimed as the source of "all true culture and civilization" by the nineteenth-century African-American pamphleteer already cited, many Armenian writers claim a primacy for Armenia's contribution to world history. A slightly less modest claim is made by the British scholar of the Caucasian region, David Marshall Lang (1978: 9) who, while conceding that the Mesopotamian civilizations and Egypt were "the main sources of civilized life in the modern sense", none the less maintains that "Armenia too has a claim to rank as one of the cradles of human culture".[8] Armenian myth invokes biblical authority to sustain this claim. According to the Book of Genesis (8: 4), after 150 days of rain, on the seventeenth day of the seventh month Noah's ark "grounded on a mountain in Ararat". Mount Ararat is, of course, in the centre of historic Armenia. As the beasts, birds and humans (i.e. Noah's family) are believed to have issued forth from this place, Armenia can be considered to be at the epicentre of the rebirth, if not the birth, of the earth.

Centre it may have been, but the Armenians subsequently had some difficulty in resisting being walked over by intruders from the periphery. One powerful colonizing group were the Medes, who first used the name "Armini" as a self-description, a name the Greeks later modified to Armenia. Cultural survival in the face of the Hellenist and Persian influences was also difficult, although Artashes I managed to encourage his subjects to retain the Araratian dialect. A brief period of expansion in the period 93–66 BC – when Armenia stretched from the Mediterranean to the Caspian Sea – was halted by the Romans in the latter year. Christianity became ideologically dominant and was adopted as a state religion in AD 301. Next, the Byzantium Emperor Maurice (who himself is popularly supposed to have been a simple Armenian peasant who made good) exerted his ascendancy by setting an ominous precedent. In AD 578 he transported 10,000 Armenians to Cyprus, 12,000 to Macedonia and 8,000 to Pergama – these deportations being the origins of the Armenian diaspora. Maurice was no great lover of his fellow Armenians. As he wrote (cited Lang 1978) to the Persian king:

> The Armenians are a knavish and indolent nation. They are situated between us, and are a source of trouble. I am going to gather mine and send them to Thrace; you send yours to the east. If they die there, it will be so many enemies that will die; if, on the contrary, they kill, it will be so many enemies that they kill. As for us, we shall live in peace. But if they remain in their own country there will never be any quiet for us.

Armenia was later subordinated by the force of Islamic arms and turned into "the Emirate of Armenia". This was followed by subordination to the Seljuk Turks and the migration west to Cicilia by many Armenians. Tartar, Mongol and Turkoman domination followed. The last significant invaders were the Russians, sweeping down in 1828 and forcing the division of Armenia into Turkish, Persian and Russian Armenia (Armen et al. 1987: 6–24).

Through all these vicissitudes Armenians maintained their distinctive language and two particular brands of Christianity – the Catholic Armenian Church and the Armenian Orthodox Church. The modern disaster and dispersion began in the late nineteenth century when a pan-Armenian nationalist and revolutionary movement trying to reunite the three parts of Armenia was met by the Ottoman Sultan Hamid ("The Red Sultan") with massive violence. Close to 300,000 Armenians were killed in Turkish Armenia between 1894 and 1896. This was, however, merely the prelude to an even greater assault by the Turks during the First World War.

The most traumatic event in Armenian history commenced in 1915 when the Turks initiated the killing of Armenians or their deportation to Syria and Palestine. On the night of 23 April 1915, political, religious, educational and intellectual leaders were rounded up and murdered. The same fate awaited Armenians who had been serving in the Ottoman army (Hovannisian 1981b: 29). It is now widely accepted (though still fiercely disputed by Turkish sources) that "close to one million" people – about one half of the Armenian population – were either killed or died of starvation during the 1915–16 period (Melson 1992: 146–7). If we add to this figure those who perished in the period up to 1922, "the number of Armenian dead may safely be put at around 1,500,000" (Lang & Walker 1987: 8). Much of the documentation recording the shocking events of 1915 was compiled by a young Oxford historian, Arnold Toynbee – subsequently to become one of the greatest scholars of world history. His services were secured by James Viscount Bryce, chairman of the Anglo-Armenian Association, who was determined to provide irrefutable evidence of the Turks' wrongdoing. Toynbee's (1916) collection of documents was given the imprimatur of the British government and was published in French the next year.

Toynbee's conclusions (1915, 1916) were both explicit and graphic. He made no bones about accusing the Turks of the perpetration of mass genocide and large-scale atrocities. "The river Euphrates changed its course for about 100 yards to a barrage of dead bodies", one witness claimed. Another, a German employee of the Baghdad Railway (quoted by Chaliand & Ternon 1983: 46), confirmed that this was not a momentary phenomenon:

> For the last month, corpses have been observed floating down the Euphrates, in twos tied back-to-back, or tied together by the arms in groups of three to eight. A Turkish officer who was posted to Djerablous, was asked why he did not have the corpses buried. He replied that no one had given him any orders to do so, and, in any case, it was impossible to establish whether the corpses were those of Muslims or Christians since their penises had been cut off. (The Muslims would have been buried but not the Christians.) The corpses stranded on the bank are devoured by dogs. Other bodies which had been cast up on the sand banks were the prey of vultures. . . . About 10,000 have arrived in Der-el-Zor, on the Euphrates, and so far there is no news of the others. It is said that those who have been

sent towards Mosul are to be sent to colonize land 25 kilo-
metres from the railway; that means they are to be driven
into the desert, where their extermination can be carried out
without witnesses.

The Turkish government's response to the mountain of testimony
describing its soldiers' genocidal actions was to suggest that the
government was merely putting down a revolt and to make the
even more implausible charge of Armenian massacres directed
against the Turks.[9] Nationalist Turkish politicians and state-
sponsored historians still vigorously refute that the genocide ever
took place. Internationally, they are joined in this absurd denial
only by Pakistan, presumably because of some misplaced sense
of Islamic solidarity.

Naturally, the Armenians who survived the massacres and forcible deportations consider themselves to have been victims of a
uniquely appalling crime. So it was. However, with the benefit of
hindsight, we can also see that 1915–16 provided a rehearsal for
the Nazi Holocaust with which it has indeed been systematically
compared.[10] The events of 1915–16 also bear some comparison
with later examples of mass displacements of peoples in the face of
intolerant nationalisms and ethnic particularisms. Although the
genocidal intentions are normally absent, there is a clear moral, if
not causal, connection between the Armenian deportations and
events like the mass displacements of the Palestinians by the Israelis in 1948, the population swaps between India and Pakistan in
1948–9, the tit-for-tat expulsions between Nigerians and Ghana-
ians, and the current "ethnic cleansing" of inconvenient groups
in the micro-states that emerged following the disintegration of
Yugoslavia.

After the massacres: Armenians at home and abroad

What happened to Armenia itself after the 1915–16 massacres?
To explain this outcome I briefly need to set the scene. The Turkish
government had been allied to Germany in the First World War,
but had made a poor showing against the Russians in the first
six months of 1916 when the tsarist armies had overrun Turkish

Armenia. Normally, this would have been a cause for Armenian celebration, but the Armenian volunteer units had been disbanded as a nationalist threat to the Russian empire, and the Armenians scattered in the victorious tsarist army found little but corpses and skeletons to greet them (Walker 1980: 243). In a secret Anglo-Russian deal, the tsar had secured British agreement to annex Turkish Armenia after the war. But all such calculations were rendered nugatory by the extraordinary events in Russia.

The Menshevik revolution in the spring of 1917 had allowed Armenians to seize a measure of self-determination and a precarious liberal-democratic state was born. However, the increasing demoralization of the Russian soldiers and the lure of the revolution led to mass desertions, while the Treaty of Brest-Litovsk, signed by Trotsky, left the Caucasian peoples to the mercies of the Germans and Turks. Bloody battles between the ultimately successful Turkish army and the desperately defending Armenians ensued, with considerable atrocities on both sides. Amid starvation, famine and deprivation, the Armenians hung on for "grim death", but by the end of 1920 all that was left of their "independent state" was Soviet Armenia, one-tenth of the imagined "Great Armenia".

The Armenians who survived the atrocities joined earlier communities in the Middle East, particularly in Lebanon, Syria, Palestine and Iran. But significant numbers were scattered further afield – to Ethiopia, the Far East, Latin America (particularly Argentina), Greece, Italy and England. By far the largest and most well established Armenian diasporic communities emerged in France and the USA. There is a confusing plethora of population statistics to choose from, but three counts of the distribution of the Armenians are shown in Table 2.1.

The discrepancies between the three columns are partly accounted for by population increases, but also by the difference in sources, with a tendency for some sources to count every last Armenian, however far they may have strayed from their grandparents' indelible identity – forged as it was in the fire of the genocide. Also not shown are the more recent movements of population from the Middle East and from the former Soviet Union after the fall of official communism in 1989. Whatever the exact numbers may be, the proportions are likely to be roughly accurate. As can

Table 2.1 Armenians worldwide.

Country	1966	1976	1985
Armenian SSR	2,000,000	2,600,000	3,000,000
Azerbaijan SSR	560,000	n.a.	560,000
Georgian SSR	550,000	n.a.	550,000
Russian SFSR	330,000	n.a.	360,000
Others	60,000	n.a.	n.a.
USSR minus			
Armenian SSR	n.a.	1,400,000	1,610,000
Total USSR	3,500,000	4,000,000	4,610,000
USA and Canada	450,000	500,000	800,000
Turkey	250,000	n.a.	70,000
Iran	200,000	n.a.	200,000
France	200,000	n.a.	300,000
Lebanon	180,000	n.a.	200,000
Syria	150,000	n.a.	100,000
Argentina	n.a.	n.a.	100,000
Others	570,000	n.a.	233,000
Total (rest of the world)	2,000,000	n.a.	2,003,000
Total worldwide	5,500,000	n.a.	6,613,000

Sources: For 1966 figures, Lang & Walker (1987: 12); for 1976 figures, Schahgaldian cited Suny 1993: Note 3 to Chapter 13); for 1985 figures, Armen et al. (1987: 33)

readily be observed, considerable numbers of Armenians live in the former USSR outside Soviet Armenia, most of them in the adjacent Caucasian states. This was because of both historical settlement patterns and the relative freedom to migrate internally in the period of the USSR's existence. Armenians continue to live in Turkey and the Middle East, while significant and increasing diasporic communities have settled in France and the United States. The US Armenians are particularly successful in economic terms and are said to have a per capita standard of living higher than any other Armenian diasporic community and one that compares favourably with other well placed ethnic groups in the USA.

I have space to comment only on the two biggest and most influential Armenian diasporic communities outside the former USSR – those in the USA and France. There are perhaps three striking features of the Armenian diaspora in the USA – the relative public silence of the community until the mid-1970s, the more public role played since that time, and the growth of a powerful set of internal social and cultural organizations. Some of the initial silence was clearly a reflection of psychosocial trauma, known in more general terms as "survivor syndrome". The survivors often felt guilty and undeserving of their chance good luck. They were laden with unresolved anger and found it difficult to enjoy their freedom and material success – it was as if their enjoyment would court another disaster and more misfortune, or would have been an insult to the dead (Boyajian and Grigorian 1991). Acute psychological states – reactive depression, anhedonia, hyperaesthesia and nightmares – have been widely reported by survivors, but even if we ignore these more extreme reactions, it is noticeable that the first and much of the second generation of Armenian-Americans adopted a privatized, inward-looking world of apparent conformity to the assimilationist ethic, *together with* a strong sense of difference, which was rarely displayed in the public domain.

Some of these confused feelings of acceptance and wariness emerge in an apparently autobiographical account provided by the Californian-born writer of Armenian descent, William Saroyan. He recalls (1962: 87–8) his school days in Fresno and a dialogue with his teacher, Miss Chamberlain. She had reprimanded him for speaking Armenian in class and making the other pupils laugh. Was he making fun of her?

> "No, we just like to talk Armenian once in a while, that's all."
> "But why? This is America, now."
> "The Americans don't like us, so we don't like them."
> "So that's it. Which Americans don't like you?"
> "All of them."
> "Me?"
> "Yes, you" . . . ["Americans always stick together"]
> "Well maybe we do, but then this *is* America, after all."
> "But we're here, too, now, and if you can't stand the only way we can be Americans, too, we'll go right on being Armenians."

The shift to a more public airing of the community's distinctive history can also be marked by a literary event – namely the publication of Michael J. Arlen (junior's) well known book *Passage to*

Ararat (1976). Michael Arlen senior (1895–1956), born Dikran Kouyoumdjian, was the son of a Bulgarian Armenian merchant who changed his name to gain acceptance in the English literary set. A friend of D. H. Lawrence and author of a highly successful novel called *The green hat* (1926), he was seen as the epitome of a successful assimilationist who had turned his back on the past and had found recognition and acceptance in his new environment.[11] The publication of Arlen junior's book is often seen as a refutation of his father's attempt at assimilation and, with it, the public passivity but private torment of the Armenian community. It helped to galvanize the US Armenian community into making the difficult journey back to the past and to assume its political identity. Some of this new found energy went into extremism and wild acts of terrorism triggered by the assassination of a Turkish diplomat in Santa Barbara in 1973 by a 77-year-old survivor of the 1915–16 massacres. Attacks on other diplomats, on the Turkish airline and on Turkish property followed. Although all rationalizations for terrorism are morally suspect, it is easy to see that the 60-year silence about the genocide and the obstinate denials of the Turkish government were at some point going to provoke open rage rather than resignation and repressed anger.

A more considered response by the emerging generation was to build on the very considerable community organizations that had survived into exile or been newly created. Of these the Armenian Apostolic Church and the Dashnak party (the "federal", anti-Soviet revolutionary party, which was in power in the brief period of independence in 1918–20) are pre-eminent. The Dashnaks threw a spanner in the works when they provoked a split in the Church in 1933, arguing that the newly elected Catholicos was a communist puppet. Most of these rifts were healed by the need for a united, non-sectarian committee to organize the commemorative events of 1975 and 1985 – the sixtieth and seventieth anniversaries of the genocide. To these inherited institutions have been added organizations that grew up in the diaspora itself, such as the Armenian General Benevolent Union, the Armenian Assembly of America, the Armenian Historical Research Association, the Zoryan Institute, the Hairenik and Baikar Associations of Boston, the Armenian Relief Society, and a host of others too numerous to mention. Much of this activity, particularly in educational and charity work, is promoted by wealthy Armenian patrons, including substantial foundations like the Calouste Gulbenkian Foundation. There are five Armenian newspapers in the USA, eleven day-schools and many clubs and recreational activities promoted by the Armenian churches.

However, perhaps the most important recent change in this organizational activity has been the growth of a powerful Armenian political lobby in Washington. Armenian organizers in the USA have sponsored a Bill in Congress to declare 24 April (the beginning of the massacres) a national day of remembrance of "man's inhumanity to man". They have learned from, and made common cause with, the Jewish-American lobby, sponsoring joint exhibitions, conferences and publications. They have, as I shall explain more fully below, taken full advantage of the changing geopolitics at the end of the Cold War and seem to have found in Senator Robert Dole (the Republican leader in Congress and presidential candidate) a powerful friend. (It is said that he was treated by an Armenian-American surgeon after suffering grievous war wounds.)

What of the Armenian diaspora in France? Boyajian and Grigorian (1991: 183) suggest that one difference between the Jewish and Armenian diasporas is that "with rare exceptions the entire Armenian Community of the world is composed of survivors or their progeny. All were touched by the massacres". This observation is less true of the Armenians in France, who have a long history of settlement. (For example, the last king of Armenia is buried in St Denis.) The pre-1915 migration history, together with the strong assimilating tendencies of the French revolutionary tradition, have led to a more complex identity-formation among Armenians in France. A subtle reading of this is provided by Martine Hovanessian (1992) who contrasts the Jacobin assimilationist tendency in France with the opposing philosophical principle, the "right to be different". This tension between these two trajectories is acutely sensed in the third generation because of the economic success of their parents and grandparents, because of the secularization of the community – few are regular churchgoers – and because 80 per cent of the current generation no longer speak Armenian.

The desire to reaffirm an Armenian identity, or more strictly to affirm a double Franco-Armenian identity, is primarily related to two exogenous circumstances. First, the French state and its social institutions began to yield a little under the impact of a substantial number of North Africans and other recent immigrants who simply refused to bow to the Jacobin tradition. This allowed earlier "recalcitrant" groups like the Jews to breathe a little more easily and also permitted at least a cultural and intellectual affirmation of Armenian identity. Secondly, in the world "out there" fundamental crises and changes were facing Armenians. The civil war in Lebanon in the 1970s generated a number of refugees who chose to come to France (France had governed the country from 1920 to 1956 and its cultural influence, particularly among the Lebanese Christians, was always strong). In 1975 and 1985 worldwide commemorations of the genocide were held. Three years later, in 1988, a massive earthquake shook Soviet Armenia, and the French Armenians were mobilized to send aid and money. Shortly afterwards, communism in the Soviet Union collapsed and by 1990 an independent state had been declared.

Young Franco-Armenians did not react by immediately identifying with the new state, affirming a "Greater Armenia", or promoting a return movement. Rather, an interesting new kind of ethnicity emerged – a kind of cultural recovery (cf. Hall 1991a) based on narrative, a memory of collective suffering in earlier generations and on a sense of empathy with Armenians outside France. The essence of this ethnicity was that it was *deterritorialized*, still affirming of France, its citizenship, culture and language, but also proclaiming a new "virtual" community that stretched beyond the French frontiers.

Soviet Armenia and after

As noted earlier, all that had been left of historic Armenia by the end of 1920 was a small impoverished Soviet Socialist Republic (strictly the SSR constitution was not adopted until 1922). It was a slim basis on which to recreate a homeland, but for once the geopolitics of the area worked in the Armenians' favour. Between the wars the Soviet Union saw Transcaucasia as a strategic area protecting its southern flank, a role that if anything was increased after the Second World War, when Turkey became a key forward point for NATO and the Cold War. While acknowledging that Beria "decimated the leading Party cadres in Armenia", as he did elsewhere, Lang (1978: 290–1) was enthusiastic about the Soviet Union's trusteeship of Armenia:

> The social and economic life of Soviet Armenia made rapid strides. ... Following World War II new factories and research laboratories have been opened up almost every month. ... No one visiting Erevan, Leninakan and other cities of Soviet Armenia can fail to be struck by the general air of bustle, and the active pace of industrial and domestic construction work continually in progress.

Are these the observations of a naïve observer? Are there some data that suggest a reasonable degree of commitment to the homeland even during the period of the communist leadership? I can adduce the following. Some 300,000 Armenians served in the Red Army in the Second World War, many with considerable distinction. After the war Armenians came "home" in considerable numbers from Turkey, Persia and the Lebanon, some 100,000 from the Middle East alone. Even during the Cold War, groups of diasporic Armenians made up the largest number of tourists. However, perhaps the clearest indication of wellbeing is in the dramatically increasing population of Soviet Armenia. Some of this is accounted for by increasing longevity (officially measured at 73 years in 1985) and better health care, but most of the increase has to be attributed to voluntary return migration. If the USSR population censuses (cited Lang & Walker 1987: 9) are to be believed, the population of Soviet Armenia increased by two and a half times from 1,320,000 inhabitants in 1940 to 3,317,000 people in 1985.

Despite this evidence of the rebuilding of Soviet Armenia, the diasporic Armenian communities remained strongly divided – impelled in one direction by a deep suspicion of an old enemy, Russia, and (particularly in France and the United States) by the anti-communist policies of their countries of settlement. A contrary pull evoked pride in the achievements of their homeland within the Soviet empire, imperfect and incomplete as that undoubtedly was. The ideological divides wrought by the Cold War were set aside, first in response to the human tragedy of the earthquake in

Armenia in 1988, when millions of dollars of aid poured into the country from the diaspora, and secondly when, with the end of the Cold War, the prospect dawned for a more open and public identification between the Republic of Armenia (proclaimed in 1990) and the Armenian diaspora. Some returned to serve in the new government; many invested in the future of the new independent state.

There is one large blot on this landscape. Unlike the benign form of territorialized identification shown by young French Armenians, some groups in the diaspora with long memories and bitter hearts decided that now was the time to recommence the long march towards Greater Armenia. First in their sights was Nagorno-Karabakh, the Armenian enclave within Azerbaijan. The pressure to reintegrate the enclave started with a demonstration in the spring of 1988 when 20,000 people walked around the streets of Erevan shouting "Karabakh, Karabakh!" The Armenian-dominated Soviet of Deputies in Karabakh voted 110 to 17 in favour of being transferred to Armenia. The cry was soon taken up in the diaspora. Telethons and political fund-raising drives were organized, and individual donations poured in. In one Californian telethon in February 1994, the Dashnaks raised $1.5 million (*Financial Times*, 16 September 1994). The donations financed not only food and clothing, but also arms and ammunition. The political lobby also cranked into action, successfully pressing the US government to impose sanctions on Azerbaijan. With money and effective political support from the diaspora, the annexation of Nagorno-Karabakh to Armenia seems inevitable. Will this be the start of an expansionist policy by an independent Armenia?

Conclusion

We have seen that both Africans and Armenians conform well to the special attributes of a victim diaspora and the more general features of all diasporas. Although there was a greater element of voluntary migration from Africa than is often adduced, and the process was rather lengthy, both experienced a decisive "break event" in their histories – slavery in the first case and the 1915–16 massacres in the second. Both diasporas were widely dispersed and both clung on to a collective memory and myth about the homeland, its location and its achievements. For Africans "homeland" centred around Ethiopia, an entity with both real and fuzzy frontiers constructed as much from legend as from history. For Armenians, although the biblical reference to Noah's ark landing on Ararat carries some significance, a great effort has been made to anchor a "great tradition" in archaeological and historical studies. Celebratory studies (for example, Azarpay 1968, Nersessian 1969, Lang 1978) have lovingly recreated the art, artefacts, buildings, churches, language, script, religious traditions and literature of a great historical nation. None the less, one more cynical account of Armenian history cites the adage that "a nation is a group of persons united by a common error about their ancestry and a common dislike of their neighbours" (cited Suny 1993: 22).

Both diasporas have sought to maintain the safety and prosperity of their homelands and have shown solidarity when they were in danger. Notable acts of solidarity were displayed by Africans when the Italians invaded Ethiopia and by Armenians in response to the events in Soviet Armenia after 1988. A substantial return movement existed in both cases, although, except when there was involuntary migration from the Middle East to Soviet Armenia, the numbers involved were not great. Most of the remaining criteria also seem to be congruous. A strong ethnic group consciousness, a troubled relationship with host societies (less evident among non-Middle Eastern Armenians), a sense of empathy with other co-ethnic members, and the possibility of an enriching, creative life in the diaspora (perhaps more evident in the African case) – all apply to the two victim diasporas considered here. This is not to say that other diasporas would not qualify for the adjective "victim" – the Irish and Palestinians are two examples that immediately come to mind. However, of the diasporas so far covered, the horrific experiences of the Armenians and Africans bear the most direct comparison with the victim aspects of the Jewish diaspora.

THREE

Labour and imperial diasporas: Indians and British

In Chapter 1, I suggested that instead of arising from a traumatic dispersal, a diaspora could be caused by the expansion from a homeland in search of work, in pursuit of trade or to further colonial ambitions. These circumstances give rise respectively to a labour diaspora, a trade diaspora and an imperial diaspora. In this chapter I am concerned with the first and third categories (trade diasporas are discussed in Chapter 4). I have taken as my central example of a labour diaspora the Indian indentured workers deployed in British, Dutch and French tropical plantations from the 1830s to about 1920. The Italians who made the transatlantic crossing, mainly to the USA and Argentina, in the late nineteenth and early twentieth centuries form another possible candidate group (see Gabaccia 1992, Baily 1995).[1] Labour diasporas were, it has been argued, also constituted by the Turks and North Africans who entered Europe in the period after the Second World War (see Castles & Kosack 1985; Cohen 1987: 111–44; Esman 1994: 176–215).

Clearly, it would be stretching the term to suggest that all groups who migrate internationally in search of work evolve into a diaspora.[2] Where essentially we are talking of individual, family or small group migration for the purposes of settlement, a diasporic consciousness may not develop, particularly if the immigrants concerned both intend to assimilate and are readily accepted. If, however, among overseas workers there is evidence of (a) a strong retention of group ties sustained over an extended period (in respect of language, religion, endogamy and cultural norms), (b) a myth of and strong connection to a homeland, and (c) high levels of social exclusion in the destination societies, a labour diaspora can be said to exist. Weiner (1986: 48) is even more restrictive, confining the notion of a labour diaspora to those who "move across international borders to work in one country while remaining citizens in another". His bifurcation works particularly clearly in the five countries of the Gulf (Kuwait, Qatar, Bahrain, the United Arab Emirates and Oman), which use vast numbers of foreign workers but resolutely deny them or their children the right of citizenship even through long residence or birth.

A more specialized use of the cognate expression "proletarian diaspora" can be found in Armstrong (1976). She uses the term in contrast to a "mobilized diaspora" whose members deploy their linguistic, network and occupational advantages to modernize and mobilize – thereby offering to the nation-state valued services and skills. By contrast, a proletarian diaspora is characterized by limited communication skills and comprises "a nearly undifferentiated mass of unskilled labor" (p. 405), with little prospect of social mobility. In a sense, Armstrong's proletarian diaspora is a negative category – a group that has proved itself incapable of becoming an entrepreneurial "mobilized diaspora".

There are two important qualifications to note here, one of which is also recognized by Armstrong. First, within all diasporas, including the most economically successful, there are (sometimes large) proletarian elements. The emigrants from the Jewish Pale of Settlement included a high percentage of unskilled workers, although they were generally successful in using the labour movement or a high level of self-exploitation, to climb out of abject poverty (Epstein 1969, Green 1995). The Armenians of Istanbul are another example noticed by Armstrong. Generally thought of as a wealthy section of the diaspora, they none the less included a large proportion of people working as porters and in other menial occupations.

The second qualification is that over time, occupational mobility can radically alter a group's profile. Two of Armstrong's exemplars of a proletarian diaspora are the Poles and Italians of interwar France who were predominantly concentrated in low-paying jobs and spoke French poorly. Although there still may be some clustering at the bottom of the occupational pile, it would be difficult to sustain this view of these two groups in the post-war period. In a similar way Italians, who were previously largely circulatory migrants, began increasingly to join the mainstream of society in the Americas after 1918 (Gabaccia 1988).

In my own principal example of a labour diaspora – the indentured Indian workers employed on the tropical plantations of the European colonial possessions – there is a more mixed picture of the changes wrought by time and circumstance. In some countries, Indians showed dramatic gains in terms of their political and social mobility. In others, dispossession and poverty continued. I anticipate my story, however. The only conceptual point to reiterate here is that diasporas are rarely uniform in class terms at the moment of their migration, nor do they remain so over time.

A new system of slavery?

The history of intercontinental migration is as much a history of the transport of unfree labourers by others as it is about the propulsion of independent labourers, employees, entrepreneurs and professionals moving by their own volition. I use the expression "as much" not in a statistical sense (because in the modern world system legally free migrants have far outnumbered coerced workers) but in terms of the political, economic and social significance of such workers.[3] Unfree labour was of crucial importance to the evolution of the modern world system. The key European mercantile powers underwrote their trading empires by the production of tropical commodities and the extraction of precious metals. The means they chose was the introduction of mass slavery and coerced labour to the Americas. The "triangular trade" between Europe, Africa and the Americas was the lusty infant that was to mature as modern world capitalism. Slave labour in the plantations of the Caribbean, the southern states of the USA and Brazil, and *repartimiento* labour in Spanish America, provided the mother's milk to the newborn baby. But after the collapse of slavery, the new milch cow was indentured labour. The switch in the form of labour also involved a switch in the sourcing of the labour supply, from Africa to Asia.

Most indentured labourers (about 1.4 million in all) were recruited from India, their time of recruitment, distribution and destinations being recorded in Table 3.1. The data also include the numbers in the countries of migration in 1980. I must make at least two interpretive comments on the table. The figures for East Africa in 1980 show a sudden fall from the previous decade because of the expulsion of Asians by President Idi Amin of Uganda in 1972. (In 1970, there were 182,000 Indians in Kenya and 76,000 in Uganda. By 1980 there were only 430 Indians left in Uganda.) Secondly, where there are dramatic leaps in numbers in the last column compared with the previous column, as in South Africa, this is sometimes accounted for by the subsequent free immigration of merchants and professionals, as well as of course by natural increases.

Table 3.1 Indentured Indian workers and Indian population, 1980.

Colony/Country	Period	Indentured workers	Indian pop. 1980
Mauritius	1834–1912	453,063	623,000
British Guiana /Guyana	1838–1917	238,909	424,400
Natal (South Africa)	1860–1911	152,184	750,000
Trinidad	1845–1917	143,939	421,000
Réunion	1829–1924	118,000	125,000
Fiji	1879–1916	60,969	300,700
Guadaloupe	1854–85	42,326	23,165
Kenya & Uganda	1895–1901	39,771	79,000
Jamaica	1854–85	36,420	50,300
Dutch Guiana/ Suriname	1873–1916	34,000	124,900
Martinique	1854–89	25,509	16,450
Seychelles	1899–1916	6,319	n.a.
St Lucia	1858–95	4,350	3,700
Grenada	1856–85	3,200	3,900
St Vincent	1861–80	2,472	5,000
Total		1,361,431	2,952,495

Source: Clarke et al. (1990: 9)

The extensive movement of Indians to faraway tropical plantations provides an instructive reminder of how far the planters were prepared to go in keeping their two desiderata for profitable production – abundant land and cheap labour. The recruiters were ruthless, the journey was horrific and the arrangements made for the legal protection of the workers were inadequate. The indenture was for a fixed period, usually for five or seven years. Many of the indentured Indians were physically moved into the slave barracks of the former African slaves – a poignant reminder of why they were there. The basic conditions are summarized by Parekh (1994: 605): the indentured worker "lived on the plantation which he was forbidden to leave without a pass, worked unlimited hours, was barred from taking any other employment, and in case of misconduct subjected to financial penalty and physical punishment. In return he received a basic pay, free accommodation, food rations, and a fully or partially paid return passage to India".

In his influential account Tinker (1974), quoting Lord John Russell, characterizes indentured labour as "a new system of slavery". Despite the evidence that the planters saw Indian indentured labour as directly substitutable for slave labour, the analogy with slavery can be taken too far. Legally, the indentured workers and their offspring could not be bought or sold. Moreover, for some poverty-stricken Indians, intercontinental migration provided a window of opportunity for social mobility that the rigid caste system inhibited, but did not totally prevent. A common in-group joke among contemporary Indo-Trinidadians is that while there were no Brahmins when the ships set out from Calcutta, by the time they arrived in Port of Spain (Trinidad) several gentlemen had assumed a haughty, priestly mien. Indenture also offered a free or sponsored return passage at the end of the contract, an option taken up by only 25 per cent of the Indians taken to the Caribbean (Vertovec 1995) and by 33 per cent in some other territories. The majority either reindentured with the promise of free land or saved their pennies to buy land at the end of their indentures.

The dual aspect of oppression and the hint of better things to come is well captured by the poet, David Dabydeen, in this extract from his *Coolie Odyssey* (Dabydeen and Samaroo 1987: 281), which graphically conjures up the arrival of the indentured Indians in Georgetown, Guyana:

The first boat chugged to the muddy port
Of King George's Town.

Coolies came to rest
In El Dorado.
Their faces and best saris black with soot.
The men smelled of saltwater mixed with rum.
The odyssey was plank between river and land,
Mere yards but months of plotting
In the packed bowel of a white man's boat
The years of promise, years of expanse.
At first the gleam of green land and the white folk and the
　Negroes,
The earth streaked with colour like a toucan's beak,
Kiskidees flame across a fortunate sky
Canefields ripening the sun
Wait to be gathered in armfuls of gold

The songs of *Ramayana* and political outcomes

Did the Indian labourers abroad constitute themselves as a diaspora? A veritable political minefield exists in trying to answer this question. Indian nationalists strongly object to any attempt to separate out the three main Indian ethnic/religious groups – Sikh, Hindu and Muslim – for they see this as feeding destructive communalist sentiments in India itself. Sikhs, by contrast, insist on their difference and, as we shall see in Chapter 5, can invoke a distinctive history of Sikh settlement abroad (mainly as soldiers in the colonial employ or as free farmers), an intimate bond with the Punjab and, for some, a commitment to an independent state of Khalistan free from Indian oppression. The Muslim/Hindu distinction was less acute in the early Indian diaspora, as both groups faced similar conditions and Muslims rarely constituted more than 15 per cent of the indentured workers.[4] Parekh (1994) hoists a flag for the argument that there were three features that were particular to Hindu indentured workers and that helped them to create a distinctive diasporic consciousness – the reconstitution of family life, their religious conviction in general and, more specifically, the adoption of the *Ramayana* as "the essential text of the Hindu diaspora".

The first aspect of the Hindu diaspora, the re-establishment of the family, was made difficult by the official policy of limiting the numbers of women allowed to between one and four for every ten men. Parekh (1994: 607) suggests that "a significant proportion of indentured women consisted of beggars, divorcees from lower castes, girls who had run away from homes, widows with low social status and even prostitutes". The enormous gender imbalance led to many breakdowns of normal family life. Women were passed around among several men, while there were endless opportunities for sexual jealousy and abuse. Wife-beatings, even wife-murders, were common. In Trinidad, over a period of just four years (1859–63), 27 Indian women were murdered by their enraged husbands. The relative scarcity of women has led one researcher to claim that under indenture "probably for the first time in their lives, [women] got an opportunity to exercise a degree of control over their sexual and social lives". However, she continued, men reasserted their control "through the reconstruction, albeit in a different setting, of the Indian patriarchal family system" (Reddock cited Beall 1990: 72–3). Given the level of abuse from Indian men, colonial officials and employers alike, it is probably an error to see the scarcity of women as that strong a bargaining counter. Scholarly consensus can be reached, however, in the observation that the Indian family was gradually reconstituted, often in an oppressive patriarchal form, but none the less in such a way as to provide a source of social cohesion and a site for reasserting communal life.

As for Hinduism as the religion of the diaspora, the Brahmins were at the forefront of the movement to reimpose a conventional ritualistic set of beliefs.[5] In some colonial settings, like that of the French Caribbean, they faced an uphill struggle in trying to confront the French demands for assimilation. The Christian missionaries also gained considerable numbers of adherents by combining their theological stick with the carrots of free education and the provision of orphanages. However, these were deviations from the norm. In general, orthodox forms of Hinduism became predominant in the diaspora and were the principal means whereby the Indian labour diaspora was reconnected to the "Great Tradition" of India. Even where the authority of the Brahmins was challenged, diasporic Hindus did not generate alternative *yogis*, ascetics, *acharyas* and pandits of their own (Parekh 1994: 612). Instead, they relied on missions from India to supply their religious needs – the Sai Baba and Hare Krishna movements, for example, gained a significant following in Fiji after that country's postcolonial intercommunal conflicts (Kelly 1995). Whether in orthodox or deviant forms, however, the vital attachment between diaspora and homeland had been re-established. "Mother India" had reached out to her children abroad.

The third constitutive aspect of the Hindu diaspora was the adoption of the *Ramayana* as the key religious text. This occurred, Parekh (1994: 613–14) maintains, for four reasons. First, the book's central theme was exile, suffering, struggle and eventual return – a clear parallel with the use of the Bible by religious and Zionist Jews. Secondly, the text is simple and didactic, with a clear distinction between good and evil, a useful simplification in the harsh world of the plantation. Thirdly, the *Ramayana* hammered home what the Brahmins and many conservative men wanted to hear. The eldest son should be dutiful, wives should be demure and obedient and clear roles should be defined for family interactions. Finally, as Hindu traditions go, the *Ramayana* was relatively casteless, but it especially stressed the virtues of the lower caste, namely physical prowess and economic resourcefulness.

While this emphasis on how the Hindu diaspora "made its world" provides a helpful contrast with the predominant scholarly concern of how the world was made for them, there were none the less some powerful extraneous pressures on the Indian diaspora that collectively, if not equally, afflicted all – Hindu or Muslim, men or women, Brahmin or Sudra. The indentured workers were housed in mass barracks, subjected to a harsh regime and separated from the rest of the society in which they found themselves. At the national level, indentured labourers and their offspring developed a troubled and often hostile relationship with the indigenous people and other migrant groups. The inter-ethnic tensions in countries like Guyana, Fiji, Uganda and South Africa provide cases in point.

Often, the issue of access to land and property started interethnic conflict, although there was a high degree of variation in the outcomes of the Indians' struggle for a "stake". In Mauritius, for example, the former African slaves were not very numerous, and at the end of slavery they scattered to small fishing villages and to the towns, leaving the plantations in the hands of the Franco-Mauritian elite. Gradually, Indians were able to extend their land claims and to promote a sizeable educated, professional class that was to inherit state power at independence. In Fiji, by contrast, when indenture came to an end in 1916, 83 per cent of the land was owned by indigenous Fijians, 10 per cent was Crown land and only 7 per cent was freehold. Indians were regarded as intruders for whom short-term leases were the most that could be conceded. In the post-independence period they suffered extensive discrimination at the hands of the Fijian political elite. In a consultation conference on the 1990 constitution, following intercommunal tensions, one of the Indo-Fijian delegates, Krishna Datt (1994: 90–1), made an impassioned plea to be allowed to have a permanent relationship with Fijian soil:

> Land has been raised as an issue very close to the hearts of Fijians. We have been told of the very special, almost spiritual, ties of the Fijian with land. For the Indo-Fijian the tie is no less. . . . A symbiotic relationship of love and balance develops between the Indo-Fijian household and the land. For four generations of Indo-Fijians, that land has now acquired a very special, sentimental and religious significance. . . . The Indo-Fijians have a saying about one's roots: "One's roots are where one's umbilical cord is buried". Mine is buried in that block of land in Mateniwai. Half of it is now "reserved", but we continue to use it. . . . The other half of the land is now on tenancy at will. If ever we were to lose that piece, something within me will have died. I will have lost my roots. That piece of land holds me here, provides me with a sense of identity.

The preoccupation of Indo-Fijians can, with modifications, be observed in the other overseas Indian communities of the Indian Ocean area (Thiara 1995). Those who found themselves in Natal were desperate to acquire urban property in Durban and Pietermaritzburg, an aspiration that was vigorously resisted by the white authorities. This was the issue on which a young Indian lawyer, Mahatma Gandhi, first cut his political teeth. While the Indian South Africans slowly secured a more agreeable economic situation, they were excluded from white political power and their relationship with indigenous Africans deteriorated, resulting in an outbreak of intercommunal violence in 1949. Indians in South African were thus thrust unwillingly into a "V", not of their own making. Turn right, towards the white regime, and they were rejecting their fellow victims of apartheid; turn left, in the direction of black solidarity, and they became frightened of losing what status, rights and property they had acquired. Perhaps, not surprisingly, many remained uneasily where they were, like rabbits trapped before the headlights of an oncoming car.

Difficult as it was, the Indian community's situation in South Africa was of a picnic compared with their plight in President Idi Amin's regime in post-independent Uganda. There they were the main targets of African economic nationalism. An emerging African petty bourgeoisie wanted their shops and houses, while the poor African customer was easily persuaded that Indian traders hoarded goods and charged high prices. The Indian community was forced into four choices: (a) stay where they were and adopt local citizenship, an option taken only by a handful; (b) return to Mother India; (c) move on to happier settings like North America (where new groups of South Asian professionals, academics and entrepreneurs were heading); or (d) throw themselves on the mercy of the imperial power, Britain. Those who chose the last option, unpropitious as it seemed at the time, have in fact made remarkable progress, such that their socio-economic profile is now well in advance of that of the indigenous British population (Robinson 1995).

Imperial diasporas

In Chapter 4 I discuss the role of the trade diasporas, a number of which flourished during the period of mercantile capital. In several instances, commercial contact was followed by the settlement and colonization of the areas the merchants penetrated. Some countries were strong enough to prevent colonization – China, for example, confined European and Japanese traders to special zones within the "treaty ports". But much of Asia and Africa was relatively easily overcome by imperialist adventurers, usually from

Europe, and often dragging their home governments behind them. A number of countries remained unsuitable for European settlement, either because of particular difficulties of subduing local rulers or because the climate was unsuitable. (At the independence day celebrations in Ghana, a toast was proposed to the mosquito, which had discouraged white settlement.) By contrast, the temperate zones were attractive to European settlers and large numbers of migrants volunteered, or were commandeered, to people the colonies. Where settlement for colonial or military purposes by one power occurred, an "imperial diaspora" can be said to have resulted.

Nearly all the powerful nation-states, especially in Europe, established their own diasporas abroad to further their imperial plans. The Spanish, Portuguese, Dutch, German, French and British colonists fanned out to most parts of the world and established imperial and quasi-imperial diasporas. "Quasi" because in a number of instances, localization or "creolization" occurred, with the new settlers marrying into the local community or turning against their homelands. The nationalist movements of Latin America were replete with leaders of Iberian descent who fought for freedom from Spain and Portugal. "The Liberator" Simón Bolívar, for example, led the independence movements of Venezuela, Colombia, Equador, Peru and Bolivia. An imperial diaspora, by contrast, is marked by a continuing connection with the homeland, a deference to and imitation of its social and political institutions and a sense of forming part of a grand imperial design – whereby the group concerned assumes the self-image of a "chosen race" with a global mission.[6]

The settlement of the British empire

Emigration from Britain from the seventeenth century onwards was one of the highest in volume and one of the longest in duration in the world. Given how extensive and lengthy this process was, it is hardly surprising that emigration took many forms. Some moved as exiles for religious or political reasons. Many, like the Irish famine migrants and those dispossessed in the "clearances" of the Scottish Highlands, were forced to leave by grinding poverty, rapacious landlords or unsympathetic officials and politicians. But the bulk of British emigrants left because new opportunities – land and work to be blunt – were available in greater measure than in the British Isles. Shepperson (1957: 6–7) put it this way: the great emigration, he suggests, cannot be explained alone by "urban confusion, rural destitution, political inequality, religious restrictions, social injustices or educational handicaps endured by a section of the populace". The British people "were sufficiently advanced to aspire to social and political recognition more commensurate with individual ability, and to demand reasonable opportunity for the fruition of their material and intellectual endeavours".

However complex and mixed the motives, there was an underlying thread of state involvement. An emigration plan was first hatched in a state paper delivered to James I by Bacon in 1606. He suggested that by emigration England would gain "a double commodity, in the avoidance of people here, and in making use of them there" (cited Williams 1964: 10). The poor rates and overpopulation would be relieved and idlers, vagrants and criminals would be put to good use elsewhere. Once established, the principle was extended to other parts of the British Isles. Scottish crofters, troublesome Irish peasants, dissident soldiers (like the Levellers) were all shipped out in pursuance of the idea that they were of greater use abroad than they were at home. Not even the reverses of British power in the United States were attributed to a design fault in its pro-emigration policies. Against the *laissez-faire* doctrine of the times, the state was prepared to be involved in emigration matters.

In the century between Waterloo (1814) and Sarajevo (1914), 17 million people emigrated from Britain, 80 per cent to North America. (The full extent of this migration can be gauged by the fact that the UK population in 1821 was 21 million.) The bulk of British migrants went to the United States and to what are sometimes described as "the colonies of settlement". These were New Zealand, Canada, Australia, former Rhodesia and South Africa. What linked these countries together was that most of them became "dominions" in a formal, legal sense between the two world wars, but the description can also be used more analytically, for it aptly captures the superordination the settlers and their metropolitan backers sought to assert over the indigenous populations.

The push for an imperial diaspora probably reached its intellectual apogee in the work of the Cambridge professor of history, Sir John Seeley, who identified emigration as the key means of effecting "the peculiarly English movement of unparalleled expansion" (Seeley 1895: 357–8). He was nevertheless critical of the inefficient way in which the movement was organized. The second part of his much-quoted aphorism is rather less well known than the first. After Britain "conquered half the world in a fit of absence of mind, it peopled it in a mood of lazy indifference", Seeley remarked. Other backers of the pro-emigration cause also urged vigorous action by the authorities. As early as 1832, the poet laureate Robert Southey argued that the Irish needed to be given emigration opportunities further afield than the mainland: "It is vain to hope for any permanent and extensive advantage from any system of emigration which does not primarily apply to Ireland, whose population, unless some other outlet be opened to them, must fill up every vacuum created in England or Scotland, and reduce the labouring classes to a uniform state of degradation and misery" (cited Shepperson 1957: 18).

While such musings were common to a number of commentators, the Scotsman, Thomas Carlyle (cited Marriott 1927: 7), provided an explicit blueprint for state-aided emigration in 1843:

> Why should there not be an Emigration Service? and Secretary with adjuncts, with funds, forces, idle Navy-ships, and ever-increasing apparatus: in fine an effective system of Emigration: so that . . . every honest willing workman who found England too straight . . . might find a bridge built to carry him into new Western Lands, there to organize with more elbow room some labour for himself? There to be a real blessing, raising new corn for us, purchasing new webs and hatchets from us; instead of staying here to be a Physical-Force Chartist unblessed and no blessing! . . . A free bridge for Emigrants . . . every willing worker that proved superfluous, finding a bridge ready for him. This verily will have to be done; the Time is big with this.

The time became even bigger with this in 1845 when the potato crop in Ireland failed, a tragic misfortune that could not easily be alleviated by importing staples from England – the wheat harvest collapsed in that year. With his repeal of the Corn Laws in 1846, Sir Robert Peel took the decisive step to open Britain to foreign food imports and in so doing started the policy of cheap imported food that has been at the heart of British politics ever since. Sir John Marriott (1927: 14), MP for York and at one time a lecturer and tutor in modern history and political science at Worcester College, Oxford, saw the negative consequences of this bold move. With the collapse of the rural economy came overpopulation, unemployment and widespread poverty and with it a massive propensity to emigration, voluntary or state-aided. But the die had been cast and more and more emigrants were needed to sustain the system:

> In the short span of 150 years England has become a land of mines, forges and factories. . . . We have become an urban and suburban people, depending for food and raw materials on imported commodities which the oversea Empire is supplying in increasing proportions, and which it could produce in much large quantity but for the lack of labour and capital.

The extent of emigration was so great that even supporters of the idea of an imperial diaspora became alarmed. One writer (cited Shepperson 1957: 67) in *Sharpes London Magazine* (1852) considered that emigration:

> is a medicine that may do a great deal of good, and which, at the same time must be administered with as much caution as any drug which poisons by gradually debilitating. Our people are our life's blood, and yet we appear to be dangerously easy on the subject of losing them . . . What is the almost universal cry of the sons and daughters of England? Emigration. What is the advice that England gives to her distressed children? Emigrate. . . . That one word rings on the platforms of public assemblies, echoes through the walls of literary institutions, stares one in the face in colossal placards, thrusts itself into one's hand in the form of tailors' outfitting advertisements. It is the consolation of the idle, the refuge of the unhappy and the industrious, the watchword alike of the agitator and the philanthropist. . . . It is

our scapegoat for everything that vice, folly, or public mismanagement had brought upon us – an Alsatian for rogues
of our own creation – a Slough of Despond, into which
England may cast a little too much.

As this author indicated, the idea and promise of migration had
filtered down to all sections of the British population. In terms of
their order of magnitude, self-sponsored migration was the most
important, followed by government-supported, charity-sup-
ported, destination country-supported and trade union-supported
movements.[7] Recent research has laid more emphasis on how, even
in the context of government-supported schemes, financial and
moral support from friends, family and the wider working-class
community were necessary to effect plans for emigration. Without
this help, Richards (1993: 253) convincingly argues, it would be
impossible to explain how "some of the poorest elements in the
British Isles were able to reach the most distant of the nineteenth-
century emigrant destinations".

Emigration studies "from below" are certainly likely to have a
greater explanatory power for migration flows than the preoccupation with official and charity schemes, but the latter none the less
illustrate official and humanitarian concerns. For example, the settlement of Australia by the British was regarded as an absolute
priority by strategic thinkers because of the virtual certainty that
Asia would be seeking what the Germans were later to call *lebens-
raum*. The race between Britain and Asia was on. Marriott (1927:
41) quotes Lord Northcliffe on his visit to Australia to this effect:
"The key to your White Australia ideal is population. You must
increase your slender garrison by the multiplication of your people. Only numbers will save you. The world will not tolerate an
empty Australia. This continent must carry its full quota of people.
. . . You have no option. Tens of millions will come to you whether
you like it or not." As to voluntary bodies, there were at least two
dozen private agencies to assist settlement of adults (including, for
example, the Catholic Emigration Committee, the Salvation Army,
the Society for the Overseas Settlement of British Women, the British Dominions Emigration Society) and 14 societies targeting juvenile emigration (including the Child Emigration Society, Dr
Barnardo's Homes, the Church Army and the Church of England's

Waifs and Strays Society). Special schemes, often endorsed and subsidized by the British and dominion governments, proliferated. One that caught my eye because of George Orwell's subsequent satirical use of the phrase, was the Big-Brother Scheme to Australia. Started in 1924, the idea was that well established Australian citizens would agree to act as a Big Brother to a Little Brother from the homeland. Boys between the ages of 14 and 19 were eligible for this scheme, but they had to have a school certificate (up to Standard 6), a health certificate and a testimonial of good character. Despite its inventiveness, by 1927 only 600 Little Brothers had made the trip.[8]

Empire settlement also provided an outlet for "distressed gentlewomen", often left penniless by the common pattern of inheritance to the eldest son. Over the period 1899–1911, 1,258,606 women emigrated from Britain, many of them single and "a surprising number in middle-class occupations, such as clerks, teachers or professionals" (Hammerton 1979: 177). The movement for encouraging emigration by respectable women had powerful supporters. Edward Gibbon Wakefield, in *A view of the art of colonization* (1849) deplored the plight of women of the "uneasy" or "anxious" classes whom he thought were the very stuff needed in the colonies. They would favourably affect the dubious manners and morals of the colonists, spread religion and avoid being condemned to a reluctant barren spinsterhood. The women emigrants themselves were rather divided in their reactions to their new opportunities. One successful woman emigrant to Australia, Mrs Charles Clacy, published a best selling book in 1853 recommending emigration to her English sisters on the grounds that they would find themselves "treated with twenty times the respect and consideration you might meet with in England" (cited Hammerton 1979: 115). This view was in marked contrast to one Rosa Payne who wrote from Melbourne in 1869 to warn that "no one with the tastes, habits, or feelings of a lady should ever come out to Australia, it may do for mediocre governesses who can put up with the roughness, or I should say vulgarity of mind and great want of intellect but I would never advise a lady to try it" (cited p. 57).

In many ways the policy-makers were naïve about the likely outcomes of fostering a successful imperial diaspora. They assumed, for example, that trade flows would always be bi-directional, between motherland and diaspora. Marriott (1927: 71) earnestly made the calculation that while "every inhabitant of Canada buys British goods to the value of £2 18s 11d, each citizen of the United States buys only 9s worth. Thus every Canadian is worth to us as a customer more than six Americans". The presumption of loyalty to Britain in times of need was also assumed. Morale-boosting claims made that there were "no fewer than 6000 old Barnardo boys" fighting in the Canadian forces during the First World War (p. 61) lent further legitimacy to the idea that homelands and dominions were one in spirit and in political allegiance.

And lest the press for mass emigration from below be diverted into the wrong direction, pro-diaspora journals warned would-be emigrants against going to the USA, in case Britons should "cut themselves off from the great and good olive tree". In 1840, the *Colonial Magazine* (cited Shepperson 1957: 254) put it like this.

> Our advice is to emigrate to one of the British Colonies. There you have the laws, language and customs of your youth; you preserve an identity of interest with the parent state, and, under a wise system of colonial government, must ere long be adopted, you are still a citizen of the British empire, and a part of that great Christian kingdom to which it is a pride and an honour to belong.

As for the wretched Americans, the same magazine rather implausibly asserted that they bitterly regretted casting off the parent country. When the *Great Western* liner anchored in New York, the magazine claimed, the:

> intelligent and noble-minded populace fell into great lamentations, crying "England! revered England!! great England!!! – land of my fathers, how I love thy very name; thy age commands my respect, thy power my admiration; I claim to be thy scion, yet feel myself to be an alien: would that I could return again into thy bosom.

The end of the dominion diaspora

Unfortunately for the imperial planners, many in the dominions could see no good reason to return, or even to stay close to Britannia's bosom. Essentially, the dominion diaspora was to fall victim to the very success of the colonial settlements. In some places, like South Africa, the British imperial diaspora was but one of the claimants for political hegemony – alongside the Boers and the indigenous Africans. Elsewhere, as British hegemony was established, powerful and wealthy farmers, professionals and industrialists began to emerge among the new immigrants themselves. They were to challenge the homeland and assert their right to tax, to trade and to legislate as they chose.

The Boston Tea Party, beloved of school history books, and the consequential loss of the American colonies, were the most celebrated and ultimately the most momentous examples of this phenomenon, but the hints of a similar rift were apparent even in more quiescent dominions. For example, during a trade dispute in 1903, six English hatters were held up in Melbourne harbour and denied permission to land. The affair was soon settled, but anti-Pommie sentiments had been aroused and they led the *Sydney Bulletin* (cited Marriott 1927: 76–7) to editorialize as follows:

> The right of Australia in fact has been established, definitely to keep out of this continent English-born citizens, if in her own interest she so chooses. . . . What is important is the fact that Australia has proved her power to keep Australia for the Australians, and for such immigrants as Australians choose to welcome and has shown that an Englishman is not necessarily welcome because he is an Englishman. The six hatters have made history.

A number of dominion diasporas established their right to self-government, although in each case (like in the USA) with deleterious effects to the indigenous population. The British settlers in Australia killed the Aborigines and virtually destroyed their way of life; the colonists in New Zealand crippled Maori culture; the Canadians forced the Inuit people into reservations. To each of these three countries the British government accorded formal

Dominion status – i.e. self-government and a franchise to the settlers – while showing only token regard for the native peoples. In all the dominions, a "British" identity became hegemonic. English and Welsh law, the English language, the Anglican Church, English sporting traditions,[9] and Westminster-style political institutions either became paramount or were accorded a high status. Settlers fared less well in the remaining colonies to which the British migrated. In Kenya, the Mau Mau put paid to a wild attempt by the tiny settler group to declare "white independence"; instead decolonization placed power in the hands of the black elite. In Rhodesia, Ian Smith managed to sustain a Unilateral Declaration of Independence for about a decade, but he too was finally laid low by the force of an armed African struggle.

In South Africa, that most difficult of countries to classify and typologize, the construction of a pure dominion society was inhibited by the contrary pulls of Boer and British ambitions (demonstrated by the Anglo-Boer War of 1899–1902), and by the counterforce of African arms. Whereas the Boers organized successful shooting parties against the helpless San and Khoi-khoi (known in politically incorrect days as the Bushmen and Hottentots), the Zulu *impi*s proved rather more formidable opponents to the British army. The fate of settler society in South Africa now hangs in the balance. Whereas the European population's political monopoly is now nearly at an end, its social and economic dominance is nevertheless likely to remain important.[10]

The relationship between the British at home and their dominion–diaspora abroad had been cemented by ties of kinship, economic interdependence and preferential trade arrangements, by sport, by visits and tourism, and by the solidarity wrought by the sharing of arms in two world wars and other encounters like the Korean conflict. Until quite recently, many New Zealanders, Canadians, Australians and white South Africans and Rhodesians/ Zimbabweans stubbornly clung on to British passports as a means of affirming their British identity and hedging their political bets. Young men and women from the British diaspora abroad still often spend a *rite de passage* year in England. (They concentrate with a remarkable lack of imagination in Earls Court in London: the nearest area between Heathrow and central London with a large rental market.) Education, legal training and certification also bonded the dominions (and the Commonwealth more generally) to "the mother country". One small example is the Rhodes scholarship programme, which draws young men from the white dominions and the United States to Rhodes House in Oxford. The programme was endowed by the famous British imperialist to celebrate the achievements of the imperial diaspora and to secure a cohort of key administrators for the empire. (After protests in the 1980s from former scholars a small number of black and female Commonwealth scholars were accorded recognition.) The attempt to cling to a unified British home and diasporic identity defined primarily by descent and racial phenotype was, however, to be severely challenged on a number of fronts. First (as was shown in the illustration of the Rhodes scholars), it proved difficult to be too racially specific – the wider Commonwealth comprised a brown and black empire as well as the zones of white settlement. Secondly, with the post-war movement of Commonwealth citizens from India, Pakistan and the Caribbean to Britain, it became increasingly difficult to uphold the idea that a British identity was exclusively a white identity. Despite various attempts in British nationality and immigration legislation designed to buttress a racially based British identity, which fused white Britons to their diaspora in the dominions, a third and final factor undercut any neat correspondence between Britishness and whiteness. I allude to seismic shifts in the post-war international political economy, which impacted both on the UK and on the white British diaspora. The UK's historic decision to enter the European Economic Community (now the European Union) swept away any realistic possibility (though not the pretence) that it could maintain an independent world role. Public rhetoric that Commonwealth interests would be safeguarded was recognized, even at the time, as empty and tokenistic.

Events of similar impact were affecting the old white dominions. For the Canadians, already heavily intermeshed with the USA, signing the North American Free Trade Agreement in 1991 was seen as a sad though inevitable result of their geopolitical situation. The minority British diasporic communities in Zimbabwe, and increasingly in South Africa, are gradually being corralled into accepting black majority rule. Thousands, perhaps even tens of thousands, may take up their opportunity to live in the UK, but over the next generation many will lose their "patrial" rights and will slowly adopt a single, local citizenship. Australia and New Zealand still have close cultural, familial, sporting and linguistic ties to "the mother country", but the entry of the UK into the European Economic Community represented a brutal familial rupture. Wool, butter and lamb exports were immediately affected, but the abandonment of the Commonwealth as an economic unit also had a profound psychological effect, particularly in Australia. Prime Minister Keating's angry outburst in April 1992 that Britain had deserted Australia in the Second World War by its precipitate withdrawal from the Far East was yet another slash at the old umbilical cord. New Australians from southern Europe and Asia rarely share the British link, republican sentiment is growing and the country increasingly relates more to the Pacific rim and its hegemonic power, Japan. At the Commonwealth conference in November 1995, the New Zealand government complained bitterly that Britain had kow-towed to the French in supporting their nuclear tests in the South Pacific against the interests of its Commonwealth partners.

As I have argued elsewhere (Cohen 1994), until these more recent events the British abroad provided a crucial expression of (and gave vital reinforcement to) the evolution of British identity itself. Like other diasporic communities, exaggerated mannerisms and demonstrations of patriotism often made the British abroad more British than the British at home. The exaggeration of metropolitan manners, particularly in the case of the English, but not forgetting instances like the "kilt culture" of the overseas Scots, derived directly from the imperial heritage – the heritage of the quasi-aristocratic rule over "the natives". Anderson (1992: 32) provided a penetrating insight into the origins of this manifestation of overseas "Britishness":

The administration of an empire comprising a quarter of the planet required its own special skills. Imperialism automatically sets a premium on a patrician style. . . . Domestic domination can be realized with a popular and egalitarian appearance, colonial never: there can be no plebeian proconsuls. In an imperial system, the iconography of power is necessarily aristocratic.

Those old enough to have observed the British colonial administration at work would be struck by the force of Anderson's observation. In remote regions of Africa, Asia and the Caribbean,
middle-class English administrators affected the manners of lords.
Even working-class Britons who fled post-war Britain for the easy
lifestyle available in southern Africa and Australia in the 1950s and
1960s soon adopted the overbearing hauteur of a racial elite.

The automatic and unthinking affinity between the British diasporic communities and "home" is now largely gone. It addressed a
vital nerve centre in the British identity, one that crucially coupled
patricianship abroad to upper-class pretensions and mannerisms
at home. The Britain to which the British diaspora looked was
dominated by English aspirations and signified by the monarchy,
the gentlemen's clubs, the benign feudalism of P. G. Wodehouse's
novels, the *Spectator* and the *Daily Telegraph* (for the "intellectuals"), *Punch* and the *Daily Mail* (for the not-so-cerebral), cricket at
Lords, the regatta at Henley, lawn tennis at Wimbledon, prepara-
tory and boarding schools, and the many other small nuances of
dress, vocabulary, accent, manner and recreation that bipolarized
the class structure. By signalling their putative association with the
English upper part of that class structure at home, the British
abroad were thereby also engaging in the much venerated, and
sometimes deadly serious, pastime of upward social climbing.
Now social and political elites are firmly anchored in the dominion
societies themselves.

Conclusion

Although they endured for a long time, the two forms of diasporas
considered here, a labour and an imperial diaspora, can best be
seen as transitional types. Few people in working-class occupations – whether they are Indian workers in the plantation colonies
or British workers in Australia – have a desperate desire to be
horny handed sons and daughters of toil forever. The idea of the
"honest workers", content with their station in life and seeking
only to do a "fair day's work for a fair day's pay", is largely an
ideological construction of the bourgeoisie. That is not, of course,
to say that dissatisfaction with one's lot is generally replaced by

revolutionary zeal (as the Marxists hoped and expected). Instead, escape from the conditions of one's oppression takes a number of forms. Sometimes people escape into the imagination, deadening their life at work while creating alternatives in their leisure, hobbies, or creative activities (Cohen & Taylor 1976). Many find solace in religious expression, as was shown by the revival of orthodox Hinduism and the *Ramayana* in the Indian labour diaspora.

However, more fundamental changes at the level of politics, educational provision and the economy were needed before the Indian labour diaspora and the British imperial diaspora could slough off their oppressive heritage. For the Indians, the predominant aspirations were to own land and property, or to become traders. Time and again bitter struggles over land rights occurred. In Fiji, the Indians were described by an Indo-Fijian writer as "marooned at home" because they remained as squatters, estate workers and leaseholders (Lal 1990). In South Africa, an offer of land in exchange for reindenturing was withdrawn, but Indians managed to cling on to small plots (sometimes held by dummy white owners) or to enter profitable market gardening.

As to becoming small traders, the bulk of the Indian labour diaspora could look to the ten per cent or so of their co-ethnics who had come as "free" or "passenger" immigrants. There was a light sprinkling of religious leaders among this minority, but most were small traders, setting up shop to service the needs of the Indian community in terms of food, clothing and their religious and traditional artefacts. The Indian traders soon saw wider opportunities. Fearing competition, white merchants in northern Natal managed to ban Indian traders between 1927 and 1986, while the Afrikaners of the Orange Free State (alarmed also at the thought of a "heathen" invasion), managed to stop all Indian settlement between 1981 and 1985 (Lemon 1990: 131). All over the Indian labour diaspora, the success of petty entrepreneurship was to provide a role model for those emerging from rural impoverishment.

The Indian labour diaspora also needed to get itself politically organized if it was to begin the long haul to collective social mobility. As religious freedom was guaranteed in their terms of indenture, power was initially exercised by the subtle transmutation of religious ceremony into a popular protest. One notable demonstration of this took place in the so-called "Coolie Disturbances" of

1984 in Trinidad when troops fired on a procession, killing 12 and wounding 107 marchers. Muslim indentured and free workers had been celebrating Hosay by carrying torches and *tadjah*s (representations of the tombs of the Prophet) to the sea. While being inspired by religious conviction, the marchers were also showing bravado by carrying lighted torches in defiance of an ordinance of the colony. The official investigator, the British governor of Jamaica, was not slow to pick up the growing self-confidence of the Indian workers: "After residence of some time in Trinidad the Coolie not only becomes a man of more independent spirit than he was in India, but according to some reliable evidence, he often becomes somewhat overbearing. . . . There can be no doubt that the Coolies feel their power, or rather, I should say, have an exaggerated idea of that power." (cited Khan 1995: 85)

Through religious, cultural and finally political organization the Indian labour diaspora was able to gain considerable leverage in some of the countries of settlement. The diasporic communities were also becoming much more socially differentiated through the dripfeed of education. The teachers, doctors, lawyers, students, clerical workers and petty entrepreneurs who emerged from this process in the Caribbean have been subjected to ruthless pillory by the great, but certainly not good hearted, Indo-Trinidadian novelist and social commentator, V. S. Naipaul. Seen as "mimic men" who imitated the ways of the West without knowing their context and meaning, the emergent Indian middle classes have attracted all the conventional opprobrium of those with a little more caste, class or education. This does not, however, diminish their considerable educational and material achievements. Of course, many Indians remain on impoverished plots or in menial occupations in all the countries to which they were taken, but there is now sufficient progress in their acquisitions of land, property, education and income no longer to see the diaspora as overwhelmingly characterized by its proletarian character.

As for the British imperial diaspora, the initial impoverishment of the emigrants was generally offset by the grant of land in the countries of settlement, the subsidization of their passages and by imperial preferences and subsidies for whatever products they were able to wrest from the land. South African fruit and gold, New Zealand lamb and butter, Australian wool, Canadian maple and furs – the very objects of British household consumption were prefaced by an adjectival association with the imperial diaspora in the dominions. The settlers were also generally fortunate in their destinations. Most of the dominions turned out to have not only abundant land, but also rich mineral deposits. Add a century or so to when the bulk of the impecunious settlers left Britain and we find that their descendants start to outstrip their metropolitan counterparts on the cricket pitch and rugby field, in terms of their longevity and health, their income and their level of education.

The British imperial diaspora is rapidly fading without the sustenance wrought by the intimate connection between the mother country on the one hand and the empire and dominions on the other. This is as much a consequence of the distancing from the side of the home country as it is from the dominions. The Fleet Street defender of the imperial idea, the *Daily Mail*, was founded by Harmsworth, as its bannerhead stated, to proclaim "The Power, the Supremacy and the Greatness of the British Empire". Its editorials now rarely rise above the narrow domestic crudities of anti-European and anti-Labour Party campaigns. *Punch*, the bland satirical voice of a greater British identity, closed in 1992. Ironically, it was relaunched in 1996 not by a scion of the British establishment, but by the Egyptian financier, Mohammed Fayad, who had been denied British citizenship.

The echoes of worldwide racial bonding are still occasionally evident – in the Falklands campaign, in the proud commemorative marches of war veterans and in the activation of the British diasporic vote for the Conservative Party in the 1992 general election. But the collapse of empire, macro-changes in the world situation facing Britain and its former dominions and the evolution of the empire into a multiracial Commonwealth have fragmented the unquestioned loyalty, and dissolved the essence, of the British imperial diaspora.

FOUR

Trade diasporas: Chinese and Lebanese

Trade diasporas in the classical world became familiar to modern western European scholars through Homer's writings. Surprisingly, both the *Iliad* and the *Odyssey* contain generally negative views about the role of commerce. The Greeks (rather like the Romans later) preferred the "noble" ideals of military conquest, plunder and colonization to trade. They relied for commercial affairs on the Phoenicians, the legendary "Bedouin of the sea", who exchanged products and knowledge as far afield as Spain, the British Isles, Greece, Babylon, Persepolis and Thebes. Used of the Phoenicians in early modern history, the expression diaspora was revived to allude to networks of proactive merchants set up to buy and sell their goods along established trade routes. This drew the meaning of the word closer to the Phoenician prototype. Curtin (1984: 2–3) argues that trade diasporas can be traced back even further, providing the "most common institutional form" after the coming of urban life. Merchants from one community would live as aliens in another town, learn the language, the customs and the commercial practices of their hosts then starting the exchange of goods. He continues:

> At this stage a distinction appeared between the merchants who moved and settled and those who continued to move back and forth. What might have begun as a single settlement soon became more complex. ... The result was an interrelated net of commercial communities forming a trade

> network, or trade diaspora – a term that comes from the Greek word for scattering, as in the sowing of grain. ...Trade communities of merchants living among aliens in associated networks are to be found on every continent and back through time to the very beginning of urban life.

In his comprehensive account, Curtin (1984) documents diasporic networks of traders in Africa, Anatolia, Mesopotamia, pre-Columbian America, Armenia and China.[1] Often vast wealth was accumulated, while in some cases a lucrative trading monopoly, combined with great diplomatic skill, allowed "middlemen" to transform themselves into the notables of small but viable city-states. The most significant example of this outcome is found in sixteenth-century Venice, which commanded the trade between Europe and Asia and supported an advanced artistic, cultural and civic life. (The power of the Turks in the eastern Mediterranean and the growth of competitive nation-states in western Europe ultimately put paid to Venice's powerful commercial position.) Allied to the trade diasporas and the imperial diasporas (discussed in Ch. 3) was an intermediate type, which might be described as an "auxiliary diaspora", a term related to Tinker's (1974) "imperial auxiliaries" or "auxiliary minorities".[2] Auxiliary diasporas profited from colonial expansion but were composed of ethnically-different camp-followers of military conquests or minorities permitted or encouraged by the colonial regimes. Often the small numbers representing the imperial power meant that local hostility was directed instead to the more visible and often more numerous auxiliaries, who were seen to be "foreigners" allied to the colonial administration. Chinese traders in the European colonies of South East Asia, the Lebanese in the Caribbean and West Africa, and the Indians in East Africa, all had some features of an auxiliary diaspora, but their arrival in the European colonies was also impelled by the autonomous expansion of their own trading networks. Not all auxiliaries were traders. A good case in point were the Sikhs, who migrated to many areas as a military force in the employ of the British colonial administrations.[3] The presence of such auxiliary minorities was later to have important consequences as nationalist movements sought to homogenize their populations – forcing the auxiliaries to choose between local citizenship, repatriation, or rescue by the former metropolitan power. Although there are peculiarities that derive from the auxiliary aspects of some diasporas that deserve special attention, I have an opportunity here to deal only with the general features of trade diasporas (taking the Chinese and Lebanese as the exemplary cases).

The making of the Chinese diaspora

Given the common stereotype in the West of the Chinese as innovative and successful traders, it is interesting to learn that historically merchants were almost totally subordinate to the mandarinate, at least up to the end of the Tang dynasty. Rather like the ancient Greeks, they also had to struggle against a Confucian heritage that left them at the bottom of the social scale. It was only after the tenth century, when the maritime trade with the southeast provinces of China became substantial, that the status of the traders began to improve. Wang (1991: 80–99) provides an informative picture of the Hokkien traders, looking in particular at their settlements in Manila from the 1570s and in Nakasaki after 1600. In response to competition with the Dutch and Portuguese, the Spanish officials in Manila welcomed the Chinese as a means of building up the colony. Within 30 years the Chinese population had reached 10,000 and a thriving trade in silks, tools, textiles, food, furniture and porcelain commenced. Those who did not convert to Catholicism retained their primary cultural links with south China and began to develop a pattern of circular migration, best described in English as "sojourning" – of which more anon. As for the Hokkiens in Nagasaki, their own effectiveness was limited by the periodic disapproval of their activities by their own government. The Japanese also gave preference to the European mercantile companies backed, as they were, by their royal charters and their capacity to negotiate treaties on behalf of impressive-sounding royal houses. Despite these handicaps, the Hokkiens showed their adaptability by adopting Buddhism and, by the middle of the seventeenth century, a substantial maritime empire had been developed, notably by the Zheng family. Because they were lowly provincial merchants, Wang (p. 98) contends, they "had to live by their wits, cultivate the fine art of risk-taking, and, at the crunch, could count only on their family–village system and strong local Hokkien loyalties to help them through hard times". The connection with "homeland" was thus both instrumental and necessary.

The story of these Hokkien trading communities can be used to make apparent one important distinction between trade and imperial diasporas. The former were not state-sponsored and state-backed, the latter were. In the case of the Chinese this led to an inner resilience and a high level of family and clan solidarity, which in turn gave birth to the famous Chinese capacity for "adaptability". One of the most propitious examples of "adaptability" was in Singapore, which when occupied by the British was nothing but a sleepy fishing village. Chinese traders were invited to come to Singapore in the nineteenth century by Sir Stamford Raffles to develop the port. They arrived in considerable numbers, quickly learned European laws and trading practices and soon began to speak English for commercial purposes. Raffles was delighted: Singapore's prosperity was "the simple but almost magic result of that perfect freedom of Trade which it has been my good fortune to establish" (cited Pan 1991: 27). Free trade plus the Chinese traders would have been a more accurate rendering of the magic formula.

As with the British, so it was with the other colonial powers. The French encouraged Chinese immigration to French Indochina, Mauritius and Réunion, while the Portuguese and Dutch followed suit in Macao and Batavia respectively. The founder of the Dutch colony in Batavia, Jan Pieterson Coen, enthused: "There are no people who can serve us better than the Chinese". Coen was so excessive in his zeal to acquire Chinese immigrants that he sent expeditionary parties to kidnap some on the mainland while blockading Manila and Macao so that the junks would be diverted to Batavia. However, a point forcibly made by Wang (1991: 170–1) of the Singaporean case, the Chinese traders were not essentially loyal either to the colonial power or to their places of settlement. They were not thus "auxiliaries" in a strict sense. Rather, they were loyal to thriving entrepôts and profitable arrangements, not caring overmuch whether the British, French, Portuguese, Malays, Dutch or Indians were in charge of the political superstructure.

The lack of commitment to local political life in the places to which the Chinese migrated was linked to the practice of sojourning rather than settling. There are a number of ways of explaining the Chinese traders' retention of a strong connection with "home". I have already suggested that sojourning was intrinsic to the group's coherence and its commercial survival. Pan (1991: 12–13) advances some additional thoughts. She suggests that a preoccupation with identity and genealogy is characteristic of a group that was intrinsically marginal, even in China – nearly all the "overseas Chinese" were not from the Han centre of the country, but from the peripheral regions of Fukien and Kwangtung. Despite being sinocized, they were also of somewhat different ethnic origins; more akin, it is said, to the inhabitants of Vietnam, Cambodia and Laos. Then too there was the almost mystical attachment to *hsiang* ("home"), which was never an immense entity like "China", but rather could mean a village, a home town, familiar countryside or simply the place of emotional attachment. Pan (p. 21) continues: "For commitment to one's native place, one's ancestral home, few people could beat the Chinese." Attachment to *hsiang* was also closely associated with filial duty. How else could one perform ancestral rites, look after aged grandparents or undertake ceremonial visits to the family grave? Although her view closely mirrors the sentiments of many overseas Chinese, it has the danger of assuming the status of a timeless and unvarying cultural norm. It is far better, I would suggest, to see how the practice of sojourning evolved and why so many Chinese were to abandon it in favour of permanent settlement. Once again Wang (1992a: 1-10) has been the key scholar in elaborating the origins and changing meaning of "sojourning". The first essential change was to persuade the Chinese authorities to move beyond a position that regarded the traders abroad as more than merely "outcasts" or "waifs". This recognition first dawned in the 1880s, when the Chinese equivalent term *hua-chiiao* appeared in treaties with the French and Japanese. In these agreements, the government of China abandoned its traditional disdain of the merchants abroad and sought to protect their rights. This was partly an expression of gratitude to the "temporarily resident Chinese people and irregulars in Vietnam" who had gained official Chinese approval by militarily opposing the French. For the Japanese it was more of a quid pro quo, with the

Chinese government feeling constrained to ask for protection of its residents in Japan in response to a similar request on behalf of the Japanese in China.

Official recognition of the overseas Chinese helped to legitimize their toings and froings. But, as happened with many diasporic groups, successful endeavour abroad often illuminated the short-comings and constraints of the home country. By the end of the nineteenth century, the Chinese nationalists, revolutionaries and republicans found a ready following among the *hua-chiiao*. One popular manifestation of this was the Song of Revolution, which appealed to their patriotism, attacked materialism without politi-cal commitment and asked for contributions to the anti-Manchu cause. Extracts (cited Wang 1992a: 10) from this song make the message transparent:

> Let me call again to the *hua-chiiao* overseas
> Compatriots to the distant ends of the earth!
> Only because of the need to feed yourself
> Did you leave home to wander the seas . . .
> You are no mandarin back in your native home.
> Your descendants remain inferior to others
> Without protection none can get very far . . .
> What use is the cumulation of silver cash?
> Why not use it to eject the Manchus?
> Ten thousand each from you isn't much
> To buy cannons and guns and ship them inland
> Buy a hundred thousand quick-loading rifles
> Aimed at Peking with easy success!
> The Manchu barbarians destroyed, peace will then surely
>   follow,
> A republican polity immediately assured!
> The *hua-chiiao* can then vent their feelings
> And the Westerners retreat to call you brothers
> Much better than building fortunes and pleasures
> Which can do nothing when death appears.
> It is hard to be happy all one's life,
> You need but little conscience to feel shame.
> What then is the most shameful matter?
> To forget one's ancestors involves the greatest hate!

If not that, to register as a foreign national
Forgetting that you come from Chinese stock.
In life, you may gain an awesome fame
After death how can you face your ancestors?

This appeal is interesting for a number of reasons, not least of which is the claim to a common ethno-nationality and an attack on the Manchu as aliens. One of the most enthusiastic supporters of this song was Sun Yat-sen (1866–1925), the founder of the Chinese Nationalist Party, whose followers had distributed hundreds of thousands of copies of it. Although born in Guangdong, Sun Yat-sen was educated in Hawaii and Hong Kong, where he trained and practised as a doctor. Sun's key commitment was to the maintenance, restoration, safety and prosperity of the homeland (to quote one of our own listed features of a diaspora), and a key means to realizing these ends was to mobilize the entire diaspora. He even wished to re-sinocize those who had been assimilated in their countries of settlement and "entered into the foreign registers". They too could be redeemed and have their "Chineseness" restored. The support of the diaspora was ultimately to prove vital to the success of the 1911 revolution, the key event that allowed Sun and his followers to make of China a modern nation-state.

The Chinese as minorities

The 1911 revolution can be regarded as marking the waning of the conventional "sojourner option" for the Chinese diaspora. The strategy of working and trading abroad but maintaining a close political, social and cultural relationship with *hsiang* was to prove difficult to sustain for three reasons. First, it was irreconcilable with the emerging nationalisms of the former colonial world, particularly in South East Asia. Secondly, as with all overseas communities, second or third generations became culturally localized and began to drop away old habits associated with the past. Thirdly, after the Chinese Revolution in 1949, the ideological rift between the People's Republic and the diaspora was often too great to be bridged and the practical arrangements for continuing an oscillating system of migration became increasingly troublesome.[4]

The story of Malaya's decolonization provides a good example of the impasse. With the end of the Second World War, the pace of decolonization rapidly increased, but the sponsored migration of trade and auxiliary diasporas by the former colonial powers created an a priori problem – who exactly was to constitute the nation? As Lian (1995: 392–6) shows, in the attempt to articulate a Malayan identity, the non-Malays – Indians and Chinese – were scapegoated as alien minorities. They were different in appearance and religion, they appeared not to want to take part in the process of nation-building and, perhaps most tellingly, they occupied positions in the economy that the nationalist elites or their clients craved. The suspicion of the Chinese by the Malays was somewhat unjust in that the Chinese population of the Federated Malay States and the Straits Settlements (Singapore) was increasingly less footloose. The figures speak for themselves. In 1911, in conformity with the sojourner pattern, less than 24 per cent of the Chinese in the Straits were locally born, while only 8 per cent were locally born in the Federated Malay States. Twenty years later, the Chinese constituted 70 per cent of the population in the Straits, 38 per cent of whom were locally born. (By 1957, 73 per cent were native born.) The Chinese could not win. If they continued with their traditions of oscillating migration, they were not showing proper commitment to the anti-colonial struggle. If they indigenized – as increasingly after 1949 they felt constrained to do – they were a threat to the Malays.

The Malays forced through a form of citizenship that insisted that a *bumiputra* ("prince of the soil") had to speak Malay, practise Islam and follow Malay custom. The Chinese demanded impartiality and an acceptance of cultural and religious pluralism. For a while, the powerful political personalities of the time, Lee Kuan Yew and Tunku Abdul Rahman, patched together some political compromises and managed to form a federated Malaysia. The federation lasted for only two years (1963–5) until, under the impact of Sino-Malay riots, Singapore withdrew to become an independent state. For the first and only occasion a section of the Chinese diaspora constituted itself not as an ethnic minority, but as a majority in its own state. Singapore is best conceived of as a "city-state", the basic business of which is anchored around the import–export trade and providing financial services to the global economy.

In this sense, Singapore remains true to the trading origins of the Chinese diaspora first invited there by Raffles. It is to the global economy what Venice was to the early modern world, not perhaps in its overall dominance, but rather in its function as the political embodiment of a successful trade diaspora.

All other parts of the Chinese diaspora constituted themselves as minorities, with significant concentrations in all continents other than Africa.[5] Over the period 1848–88 alone, over two million Chinese found their way to such diverse destinations as the Malay Peninsula, Indochina, Sumatra, Java, the Philippines, Hawaii, the Caribbean, Mexico, Peru, California and Australia. The Chinese diaspora today comprises 22 million people, compared with 1,000 million at home. I have laid emphasis on the Chinese as a trade diaspora, but in fact the Chinese emigrants fell into three distinct classes – indentured workers (the so-called "coolies"), free artisans and traders.[6] We are not centrally concerned with the first two groups here, but it may be helpful to say a little about the "coolie trade", for it impacted on the other two parts of the diaspora.

Comparatively little has been written on this theme by Chinese authors because the experience was a source of some embarrassment to China, indicating its weakness in the face of imperialist labour recruiters. However, Ong (1995) breaks new ground by taking a much more positive view of the achievement of the indentured labourers. Their endurance, he submits, was a copybook demonstration of the virtues of deferred gratification. Endless backbreaking work laying the railways across the USA or working in tropical plantations and mines was better than starvation at home. Moreover, those who decided to stay after their indenture formed the nucleus of the Chinatowns that are so evident in many large cities. To the former indentured workers were added the artisans like tailors, blacksmiths, ships' chandlers, cobblers and carpenters. Those merchants who abandoned or modified their practice of sojourning thus had a ready-made ethnic enclave in which to trade.

The growth of Chinatowns became the unique institutional vehicle for the Chinese to be in, but not necessarily to become of, the societies in which they settled. The beginnings of the biggest of the world's Chinatowns, in New York, can be traced to one shop; as late as the mid-1960s it covered only six blocks with 15,000 people.

By 1988 there were 300,000 residents; 450 restaurants employed 15,000 people, while 500 garment factories hired about 20,000 Chinese women (Kwong 1987: 25–6). Pan (1991: 305–6) describes the area in these terms:

> Chinatown has stuck to its own ways the longest, a classic, self-contained ghetto that was haunted by the Exclusion Acts and little freshened by new blood.[7] The residents huddled together for comfort and let the rest of the world go by, a world which merely seemed a place apart in the eyes of some and loomed up to frightening heights in the eyes of others. . . . Those who gravitated towards Chinatown found an enclave clad in the whole paraphernalia of immigrant Chinese communities, from secret societies to clan associations, each group looking after its own, the whole presided over by the Chinese Consolidated Benevolent Association (CCBA), a staunch supporter of the Kuomintang. . . . The last thing [the CCBA leaders] wanted was to engage with the larger world, the world of city politics and administration – for so long as the Chinese community kept to itself, so long as the Chinese looked to the traditional associations for all their needs, these men rule the roost in Chinatown.

Kwong (1987: 8), a social scientist who lived for many years in New York's Chinatown, is also sceptical about whether integration into the larger society will take place: "Powerful interests in and out of Chinatowns are served by keeping the majority isolated from American society." The functions of Chinatowns are none the less changing radically. Overseas Chinese in precarious situations (for example, Hong Kong and Taiwan) used New York's Chinatown to shift their money. Kwong (1987: 45) argues: "While the rich moved part of their business operation to the United States, the less wealthy put their savings in the care of relatives, who made deposits in Chinatown banks to avoid complicated rules governing non-residents. Many banks were set up precisely to facilitate such transactions." Investments in property and their relatives' businesses, as well as speculative ventures, have created a hothouse economy in the Chinese enclaves.

As far as outsiders are concerned, Chinatowns are also transmuting as global tourism finds in them what the guidebooks call "authentic", but what we know are often newly socially constructed versions of ancient Chinese practices. Tourist buses, herbalists, acupuncturists, kitchenware shops, sages, masseurs and restaurants proliferate as the Chinese learn to offer yet another commodity to the global market place – their ethnic quaintness. However, beyond the tourist gazes and the bubble worlds of the Chinatowns, the new generations of the Chinese settlers, as well as those joining them from Hong Kong and Taiwan, are entering into professional and business life in significant numbers. Sometimes known as "the uptown Chinese", their presence in the occupational profile in two major US cities is shown in Table 4.1.

Table 4.1 Occupations of Chinese in Los Angeles and New York, 1980 (%).

	New York	Los Angeles
Managers	8.8	16.5
Professionals	8.6	16.3
Technical workers	2.7	6.8
Sales	6.4	9.4
Clerical workers	10.1	14.1
Private household	0.8	1.1
Service workers	25.1	12.4
Operators	30.6	12.4
Labourers	1.3	1.5

Source: Waldinger & Tseng (1992), using 1980 US census data.

At first sight, our old friends the sojourning traders seem to have disappeared from the US classifications. However, as Waldinger and Tseng (1992: 23–4) explain, this is only apparently so. Because of the growing interdependence of the US economy with the Chinese Pacific economies of Taiwan, Hong Kong and China, many west coast Chinese in particular are becoming "hypermobile" migrants, who establish a family in one society, start a business in the other and are constantly moving between the two. These *Tai Ku Fe En* ("spacemen") may have a professional practice or business in (say) Taiwan, yet locate their families in Los Angeles to maximize educational opportunities or as a safe haven in the event of political instability. Others are more explicitly traders, facilitating commerce across the Pacific Ocean and using their homeland and diasporic networks to do so. The increased mobility arising from the regionalization and globalization of the market place, together with the neoliberal turn in the People's Republic, has greatly invigorated, rather than diminished, the Chinese trade diaspora (see Ch. 7).

The great Lebanese emigration

The Lebanese trade diaspora comprised two initially distinct groups, merchants and labourers, whose fates converged in the countries to which they emigrated. From the seventeenth to the nineteenth centuries, relatively prosperous independent merchants had set up networks spanning the burgeoning trade between the Middle East and Europe. Significant settlement took place in Egypt and in Livorno, Marseilles and Manchester. If we discard the somewhat fanciful connection with the Phoenicians, the pioneer Lebanese emigrants were Greek Catholics (Melkites) who controlled the trade with Egypt. Mount Lebanon,[8] the area round Beirut, was highly integrated into the modern world economy and stood at an important axis of trade, transport, communications and finance. Beirut itself was the financial capital of Syria and foreign banks and insurance companies proliferated. Railway and port companies, silk-reeling industries, banks, hotels and educational institutions all constituted the basis for a bourgeoisie, the size of which had no parallel in other Middle Eastern countries.

As the massive flows of emigration were to confirm, this picture of a thriving community was, however, somewhat superficial. Christians had always shown a great propensity to migrate, partly because of the communal clashes of the 1840s and 1850s and the sense that the Ottoman government was unsympathetic to their religious beliefs. To this sense of insecurity was added an underlying economic cause for emigration. The population of Mount Lebanon had increased dramatically, without a corresponding increase in local jobs. Indeed, the economy was distorted by its excessive dependence on finance and trade at the expense of industry and agriculture. What little industry there was turned on the trade in silk, which was subject to periodic decline as world prices fluctuated. Hashimoto (1992) advances an interesting hypothesis that those who acquired foreign currency in exporting silk thread and cloth in the good times were in a better position to go abroad later when prices collapsed.

By the turn of the century, "emigration fever" had gripped Lebanon. Figures from 1900 suggest that 120,000 had left the Syrian province, the vast majority from Lebanon. In the same year the American consul put the number of Syrians in the USA at "over 50,000". At the turn of the century there was a new census ordered for Lebanon, which some, probably correctly, thought was intended as a source of information to start the recruitment of Lebanese Christians as conscripts in the service of the Ottoman empire. When the Balkan wars flared up again the threat of conscription produced a strong impulse to emigrate. By 1914, emigration was estimated at 15,000–20,000 people a year. Some 350,000 Lebanese had left by that year, over one-quarter overall and, in some districts, one-half of the home population (Issawi 1992: 31).

In the literature on the various Lebanese communities abroad, there is considerable confusion over how many of their number left for voluntary reasons and how many were impelled by "push" factors originating in the Lebanon. This description of the Lebanese in the USA (Naff 1992: 145) is typical in its ambiguity:

The Syro-Lebanese were not driven to America on a mass scale from either economic desperation, religious persecution, or political oppression although something like these conditions were more likely in Syria than in Mount Lebanon. By their own testimony, the immigrants came to improve their economic condition and to return home in a year or two, wealthier and prouder than when they left. It was while they were pursuing their get-rich-quick goal that they discovered the ideals of freedom, democracy and opportunity and they embraced them fervently. Later others would join the "gold-seekers", for a variety of reasons such as evading personal problems or joining relatives. Muslims, Druzes, and some Christians escaped military conscription after 1908 and many who have suffered through the famine of the First World War also emigrated.

95

The divided motives of the emigrants can be seen in the very dramatic switches in their occupational background. For example, data from Argentina show that over a 40-year period the ratio of merchants to labourers virtually reversed (see Table 4.2).

Table 4.2 Declared occupations at point of entry: Middle East arrivals in Argentina (% in brackets).

	1876–9	1900	1909	1913
Merchants	8135 (81.9)	1146 (72.3)	5763 (49)	904 (4.6)
Labourers	437 (4.4)	111 (7)	1906 (16.2)	9506 (48.6)

Source: Klich (1992: 265).

Although these data include all Middle Easterners arriving in Argentina, the overwhelming majority were Lebanese. While the change from merchants was steep enough until 1909, it became precipitant thereafter, probably indicating the consequences of the 1908 conscription. The data are, if anything, more impressive if we bear in mind that the Ottomans were reluctant to give travel papers to any Lebanese other than those in "good standing" who were engaged in commerce and business likely to benefit the empire. Several documents subsequently uncovered by scholars talked of the embarrassment that would be caused to the Ottoman government by the arrival of impoverished or destitute emigrants. It is likely therefore that a number of Lebanese from modest backgrounds declared themselves to be merchants.

Even if the motives for emigration varied, aspirations did not. The two broad strands of Lebanese migration coalesced in the diaspora with very few of the immigrants accepting unskilled industrial employment. Instead, most preferred to establish themselves as itinerant traders – pedlars. A number of case studies in Hourani and Shehadi's (1992) massive collection of case studies can be cited to confirm this general pattern:

- *Bishmizzini villagers*: "Most became merchants, generally starting as itinerant pedlars" (p. 42);
- *Lebanese in Brazil*: "The stories of wealthy former pedlars now retired to São Paulo or Rio de Janeiro encouraged more Syrians and Lebanese to move to the Amazon basin" (p. 293);
- *A Lebanese in Jamaica*: "To the end of his life old Elias Issa, who

had arrived in Jamaica in 1894, could show the mark on his back made by the box he has carried as a pedlar. After some years he was able to buy a donkey and then set up shop in Princess Street, later moving to Orange street" (p. 343);

- *Lebanese in the USA*: "The vast majority of the pioneers – men, women and children – were drawn by the magnet of pack peddling. Despite its hardships, they preferred it to the drudgery of the factory and the isolation of American farm life" (pp. 145–6). "Before the First World War a pedlar could average $1000 a year while white American labourers earned $650" (p. 147);

- *Lebanese in Montreal*: "Of all the occupations in which the early Lebanese immigrants were involved, peddling was to have the most profound effect not only on their economic well-being, but also on their geographical distribution. Later Lebanese wholesalers opened up to replenish the pedlar's merchandise" (p. 27).

The reference to "wholesalers" is a useful reminder that very large distinctions exist within the category of "traders". At least in his early life, "old Elias Issa" and his ilk were certainly dependent on importers and wholesalers who were operating on a totally different scale. While many of the Lebanese continued in trade related activities, the second and subsequent generations abroad became increasingly occupationally differentiated.

In his richly researched study of the Lebanese in West Africa, van der Laan (1975: 222–4) also warns against seeing his subjects in too simplistic a way. He prefers the word "trader" to "middleman", explaining that not all trade was conducted between Africans and Europeans, with the Lebanese in the middle. With respect to the rice and kola trade, in which the Lebanese were heavily implicated, the buyers and sellers were all Africans. Again, after the 1930s the structure of foreign trade in Sierra Leone changed. The produce trade was faltering, but the trade in general merchandise continued, partly in response to the increased prosperity brought about by the mining of diamonds on a significant scale. "Shopkeeping became more important than produce buying and there was ample justification for describing the Lebanese primarily as shopkeepers" (p. 223).

Whether shopkeepers or middlemen, by the late twentieth century, as a distinguished Lebanese scholar, Albert Hourani, remarks (1992: 5–9), the descendants of the Lebanese migrants boasted a president of Colombia, a prime minister of Jamaica, a majority leader in the US Senate, a Nobel prize winner for medicine, a president of the (UK) Royal Society, a world famous heart surgeon and a prizewinning Lebanese-Australian novelist.

The Lebanese diaspora: butterflies and caterpillars

Were the Lebanese abroad no longer part of the society they had left behind? Hashimoto (1992 citing Chiha) vigorously contests the idea of a divorce between home and abroad and uses an expressive metaphor to capture the sense of continual goings and comings. "A butterfly", he declares, "becomes a caterpillar again". People leave Beirut and the villages, then return from abroad, only to depart again not too long later. One illustrative figure of this tendency is that the percentage of return migrants between 1926 and 1933 was 41 per cent of the total number of emigrants (Hashimoto 1992: 66n). The volume of this "continually reversible population flow" is virtually unprecedented in populations that are so widely dispersed. The extent of the dispersal of the diaspora itself is demonstrated in Table 4.3.

The movement back and forth from the diaspora to Lebanon makes the distinction between stocks and flows of migrants difficult to gauge. The data are therefore imprecise, but adequate to illustrate that over two-fifths of self-declared Lebanese do not live in the Lebanon at any one time. Such a proportion abroad is unusual, if not unprecedented. Puerto Ricans, for example, are split half-and-half between the island and the mainland, often with several crossovers over an individual migrant's lifetime. However, Puerto Rico is contiguous with the USA and, since 1917, despite their special status as a "free associated state" of the USA, Puerto Ricans have been entitled to US citizenship. Circulatory migrants from the Dominican Republic to and from the USA and from the neighbouring states to and from South Africa are also very common, but again the feature of contiguity looms large.

What draws the Lebanese overseas back to the Lebanon from such far flung destinations? One important explanation is, despite

Table 4.3 The Lebanese diaspora by country of residence, 1990.

Country	Number	Note
France	800,000	includes those with dual nationality
Brazil	200,000	since 1945
West Africa	200,000	many dual nationals in Nigeria, Sierra Leone, Ghana, Ivory Coast, Zaire and other countries
Argentina	200,000	
Australia	100,000	
Canada	100,000	
Gulf/Saudi Arabia	200,000	includes some Palestinians
USA	400,000	since 1945 (300,000 pre-1914)
Total	2,200,000	Cf. 2,897,000 in Lebanon (1991)

Source: Segal (1993: 102)

frequent memories of bitter ethnic conflict, the extraordinary hold that the imagined homeland has over the diaspora. Some of the ancient cedars of Lebanon were felled to build King Solomon's fabulous temple. In the nostrils of the poor Lebanese pack pedlars remained the scents of cedars and mint, while their palates recalled the taste of mulberries, *kippi*, the fiery red and soft white wine. An almost physically palpable nostalgia is evident in the survival and spread of Lebanese cuisine and in the literature and art of the Lebanese diaspora. The *mahhar* movement, founded in New York around the turn of the century, formalized the cultural movement; it included such notables as Khalikew Jibran (author of *The Prophet*). More recently, the Australian novelist David Malouf recalled his grandfather in this evocative poem (cited Hourani 1992: 11):

I find him in the garden. Staked tomato plants are what
he walks among, the apples of paradise. He is eighty
and stoops, white-haired in baggy serge and braces. His
    moustache
once warrior-fierce for quarrels in the small town of Zable,
where honour divides houses, empties squares, droops and
    is thin
from stroking, he has come too far from his century to
    care . . .
This is his garden,
a valley in Lebanon; you can smell the cedars on his breath

and the blood of the massacres, the crescent flashing from
  ravines
to slice through half a family. He rolls furred sage between
thumb and forefinger, sniffs the snowy hills; bees shifting
gold as they forage sunlight among stones, church bells
  wading
in through pools of silence. He has never quite migrated.

To the cultural movement in the diaspora were added many magazines, newspapers and social and quasi-political homeland organizations. The Lebanese League of Progress, for example, was founded in the Americas in 1911, although it tended to promote a Maronite-Lebanese nationalist position. Kindling the putative association with their ancient role models, Phoenician clubs all over the diaspora helped to cement the ties with the homeland, bridged the generation gap and supplied practical assistance with travel costs. The Lebanese airline, MEA (Middle East Airlines), provided a modernized, cheap form of transport that linked all parts of the Lebanese diaspora, often in very difficult circumstances.[9] Trading links and cultural nostalgia may in themselves have been insufficient to prevent the gradual erosion of a Lebanese identity in the diaspora had not the politics of the Middle East intervened to reactivate an interest in the homeland. Three particular blows fell hard on the Lebanon and ramified throughout the diaspora. The civil war, beginning in the 1970s, reactivated the horrors of the 1850s and 1860s, this time with the landmine and submachine gun replacing the sabre and the muzzle-loader. The beautiful trees and buildings of the Mount could be seen disintegrating on the television screens of the diasporic communities. Politicized and bitter refugees fuelled emigration once again and renewed a diasporic consciousness. To the blow of the civil war was added the contemptuous invasions and bombings of the country by the Israeli army and air force. For some Lebanese this provoked an identification with the Palestinian cause and with Pan-Arabism. The very existence of Lebanon seemed bound up with the creation of a viable Palestinian homeland. Finally, for some Christian Lebanese the invasion of Syria raised echoes of the Ottoman past. Fortunately, the impress of the Syrians has been much lighter than many feared; the country is rising from the ashes and from the bomb craters of civil war. Despite renewed Israeli attacks, Lebanese can once more be both butterflies and caterpillars.

Conclusion: ethnic entrepreneurs and trade diasporas

I chose not to introduce this chapter with an extended theoretical discussion because I wanted first to describe the contours of the Chinese and Lebanese trade diasporas before drowning the reader in a welter of contending theoretical positions. However, it is now necessary to recognize that our understanding of the experience of these groups comes from a wider theoretical and comparative literature that tries to explain the extraordinary commercial success of some immigrant groups relative to the native born populations or to other immigrant groups.

One comparative starting point is Max Weber's discussion of "pariah-people" such as the Jews and gypsies. These two peoples, Weber noted, had lost their territories, were confined to particular occupations and were endogamous in respect of dietary prohibitions, religious practices and social intercourse (Bendix 1973: 150). The Jews developed a form of "pariah-capitalism", which started with moneylending and built to speculative investment and thence to banking and high finance. The caste-like attributes of these groups provided the basis for complete trust inside the group and an acute need to create some security against the threatening outsider. Clearly, there are some analogies between the pariah people and the auxiliary trade diasporas like the Chinese, Lebanese and Indians, who were permitted to engage in commerce by the colonial regime but had a similar fear of being absorbed by the native populations. The combination of blocked opportunities, hostility from others and ethnic cohesiveness seem to create an advantageous sociological and commercial ethos in the ethnic group concerned (Chan & Ong 1995).

While these factors may be important, they are also insufficient. Is there a set of norms and values that has developed and prevails to predispose the group concerned towards commerce and entrepreneurship? Once again, Weber's fertile mind kicked off this debate with his much discussed thesis that there was an "elective affinity" between Protestantism (especially its Puritan and Calvinist variants) and capitalism. I have already touched on this discussion in Chapter 3 in examining the British imperial diaspora. Weber's discussion of non-European religions (Confucianism, Hinduism, Islam and prophetic Judaism) is less flexible and more schematic than his analysis of Protestantism, with a tendency to freeze past practices as if they were a contemporary anthropological present (Bendix 1973: 98–256).

None the less, many scholars of non-European societies find support for a modified Weberian thesis, not through exact textual reference to the eminent sociologist, but rather by finding Puritan-like countercurrents within the non-European societies and religions he described in such monochromatic terms. For example, Kennedy (1988: 141–3) shows how in a number of African societies private accumulation and economic experimentation, at the expense of kin loyalties, was encouraged by conversion *either* to Christianity *or* to Islam. It was the movement towards an outsider status – it did not matter much which – that was decisive. In Japan, the Confucian, Shinto and Buddhist legacies were all overcome in the Tokugawa period, which "saw the full flowering of an emerging class of commercially oriented outsiders who would create the mould for Japan's economic culture" (Kotkin 1992: 129–30). In the case of the two trade diasporas discussed in this chapter, I have already made clear that the Hokkien merchants were ethnically distinct and successfully fought against the Confucian hierarchy that left them near the bottom of the social order. Finally, though I have made less of the connection between a particular religion and trading success, in the Lebanese case there is a broad congruence between those professing one or other of the Christian faiths (Maronite, Greek Orthodox, Greek Catholic and Armenian Orthodox) and the likelihood both of migrating and of succeeding economically.

Besides Weber, another great scholar of comparative social systems, Arnold Toynbee, sees diasporas as service agents filling the cracks and crannies between the great civilizations with which he is preoccupied. Toynbee's world comprised a progression of civilizations dominant until their deaths, a fate often brought about by self-inflicted wounds. He saw diasporas as "abortive civilizations" or "fossil societies" that none the less clung tenaciously on to their communal identities without the convenience of a physical frontier like a mountain fastness. Jews, Scots and Lebanese are mentioned in passing as examples of diasporas, but Toynbee's most arresting comment (1957: 217) captures the psychological need to succeed in an economic niche:

> In the life of a diaspora, its psychological self-isolation would prove impossible if those who practised it did not, at the same time, develop on the economic plane a special efficiency in the exploitation of such economic opportunities as had been left open to them. An almost uncanny aptitude for economic specialization and a meticulous observance of jots and tittles of a traditional law are a diaspora's two main devices for providing itself with artificial substitutes for impregnable frontiers or military prowess.

The unfortunately sexist but otherwise well conceived concept of a "middleman minority" is a somewhat similar notion to that advanced by Toynbee. Like the notion of a diaspora (in general) or a trade diaspora (in particular), the expression "middleman minority" has been used to describe Jews, Indians, Chinese, Lebanese and Greeks. Rather than seeing middlemen minorities as being uncomfortably sandwiched between such grand categories as "civilizations", Bonacich (1973) sees them as being lodged between, in principle, any two ethnic groups that stand in a class-like relation of superordination and subordination. The dominant elite of the dominant group uses the middleman minority to foster economic development, but turns it into a scapegoat when things go wrong. The subordinate group benefits from the services the middlemen provide, but sees them as competitors or "sojourners" who owe no fealty to their society of settlement.[10]

Are the Chinese and Lebanese trade diasporas to be discussed in terms of their pariah status, their auxiliary character, their religious distinctiveness or their role as service agents or "middlemen minorities"? All these aspects are salient to their situation in some respects. However, one cannot help sensing throughout this array of cognate theory the siren voice or the unstated assumption of the superior validity of the nation-state (or, in Toynbee's case, the great civilization). Trade diasporas are presented as anomalies with unfortunate or intractable qualities that are puzzling and inconvenient. I would instead submit that the trading diaspora can be seen as an enduring and perhaps innovatory model of social organization that may be advantageous to the diaspora itself, its homeland and its place of settlement.

FIVE

Diasporas and their homelands: Sikhs and Zionists

A "homeland" is imbued with a sentimental pathos that seems to be almost universal. Motherland, fatherland, native land, natal land, *Heimat*, the ancestral land, the search for "roots" – all these cognate notions invest homelands with "an emotional, almost reverential dimension" (Conner 1986: 16). Often, there is a complex interplay between the feminine and masculine versions of homeland. In the feminine rendition, the motherland is seen as a warm, cornucopian breast from which the people collectively suck their nourishment. One Kirgiz poet (cited Conner 1986: 17) suggested that the relationship between homeland and human preceded birth itself: "Remember, even before your mother's milk, you drank the milk of your homeland," he wrote. Similarly, the biblical promised land was said to be "flowing with milk and honey".

In other interpretations, the nurturing white milk of the motherland is replaced by the blood of soldiers valiantly defending their fatherland. Their blood nourishes the soil, the soil defines their ethnogenesis. *Blut und Boden* (blood and soil) was Bismarck's stirring call to the German nation, an evocation that was renewed by Hitler two generations later. Even now, in the wake of the post-1945 liberal-democratic constitutional settlement, the Germans are unusual in insisting on a definition of citizenship and belonging – *jus sanguinis*, the law of blood – that emphasizes descent, rather than place of birth or long residence. Thus, third and fourth generation "ethnic Germans" from the former Soviet Union, many of whom no longer speak German, are accorded instant citizenship in preference to second-generation Turks who have been born and educated in Germany. Sometimes the images of motherland and fatherland are conflated. The British conceptions of homeland, for example, evoke the virile John Bull character exemplified in modern times by the indomitable wartime hero, Winston Churchill. They are also derived from the received history of Boudicca, Britannia, Queen Victoria and, perhaps more fancifully, Prime Minister Margaret Thatcher. The last was fond of denouncing her fellow citizens as being overdependent on the "nanny" welfare state. However, she too (as she accepted in a rare moment of self-awareness) was a nanny in another sense, administering to all, the purgatives and punishments previously supplied only to the British upper classes by unforgiving governesses.

Given the powerful sexual, psychological and affective functions of "homeland", it is hardly surprising that "foreigners", "strangers", or "newcomers" are often identified negatively as "the other" and used to construct the collective identity of "the self" (cf. Cohen 1994: 192–205). This is not to justify racism or xenophobia, merely to suggest that the social construction of "home" uses fears and passions that are deeply etched in human emotions and weaknesses. Of course, there are a number of immigrant societies (the USA, Canada, Australia and Brazil among them) where an ideology has been advanced that a new national identity can be forged with people of diverse origins. Even these societies, however, have periodic outbursts of nativism and imperfect social integration.

Just as the evocation of "homeland" is used as a means of exclusion, so the excluded may see having a land of their own as a deliverance from their travails in foreign lands. A homeland acquires a soteriological and sacred quality. In Chapter 1, I suggested that one of the common features of all diasporas is the idealization of the real or putative ancestral home and a collective commitment to its maintenance, restoration, safety and prosperity, even to its creation. In this chapter I want to focus on two cases in which the homeland was invented or reinvented. I shall show how the Sikhs' ambition to create an independent Khalistan emerged both as a solution to oppression within India and as a response to the demands of the Sikh diaspora. However, whereas their diaspora failed to achieve a homeland, my second case considers the post-homeland situation of the Jews. Here, I continue the story started in Chapter 1 regarding the origins and character of the Jewish diaspora to look at its relationship to the state of Israel, now nearly 50 years old. I also explain the arguments of the "post-Zionists" in the diaspora who reject the territorialization of Jewish identity.

The origins of the Sikh diaspora

Like the Jews, the Sikhs are ambiguously a nation, a people, an ethnic group and a religious community. The religion was founded by Guru Nanak (1469–1539) in the Punjab area of north India. Under his leadership, and that of the following nine gurus, a distinctive religious community emerged. Its theology was syncretic, drawing freely from its parent religions, Islam and Hinduism, but in the process many elements were jettisoned. Caste, for example, was effectively abolished. The extent of egalitarian relations between all Sikhs, men and women, is also notable, but so too is the masculine, militaristic ideology of Sikhism. This last feature seems to have arisen from the forcible conversion to Sikhism of another Punjabi-speaking people, the Jats, over the period 1563–1606.

Apparently, the guru at the time, Arjun Dev, thought that proselytizing was best done in the form of a holy war. From this experience emerged the central Sikh ideal of a soldier-saint, a concept not unlike that of a Christian crusader. Collectively, the soldier-saints were enjoined to form a brotherhood (no sisters here) to advance the cause of Sikhdom. The brotherhood was called the Khalsa. (The imagined homeland of the Sikhs was later to be named Khalistan.) As with the Khalsa itself, Sikhs are rather fond of naming their icons with an initial "K". Uncut hair, curled under a turban, is called *kes*. Other symbols of difference include an iron bracelet, worn on the right wrist (*karha*), a ceremonial sword (*kirpan*), a comb in the hair (*kangha*) and rather unusual breeches (*kachha*). Other groups lived in the Punjab and also spoke Punjabi (see Helweg 1979: 2–3), so the adoption of the five Ks, as they are known, is best understood as a form of "social marker", forcing a recognition of difference on the non-Sikh as well as affirming a sense of community between the Sikhs themselves.

At the political level a complex set of localized loyalties were welded together under the leadership of Maharajah Ranjit Singh, who died in 1839 after 40 years on the throne. Kushwant Singh (1977: 3), in his well known history of the Sikhs, described the Punjab at that time as "one of the most powerful states in Asia". The Punjabis controlled the fate of the Afghan throne, contained the Chinese in Tibet and stopped British expansion from the southwest. The crucial strategic importance of the Punjab was well understood by all the principal players. Cut off by the Himalayas to the northeast, the Punjab valleys were the crucial axial point between central Asia and Hindustan. Later the Russians also sought to penetrate the area. Kipling's famous novel *Kim* (1901) is all about how an abandoned Anglo-Indian boy was trained to become a secret agent to spy on Britain's enemies in the Punjab.

I digress. The narrative needs to recommence with the decline of the Punjab state in the period after 1839. The struggles over Ranjit Singh's succession were chaotic – with misfortune, miscalculation, venality and brutality (one maharaja was manually disembowelled by his rival) seriously weakening the political and military capacities of the Punjabis. The British spotted their opportunity. They invaded in 1845, and four years later the Punjab was theirs. The very suddenness of the collapse – from kingpins to underdogs in a decade – led to a fabulation and reconstruction of the Ranjit Singh period as a golden age. The lustre assigned to his rule has been further burnished by time and distance. Then, so the legends state, all Sikhs were united and powerful. Then, their ideal of the soldier-saint was consummated.

On this occasion the British had the sense not to throw sand into Punjabi faces. They demilitarized the Punjab, restored law and order, stimulated agriculture and favoured the Sikhs for employment, particularly in the army.[1] In the Sepoy Mutiny of 1857, when the rest of northern India turned on the government, the Sikhs sided with the British.[2] As one British governor-general remarked, the future of the Sikhs "was merged with that of the British empire in India" (Singh 1977: 83–4). Although the British administrators made a positive economic contribution, the distinctive cultural and religious identity of the Sikhs began to erode. That gentle but omnivorous religion, Hinduism, began to reassert itself, while the disbanded Khalsa soldiery became dacoits engaged in "thuggeeism" (from which the English word "thug" was derived). One of Ranjit Singh's sons, the five-year-old Duleep Singh, who had been officially proclaimed maharaja in 1843, was despatched to a sad exile in Britain. He was educated in Scotland, became a Christian and was given a sufficient allowance to set up as a Norfolk country squire. However, his past never quite left him. In a long letter to *The Times* in 1882 he denounced British rule in the Punjab and rediscovered his Sikh faith. Denied the right to return to the Punjab, he was arrested in Aden, then exiled to Paris where he died in 1893 (Visram 1986: 71–3).

As to the soldiers recruited, the British colonial army provided a window of opportunity to serve and sometimes to stay in various parts of the empire. Malaya was one of the first ports of call for Sikh soldiers; then they found their way to Fiji, New Zealand, Australia and Canada. In the Canadian case, a detachment of Sikh soldiers returning indirectly to the Punjab from Queen Victoria's jubilee in 1897 landed in British Columbia. These soldiers spread the word to the rural districts of the Punjab that there were opportunities for agricultural workers on the railways and in the lumber mills. In response, 5,000 Sikhs arrived in Canada between 1904 and 1907 (Chadney 1984: 26–7). Although Sikhs, as equal subjects of the king, were technically free to migrate anywhere in the empire, racists in Australasia and Canada soon made their lives hell. They succeeded in halting immigration from Asia by deploying popular prejudices and mobilizing white opinion against the newcomers. One popular song in British Columbia (cited Singh 1977: 169) ended with this chorus:

> Then let us stand united all
> And show our fathers' might,
> That won the home we call our own,
> For white man's land we fight.
> To oriental grasp and greed
> We'll surrender, no never.
> Our watchword be "God save the king"
> White Canada for ever.

Despite this campaign of hatred, Sikhs excluded from Canada found their way to the USA and also to many parts of the British empire, including the metropolis itself. Although the bulk of the movement to Britain was after 1960, even in the 1920s and 1930s

Sikhs were evident in the Midlands, Glasgow, Peterborough and London in the role of door-to-door sellers of hosiery, knitwear and woollens (Visram 1986: 192). The number and global distribution of the Sikh diaspora by the late 1980s is listed in Table 5.1.

Table 5.1   The Sikh diaspora, by country of residence.

Place	Date of arrival	Population
Europe		
United Kingdom	1960–90	300,000–400,000
Denmark	1981–	3500–5000
Germany	1981–	15,000–20,000
France	1982–	2500–3000
Belgium	1984–	3500–5000
Netherlands	1984–	1500–2000
Americas		
Canada	1905–13	7500–10,000
	1960–90s	100,000–125,000
USA	1905–13	7500–10,000
	1960–80s	100,000–125,000
Mexico	1930–	1000–1500
Argentina	1950s	500–2000
The Far East		
Malaysia	1865–1940	30,000–45,000
Singapore	1865–1940	25,000–30,000
Australia	1890–1910	5000–7500
New Zealand	1890–1910	2000–3000
Fiji	1890–1910	1200–2500
Philippines	1910–30	2000–5000
Thailand	1920–40	2500–5000
The Near East		
Afghanistan	1900–30	2000–2500
United Arab Emirates	1970–80	10,000–25,000
Iraq	1970–80	7000–10,000

Source: Tatla (1993: 68) citing a wide variety of data collected over the period 1969–88.

Sikhs: the lure of homeland

The loyalty of the Sikhs to the British empire was poorly rewarded. Not only did they have to suffer immigration restrictions, but also the 100,000 troops in the First World War were paid less than

British servicemen and were restricted in their duties. British privates sometimes did not salute their superior Sikh officers, which caused great offence. These insults did not prevent the Sikhs winning a hugely disproportionate number of awards for gallantry in the field. The Sikh reverence for honour required no less.

To the racism of the white dominions and the battlefields was added another grievance – repression in the Punjab. Returning soldiers are nearly always a force for radicalism. Coming home after arduous and dangerous service, they are confronted with the contrast between the high ideals used to build fighting morale and the realities back home. Thus it was with the Sikh heroes of 1914–18. They found the revolutionary Ghadrite movement (acting partly in sympathy with the Bolsheviks) had been ruthlessly suppressed; the summer monsoon had failed; new taxes had been imposed; while a virulent strain of influenza had wiped out 100,000 people.

On 13 April 1919, at Amritsar, six people were killed and 30 wounded after peaceful protests. The mob turned on the British banks and the Christian clergymen who had been trying to proselytize in the area. The killing of five Englishmen and an assault on a missionary provoked the British to a frenzied response. They surrounded a large crowd near the Golden Temple and opened fire without provocation, killing 379 and wounding over 2,000 people.

The Amritsar massacre is probably the most notorious act of colonial oppression in any part of the British empire. The rage of the Sikhs was augmented by the horror felt all over India at this attack on unarmed civilians. An all-India nationalist, rather than sectarian, consciousness was the primary reaction to Amritsar, but the event also marked the reawakening of Sikh political activism and religious enthusiasm. The old litany *rāj karey gā Khalsa* (the Khalsa shall rule) was loudly proclaimed again. As it became evident that the British would have to go, Sikhs reasserted their historic "right" to rule the Punjab, even though they constituted a minority within the area. The demand for a Sikh state paralleled Muslim calls for a separate Pakistan. The entreaties of the Sikhs were successfully resisted by the powerful and popular Indian nationalist party, known in short as "Congress", which feared that irredentism, secession and separatism would fragment the unity of the anti-colonial struggle.

In the Sikh diaspora, the post-1948 disposition was, however, rarely accepted without demur. Many Sikh community associations were absorbed in the politics of their host societies, forming self-help groups and seeking forms of political representation, often in alliance with other Indian groups. Nevertheless, the politics of the Punjab were never far away. In addition to the Congress Party, the Akali Dal and various communist bodies all had close allies in the diaspora. In particular, the Akali Dal took on the role of articulating the idea of a separate Sikh identity, although, unlike the Khalsa and temple management organizations, Akali supporters were often turbanless and clean-shaven secular leaders. The Akali Dal developed effective and well supported organizations in Britain, Canada and the USA, which kept in touch with one another as well as with the Punjab. The International Golden Temple Organization was set up to collect money for the central shrine of Sikh belief, while a World Sikh Festival was held in 1982. These connections provide further evidence of one of the features of all diasporas, namely a sense of empathy and solidarity with co-ethnic members in other countries of settlement.

The expressed need for a separate Sikh homeland was notably articulated in the 1950s and 1960s by a former finance minister of the Punjab government, Jagjit Singh Chohan, who raised the issue of a Sikh homeland in Britain, Canada and the USA (Tatla 1993: 171–2). He also placed a half-page advertisement in the *New York Times* (12 October 1971) claiming that the Sikhs had been misled at the time of independence:

> At the time of the partition of the Indian subcontinent in 1947 it was agreed that the Sikhs shall have an area in which they will have complete freedom to shape their lives according to their beliefs. On the basis of the assurances received, the Sikhs agreed to throw their lot with India, hoping for the fulfilment of their dream of an independent, sovereign Sikh homeland, the Punjab.

In fact a few of the supporters of a Sikh homeland had already begun using the expression "Khalistan", rather than "Punjab", as their rallying cry. A consul-general's office for the non-existent republic of Khalistan was set up in Canada, while a monthly magazine, *Babbar Khalsa*, was issued alongside a Khalistani passport and Khalsa currency. The lure of a homeland was that it appeared to offer an escape from what was represented as Hindu domination. In one supporting magazine in Britain (cited Tatla 1993: 173) the author implored Sikhs to:

> realize that there is no future for them in an India dominated by Hindus. The honour and prestige of the community cannot be maintained without state power. The sooner we realize this challenge the better it will be to set up our objective of establishing a sovereign Sikh state in the Punjab. We cannot keep ourselves in bondage for ever. Our leaders are like beggars in New Delhi asking for this or that.

The movement for Sikh autonomy or for a separate homeland might have slowly dissipated but for the storming of the Golden Temple in July 1984 by Indian security forces. The temple not only is the highest seat of religious and temporal authority for the Sikhs (analogous to the significance of St Peter's for Catholics), but also was the symbolic centre of a world without boundaries. Unlike the overseas Chinese or caste Hindus, who attracted a high level of disapprobation for leaving their homeland, Sikhs "suffered no loss of rank or merit from travel overseas" (Dusenbery 1995: 24). Sikhs could constitute themselves as a viable congregation wherever there were five worthy members, but the Golden Temple none the less retained its importance as a site for pilgrimage and a home for the *Akal Takhat* (the "throne" of the Sikhs), an artefact that was destroyed by the Indian army in 1984.

What precipitated this extraordinary event? By early 1984 Sikh separatist unrest had led to a severe clampdown by the Indian government and the declaration of emergency rule. After the separatists were said to have stockpiled arms in the complex of the Golden Temple, Delhi sent in troops. They killed the leading Sikh militant and about 700 of his followers. The horrors did not stop there. Three months later Prime Minister Indira Gandhi was assassinated by two of her hitherto utterly loyal Sikh bodyguards. The bond of trust between Hindus and Sikhs had snapped (see Bobb & Raina 1985). Some 2,000 Sikhs were killed in communal riots and Sikhs responded by terrorism and violence, adding several thousand more to the casualties.

Sikhs in the diaspora were not slow to pour petrol on the flames. The most notorious episode, which was blamed on Canadian Sikh extremists, was the crash of an Air India plane off the Irish coast on 23 June 1985, killing its entire complement of 329 passengers and crew. Members of the Babbar Khalsa in Canada were immediately arrested, but suspicion soon fell on one Inderjit Singh Reyat, who was extradited from Coventry to Vancouver, where he was convicted of placing bombs at Narita airport in Japan and on the fateful Air India plane.

The more constitutional Sikh parties and associations desperately tried to distance themselves from terrorism and managed to win some political support in Canada, the USA and Britain. The World Sikh Organization and the International Sikh Youth Federation, in particular, mobilized tens of thousands of Sikhs in peaceful demonstrations for an independent Sikh state. New organizations, like the Khalistan Council, sprang into being and there was a general shift to the youth and the militants in the *gurdwara* (temple) management committees and political associations. In the wake of the storming of the Golden Temple, the editor of a New York publication *Sikh News* (cited Tatla 1993: 187–8) made a suggestive comparison between the Sikh, Jewish and Palestinian diasporas. All three, he argued, were subject to oppression and injustice (in my terms they were "victim diasporas"), but:

> the Jews have transformed their dreams into a reality. The Palestinians' cause, though equally just, has been poorly served. . . . Now the question arises, "How do the Sikhs appear to the world?" The Indian government would like nothing better that the international community should brand us "terrorists". The Sikh nation's cause has to be fought simultaneously on three fronts: (a) the hearts and minds of our people; (b) the international community; and (c) the Indian government. Are we like the Jews struggling to right a momentous wrong or like the Palestinians with little sense of their past, a chaotic present and little hope for the future? If the shoe fits, wear it.

Though this is a cruel parody of the Palestinian cause, the author captures the sense of incoherence in Sikh responses to the events of 1984. The reactions in the diaspora were ones of shock, fury and outrage, but they lacked a clear focus or any inspired leadership from the Punjab itself. The Sikhs in India began to disintegrate into rival factions. In particular, the urban based Delhi intellectuals distanced themselves from the "dung-heap" politicians in the Punjab. In one notable *volte face*, the historian Khushwant Singh (1992) denounced the continuing militancy in the Punjab as "thuggery" and condemned the assassination of Indira Gandhi. In the first (1977) edition of his *History of the Sikhs* he had insisted that "the only chance of survival of the Sikhs as a separate community is to create a state in which they form a compact group, where the teaching of Gurmukhi and the Sikh religion is compulsory, and where there is an atmosphere of respect for the tradition of their Khalsa forefathers". In marked contrast, the 1991 edition denounced the "lumpen sections of Sikh society mindlessly propelled by the Khalsa death wish". His other statements on self-determination had also been toned down and sanitized (see Singh 1993).

"Amritsar" has come to haunt the Sikhs, first because of the events in 1919, then in 1984. The dream of an independent homeland is structured around those two dates – which have provoked determined resilience as well as a sense of despair. For the moment, advancing the Sikh claim for a nation-state looks unlikely to bear fruit. But memories are long and the desire for this expression of modernity and territoriality is great. It is possible, as is suggested below, that with the general deterritorialization of all social identities, Sikhs may find they are able to develop functional international alternatives to a state. This solution is, however, unlikely to have much appeal to the diehards who continue to nurse their grievances and bitterly resent the failure of their cause.

Can Israel be a "normal" state?

I now turn to my second key example: that of a diaspora that has been successful in creating a homeland. Israeli politicians and Zionists alike assume that the creation of the state of Israel in 1948 was the logical development of Jewish aspirations since the original dispersal. Like the Sikh nationalists, Zionists imagine a Golden

Age when Kings Solomon and David ruled and the Jews were united. The defining characteristics of the Jewish diaspora and the fulfilment of the Zionists' dreams of a state of their own have been discussed in Chapter 1. Here I want to look at the special peculiarities that marked the creation of Israel before turning to the reactions to this event in the diaspora. Despite the desperate attempt on the part of its Zionist founders to foster "normality", to be like other nations, the circumstances that surrounded the birth of the Israeli state were far from normal. Let me illustrate these entanglements by making just six points:

1. The founding mythology of the state of Israel suggests that its leaders were engaged in the "ingathering" of dispossessed exiles. While this was partly true, it is not the whole truth. A "revisionist" group of Israeli historians (for example, Shafir 1989) has questioned nationalist hagiography through demystifying the personalities, political positions and ideological pronouncements of the founding fathers and mothers of the Zionist enterprise. Yes, the migrant Jews were victims of oppression in the Eastern Pale of Settlement. But they were also the bearers and willing accomplices of Western ideas of colonization held particularly by those like the Rothschilds and the Palestinian Land Development Company who bankrolled Zionist settlement. In this respect, the Zionist project was similar to the British chartered companies or the Dutch East India company financing white settlement in far off places. Less, in short, of a victim diaspora and more of an imperial one.

2. In their quest for help in establishing a state, the Zionists arrived at some rather uncomfortable conclusions and picked up some rather unsavoury supporters. Herzl, for example, thought that anti-Semitism would serve his cause while British diplomats and statesmen such as Shaftsbury, Palmerston and Balfour were opportunist allies rather than true friends. In fact they were interested in getting rid of what they saw as an alien race and in the advantages of a Jewish Palestine for British strategic calculations (Sharif 1983: 122 and *passim*).

3. The founders of the state of Israel were largely secular Jews from the Polish–Russian Pale who reflected simply one of

four political trajectories commonly articulated there at the end of the nineteenth century: (a) to stay and fight for justice through social-democratic and revolutionary parties; (b) to migrate to other parts of Europe and the USA (by far the most popular option); (c) to abandon themselves to inward looking religious reflection; and (d) to emigrate to Palestine. Although time has softened these profound and bitter disagreements, ultra-Orthodox Jews, even in Israel, do not accept the state of Israel. They regard its secular character with loathing and refuse to serve in its army.

4. Perhaps the most controversial and difficult issue for Zionists to accept is that while the founding of the Israeli state provided a modicum of justice to the Jews, it occasioned serious injustices for the local Palestinians. The displacements of the Palestinians have caused endless recriminations and soul searching among all Jews, but in terms of my present concern with "normality", this was a less unusual feature of nation-state formation than is sometimes supposed. As we saw in Chapter 2, it happened thus in the First World War when 1.75 million Armenians were displaced by the Turks. It happened with the separation of India and Pakistan in 1948. It is currently happening with a vengeance in the former Yugoslavia and the former Soviet Union.[3]

5. Because the Israeli state was established in the traumatic aftermath of the Second World War as a homeland specifically for Jews (and no others), it adopted a descent-based definition of citizenship, *jus sanguinis*, which had embarrassing similarities with the notions proposed by the Nazis. All immigrant Jews were given immediate recognition under the "Law of Return", while resident Palestinians were only grudgingly and slowly given civic rights. As Haim Cohen, a former Israeli Supreme Court judge, remarked: "The bitter irony of fate has decreed that the same biological and racist arguments extended by the Nazis, and which inspired the inflammatory laws of Nuremberg, serve as the basis for the official definition of Jewishness in the bosom of the state of Israel" (quoted Sharif 1983: 5).

6. Finally, although Israeli political leaders lay great emphasis on the sovereignty and independence of their state, it is

unlikely that it could have thrived (perhaps it might have survived) without three external supports: (a) German war reparations paid in repentance of the Holocaust; (b) huge sums of money from the Jewish diaspora for development projects; and (c) the diplomatic, military and financial help of successive US governments, their attitudes influenced by the powerful US Zionist lobby.

To make my position clear, I conclude that none of the six points together or separately constitute the basis for some naïve, counterfactual speculation that the Israeli state should not exist. Without it the remnants of the Holocaust Jews and the refugees from intolerance and famine in Ethiopia, North Africa, Russia and many other places would have perished. None the less, the particularities that marked the rebirth of the Jewish homeland go a long way towards providing an explanation of why, even after 50 years, its legitimacy continues to be questioned by the states and peoples surrounding it. These birth traumas also clarify why the fervent desire for "normality", in effect a desire for full acceptance by other nation-states, is unlikely to be realized in the intermediate future. Rather, it seems likely that the Israeli state will be regarded as anomalous, destabilizing and deleterious to the region for many years to come.

Israel and the diaspora

Just as the re-creation of a Jewish homeland triggered a complex set of relations within Israel and the Middle East, so the very fact of Israel's existence posed a challenge to Jews in the diaspora. "It bestowed on them the freedom to choose between their countries of birth and their ancient homeland" (Gorny 1994: 41–2). As I have made clear before, it would be better to say that the choice was between their countries of birth and a reinvention of their ancient homeland.

To insist on this point is to flag up the whole range of existentialist, essentialist, theological, political, cultural and psychological questions that marked the responses in the diaspora to the foundation of the state of Israel.[4] I shall say something in turn about groups that I characterize respectively as Zionists, patrons and proto-Zionists, zealots, the religious Reform groups, and assimilationists. The special situation of those who leave Israel will also be considered.

Zionists

Probably the most common response in the diaspora to the creation of Israel was a sense of pride and fulfilment, and perhaps a feeling of relief that the remnants of European Jewry had been saved. Prior to 1948, when all energies were focused on the consolidation of the Zionist project, there was no direct conflict of loyalty between the state of residence and the reinvented homeland. What, however, was the role of the Zionist movement in the period after 1948? Some leaders advocated a three-tiered structure – with the Israeli state at the top, Zionist organizations in the middle and the Jewish masses at the bottom.[5]

This trisection was often endorsed by Israeli politicians, like Ben-Gurion, who wanted to assert their political primacy but not lose their sources of support. Some associated problems arose. If Zionists in the diaspora were to defer to Israel, they were exposing themselves again to the charges of dual loyalty, which marked the most corrosive forms of conflict between Jews and the modern nation-state. On the other hand, the Zionist organizations proclaimed a kind of Leninist conviction that they alone were fit enough and perceptive enough to lead the Jewish masses. Like those who were subjects of the dictatorship of the proletariat, most of the Jewish masses in the benign countries of settlement showed little sign of wanting to be led anywhere else.

The most compelling demand made by the Zionists was that young people, or those with skills, should abandon their life in the diaspora, however easy or profitable, in favour of *oleh* ("one who goes up" or voluntary migration) to the homeland. The youth movements were particularly audacious in their claims on youthful idealism. One movement (which I joined as an adolescent in South Africa in the 1950s) provided a curious blend of scouting *à la* Baden-Powell, Germanic rural heartiness, Marxism and strident Jewish nationalism. There was also a soupçon of Russian revolutionary "free love", which proved a good stratagem for recruiting. The movement was wholly secular and barely tolerated religious Jews. Those who were accorded the highest status in the movement would be expected to join Kibbutz Tzorah, established by

South African Zionists, to give unstintingly of their mental and manual labour.[6]

Patrons and proto-Zionists

Unlike these youthful idealists, for many wealthy and powerful Jews in the diaspora, the politics of homeland was the politics of the chequebook, the Jewish National Fund and occasional tourism. Established dynasties, like the Rothschilds and Montefiores, were spectacularly generous in funding or endowing agricultural settlements, hospitals, schools and universities. Education provided a particularly attractive target for donations, with a proliferation of buildings all scrupulously inscribed with the names of the benefactors. Sometimes the more attractive veil of philanthropy covered a rather seedy past in profiting from Prohibition or trading in arms.

The "big givers" were, however, also followed by hundreds of thousands of those who responded to particular campaigns, bought trees for Israel ("to make the desert bloom again") or plopped notes, coins and cheques into the collection boxes dutifully taken around by volunteers. No doubt many of this group were committed Zionists who, perhaps through age or circumstance, felt unable to emigrate to Israel. But the bulk of the "small givers" were probably responding to a more diffuse set of moral imperatives. As in the case of the Armenians who survived the massacres (see Ch. 2), those who survived the Holocaust often felt guilty and blemished because of their chance good fortune. One way of expiating this guilt while enjoying their material success and upward social mobility was to give generously to Israel. Besides, in the often tightly knit Jewish diasporic communities it would attract disapprobation if one were not seen to be open handed. This group, in short, comprised proto-Zionists, rather than Zionists proper. Their eyes did not burn with a messianic zeal.

Zealots

Just such a description can be applied to my next category, the religious zealots. I have already mentioned the group that lived in Israel yet refused to recognize the secular state of Israel. For them, only the messiah could reunite the diaspora with the homeland. The secular Zionists who jumped the gun were to be despised rather than commended. Locked in little urban ghettos in Jerusalem, bent over the Talmud, the zealots emerged from time to time to stone women they thought improperly dressed or to turn back buses that ran on the Sabbath. As some of this group began to participate in Israeli politics, some kind of *modus vivendi* with the nation-state began to emerge.

This was to be ruptured by the arrival of new recruits from the American diaspora, zealots who combined their American love for big power politics with a chiliastic determination. The object? None other than the reinvention of a Greater Israel said to be sanctioned by biblical boundaries and including the area known as the West Bank (west of the Jordan river). The result? Intractable contests of authority between the state authorities, who have finally recognized the need to accommodate some of the Palestinians' demands, and the new zealots – trying to create a reality on the ground by establishing settlements of their own.

Religious Reform groups

It is worth making clear that religious hostility to the state of Israel existed beyond the ranks of the ultra-Orthodox Jews. A Reform (i.e. liberal or progressive) rabbi, Elmer Berger, delivered a crucial speech in 1942, in which he provided an "ideological platform" for a position that asserted that Judaism was by its nature anti-nationalist and had survived only because of its universal principles. These "could be transmitted from country to country and era to era", while other peoples and nations disappeared from the face of the globe. He had little time for the Golden Age of Israel, regarding the much-lionized periods of Kings David and Solomon as marked by moral turpitude rather than spiritual achievement. He bluntly maintained that the Zionists had sanctioned and perpetuated those racist and fascist theories that wrongly claimed Jews had no place outside a homeland (Gorny 1994: 12–13).

The Reform groups, on the contrary, vigorously asserted that it was possible and necessary for a viable, creative and intellectually challenging life to exist outside the homeland. This involved the continued assertion of the universal principles of Judaism. In practice, the Reform groups developed a rather anodyne version of Judaism, with less emphasis on the prophetic parts of the Bible, less interest in following intricate religious observances and much more emphasis on "fitting in" with neighbours and host societies.

The general thrust of their position was to "normalize" within the diaspora rather than the homeland and to become a model minority while still retaining the right to worship in their own way.

Assimilationists

Many Jews in the diaspora have, of course, gone much further than the Reform Jews – having abandoned Judaism, or indeed any religion. Even a loose connection with their ethnic background and history is slowly beginning to erode. This phenomenon has been particularly pronounced in France, the UK and the USA, which together contain more than half the world's Jews outside Israel. About 40 per cent of UK Jews are marrying exogamously – a key indicator of assimilation. In the USA, the 1991 National Jewish Population Survey concluded that more than half the country's young Jews were marrying Gentiles, while only a small proportion of their spouses were converting to Judaism. Again, "most alarmingly from the standpoint of community cohesion, only a minority of Jewish children live in households where all the members are Jews" (Waldinger 1996: 174).

The assimilationist position is especially damaging to the Zionist view of the diaspora because people are simply voting with their feet – and these are pointed towards the affluent suburbs in affluent countries, rather than in the direction of Jerusalem. As I made clear earlier, there have always been Jews who have been keen to escape the confines of their ethnicity and their religion. However, many of them were consciously identifying with a political struggle in their countries of settlement, which they saw as more salient to their lives than the assertion of their Jewish identity. A conspicuous minority among those who worked for revolution in Russia, for labour unions in New York, for the anti-apartheid movement in South Africa, or for progressive social movements in France were of Jewish descent.What is more threatening in the current context is that Jewish identity is threatened not by a sense of rebellion, but by one of indifference. This is the obverse side of succeeding in a pluralist and tolerant society. As Waldinger (1996) records, the USA has been kind to the Jews – 40 sit in Congress, and they form a disproportionate part of the professoriat in the elite universities, a number of which are governed by Jewish presidents. These same institutions excluded Jews only two generations ago. Of the 400 richest Americans, 25 per cent are Jewish, while the group's income is twice that of the national average. Political participation, professional prowess and personal property may not be everything, but they do attest that, in the more favoured parts of the diaspora, life for assimilated Jews is more fulfilling than the Zionists assumed was possible.

The post-Zionists

In a number of seminal publications, written separately (D. Boyarin 1994, J. Boyarin 1992, 1995) and together, Daniel Boyarin and Jonathan Boyarin (1993) have mapped out the terrain of a post-Zionist Jewish identity. They start with the telling point that a Jewish culture was initially constructed in the diaspora. Abraham, supposedly the first Jew, had to leave his native land to find the promised land. The land of Israel was *not* therefore the birthplace of the Jewish people. This observation provides the starting point for an alternative rendering of Jewish history and, in particular, the suggestion that one of its most enduring characteristics is "the impossibility of a natural association between this people and a particular land – thus the impossibility of seeing Jewish culture as a self-enclosed, bounded phenomenon" (1993: 721).

Despite all the dangers of antagonizing the host societies in which they find themselves, the Jewish diaspora tradition must, the Boyarins proclaim, continue to insist on the respect for difference within "a world grown thoroughly and inextricably interdependent" (p. 723). Jewish identity can never anchor itself in a self-satisfied resting place, or manifest itself as a form of nativism; it has to find expression through a perpetual, creative diasporic tension. The Boyarins find in this deterritorialized notion of Jewish identity a new idea as powerful as the Jews' contribution to the notion of monotheism. This idea is simply that *peoples and homelands are not necessarily and organically linked*.

In rather evangelical terms they aver that if this message is understood it could help prevent the bloodshed produced by the ethno-nationalist struggles of recent years. They even proclaim that far from the Israeli state being hegemonic over the rest of Jewry (as the Zionists demanded), Israel should reimport a diasporic consciousness. This would mean that the Israelis would understand that the bona fide Jewish tradition requires sharing space with others, that there needs to be a complete separation of religion from state, that the Law of Return needs to be revoked and that they should seek to build a multinational and multicultural society. Thus the wheel comes full cycle.

Yordim, sabras *and transients*

Zionists assumed that the migratory flow would be unidirectional, from the diaspora to the homeland. It was therefore particularly galling that there were some who wished to leave Israel. Return migration has proved especially painful for those who have once gone on *aliyah*, but have now returned to the *golah*. This group is pejoratively known as *yordim*.[7] The Zionists argue that while life in Israel is one of normality, health and independence, life in the diaspora is neurotic, deficient and schizophrenic. Shusterman (1993) provides an instructive account of the philosophical journeys paralleling his decision to return to the USA after 20 years in Israel. As with many other writers, he associates the creation of the nation-state with modernity (p. 299) and suggests that the Zionists have grafted on to this coupling the idea of normality:

> We find in all these premises a modernist faith and privileging of the normal, the autonomous the essential and the authentic. Not surprisingly, the radical Zionism these premises support – that only life in Israel can be fully and authentically Jewish, can definitively and decisively resolve our problems of Jewish identity and unity – is a very modernist view. It is one guided by a goal of stable unity and definitive closure with the final return of all Jews to Israel.

Experientially, Shusterman resorts to a postmodernist argument to defend his own arguments. He commends the notions of Lyotard, who "attests to postmodernism's dissolution of authentically national cultural life into multinational eclecticism" (p. 302). This blurring of national cultures, he continues, "virtually vitiates the cultural argument for Zionism".

Others have simply left Israel for personal, professional or economic reasons without the benefit of such elaborate reasoning. In particular, those who were born in Israel, the *sabras*, often study, work and live abroad without self-consciousness.[8] A large number of new immigrants to Israel, for example those from the former Soviet Union, also have more instrumental attitudes to their period of residence in Israel, often seeing the country essentially as a transit camp. Their entry is assured under the Law of Return, a reasonably comprehensive welfare system has been established, skills can be upgraded and qualifications sought. The preferred ultimate destination is the USA, not Israel.

Conclusion

I have suggested in this chapter that the relationship of the diaspora to the homeland is both complicated and fraught. That relationship is represented by nationalists (in our case studies of the Khalistani and Zionist movements) as basically unproblematic. Nobody of course imagines it is easy to create or reinvent a homeland – international support, armed intervention, a propaganda war and community mobilization – are accepted as necessary parts of a successful attempt. But nationalists implausibly believe that once their goal has been attained all will be well.

Of course this is far from the truth. The manner and consequences of achieving statehood may be complex and controversial. For example, if terror accompanies the struggle for statehood (as it did with the Stern gang in Palestine and the Babber Khalsa in Canada) this cannot but mark the character of the state. If Khalistan were ever established, it would face an identical dilemma, with respect to the people already living there, as that which faced the neophyte state of Israel. What would happen to the 65 per cent of the population of the Punjab who are not Sikhs? Given that there are no "empty lands" left in the world, can statehood for one people ever be achieved without perpetrating injustice to other peoples, thus bringing into being new victim diasporas with new grievances.

One unacknowledged problem for the nationalists is that contemporary demands for statehood are essentially anachronistic. To demonstrate this we need for a moment to return to the crucial historical conjuncture when the nation-state emerged. Jacobson (1996: 128–34) puts forward a compelling argument that the idea of a deterritorialized universal (Catholic) Church was "flattened" by the rise of Protestantism. This placed a premium on the linking of specific peoples, affiliated with distinct Churches, to demarcated lands – thus the Church of Wales, Church of Ireland, Church of Scotland, Church of England, Dutch Reformed Church, and so forth. This nationalization of the Church was reinforced by economic and ideological imperatives. One often cited writer, Nairn (1977: 96–8), has traced the origins of the nation-state to the development of a successful bourgeoisie and active intelligentsia seeking to reconcile their relative political weaknesses with their relative economic power.

This potent vinculum between territory, polity, economy, ideology and religion was historically far more delimited than contemporary nationalists concede. This is not to say that there are not other historical conjunctures that give rise to nationalism, such as an anti-colonial struggle or the implosion of an empire, although these circumstances are rarely as propitious. It is true, for example, that there is a proliferation of internationally recognized nation-states: nearly four times the number that comprised the United Nations membership in 1945. Yet many of these are flag-and-postage-stamp states with no prospect of wielding international influence, or, in some cases, effectively governing their populations. Irredentism and ethnic conflict are common.

Brutal as it is to say this of the Khalistanis, they may have boarded the historical train too late. In the Israeli case, the quest for national sovereignty was driven through *against* the tide of history, and the ideological and practical penalties for establishing a nation-state without the favourable nexus mentioned earlier are still onerous burdens. Fifty years after its establishment, the Israeli state continues to struggle for legitimacy. Equally, the Jewish diaspora is hopelessly fragmented in its attitudes to the homeland. While the Zionists occupy many public platforms, the extent of indifference, challenge or hostility to their position is often underestimated. Although, at the moment, the post-Zionist position is barely known, its protagonists are probably articulating the wave of the future. In short, the endless quest and bitterly fought campaigns for statehood may be like trying to imprison the butterfly of ethnic identity in too small a net with too dense a mesh. Perhaps the butterfly should be permitted to fly in its own direction at its own whim?

SIX

Cultural diasporas:
the Caribbean case

Migration scholars – normally a rather conservative breed of sociologists, historians, demographers and geographers – have recently been bemused to find their subject matter assailed by a bevy of postmodernists, novelists and scholars of cultural studies. A reconstitution of the notion of diaspora has been a central concern of these space invaders. For example, the editor of the US journal *Diaspora*, Khacha Tölölyan, a professor of English at Wesleyan University, announced its birth (1991: 3) with the following statement:

> The conviction underpinning this manifesto disguised as a "Preface" is that *Diaspora* must pursue, in texts literary and visual, canonical and vernacular, indeed in all cultural productions and throughout history, the traces of struggles over and contradictions within ideas and practices of collective identity, of homeland and nation. *Diaspora* is concerned with the way in which nations, real yet imagined communities, are fabulated, brought into being, made and unmade, in culture and politics, both on the land people call their own and in exile.

For postmodernists the collective identity of homeland and nation is a vibrant and constantly changing set of cultural interactions that fundamentally question the very ideas of "home" and "host". It is demonstrable, for example, that unidirectional – "migration

127

to" or "return from" – forms of movement are being replaced by asynchronous, transversal flows that involve visiting, studying, seasonal work, tourism and sojourning, rather than whole-family migration, permanent settlement and the adoption of exclusive citizenships. These changing patterns have important sociological consequences. As Vertovec (private correspondence 1996) puts it:

> Aesthetic styles, identifications and affinities, dispositions and behaviours, musical genres, linguistic patterns, moralities, religious practices and other cultural phenomena are more globalized, cosmopolitan and creolized or "hybrid" than ever before. This is especially the case among youth of transnational communities, whose initial socialization has taken place within the cross-currents of more than one cultural field, and whose ongoing forms of cultural expression and identity are often self-consciously selected, syncretized and elaborated from more than one cultural heritage.

One way of conceptualizing the social and cultural outcomes described is to loosen the historical meanings of diaspora once more, this time to encompass the construction of these new identities and subjectivities. Earlier in this book I suggested several adjectival modifications to a monochromatic idea of diaspora (when I talked of victim, trade, labour and imperial diasporas). In like manner, I propose adopting the expression "cultural diaspora" to encompass the lineaments of many migration experiences in the late modern world.

In the rest of this chapter I shall, first, explore the somewhat labyrinthine trails of postmodern understandings of diaspora, considering, in particular, whether cultures can be thought of as having lost their territorial moorings, to have become in effect "travelling cultures". Secondly, I shall consider one of the paradigmatic cases of a cultural diaspora, namely that of migrants of African descent from the Caribbean. Finally, I shall explore the common experiences, intellectual and political visions and religious movements that cement Afro-Caribbean cultural and migratory experiences.

Postmodern views of diaspora

A starting point for many postmodernists is that conventional sociological and political categories have become too ossified to capture the fluidities of the contemporary world. For example, Bhabha (1994: 269–72) argues that, in addition to the need to abandon a belief in the exclusiveness of national languages and nation-states, we must also abandon the singularities of class and gender as "primary conceptual and organizational categories". Instead, we must be aware of the "multiple subject positions" (including race, gender, generation, institutional location, geopolitical locale and sexual orientation) that form the building blocks of identity in the postmodern world. Although not fully beguiled by post-modernism, I have myself previously suggested that the old essentialisms, such as the Marxist idea that social identity could be reduced to class identity, are now redundant. Rather, "gender, age, disability, race, religion, ethnicity, nationality, civil status, even musical styles and dress codes, are also very potent axes of organization and identification. These different forms of identity appear to be upheld simultaneously, successively or separately and with different degrees of force, conviction and enthusiasm" (Cohen 1994: 205).

My suggestion that identity is built in a different and more complex way, from a greater variety of "building blocks", presupposes that some solid structures of identity can or will emerge. Bhabha (1994) and others question this assumption, suggesting rather that we need to focus on the interstitial moments and processes where "difference" is articulated. Somewhat confusingly, these "moments" are also understood as "spaces" (thus conflating the two aspects of relativity); but whether time or locale are involved, this makes little difference to the argument. Selfhood, the representation of one's own community and other communities, as well as the difference between the two are, so the argument runs, negotiated in strange, hitherto unexplored and fluid "frontlines" and "borderposts" of identity.

We are asked to investigate and, although this is not always explicit, to celebrate the overlapping edges, the ambiguities, the displacements of difference, and the mixing of cultures, religions, languages and ethnicities. In the following passage, in defence of his controversial novel *The satanic verses* (1988), the writer and critic Salman Rushdie (1991: 394) vehemently proclaims the virtues of difference and "hybridity":

> Standing at the centre of the novel is a group of characters most of whom are British Muslims, or not particularly religious persons of Muslim background, struggling with just the sort of great problems that have arisen to surround this book, problems of hybridization and ghettoization, of reconciling the old and the new. Those who oppose the novel most vociferously today are of the opinion that intermingling with different cultures will inevitably weaken and ruin their own. I am of the opposite opinion. *The Satanic Verses* celebrates hybridity, impurity, intermingling, the transformation that comes of new and unexpected combinations of human beings, cultures, ideas, politics, movies, songs. It rejoices in mongrelization and fears the absolution of the Pure. *Mélange*, hotchpotch, a bit of this and a bit of that is how newness enters the world. It is the great possibility that mass migration gives to the world, and I have tried to embrace it. *The Satanic Verses* is for change-by-fusion, change-by-conjoining. It is a love song to our mongrel selves.

Although I do not want to be seen to be defending intolerance of any description, this quotation makes it more evident why a *fatwa* (death sentence) was issued against Rushdie by some fundamentalist mullahs in Iran. He may intermittently have invited their charge that he committed blasphemy against the prophet Muhammad. But worse, he was suggesting that their single-minded obsession with purity was both futile and out of date.

One historical analogy with the mullahs' preoccupation is Hitler's frantic attempt to maintain the purity of the German *Volk* in the face of the people without a nation, the "cosmopolitan" Jews. These perverse people wrote German poetry and played German music, but refused to abandon their Jewishness. The notion of a "cosmopolitan" was deployed then to describe someone who stood outside existing cultures, observing them somewhat at a distance, while being able to move in and out of them at will. Later, the word implied refinement, the command over a number of languages, even a certain raffishness and charm. (Little wonder it was selected as the title for an upmarket women's magazine.) In contrast, but curiously allied to cosmopolitanism, is the term "hybridity", which has been used by Rushdie, Stuart Hall (1992) and many other postmodernist authors to denote the evolution of new, dynamic, mixed cultures. This may have been an unfortunate expression to adopt for, as plant breeders know, hybrids have marked tendencies towards sterility and uniformity, precisely the opposite meaning those who used the term "hybridization" intended to convey. I prefer myself the long established concept of syncretism – the evolution of commingled cultures that are different from two or more parent cultures. There is little use, however, in playing the role of a frantic semantic. Misnomers are common in the English language and eventually acquire their intended meaning through the sheer weight of repetition. Thus it will be with "hybridity".

Hall (1992: 310–14) makes a strong link between the development of hybridity and the changing character of diasporas. For him, the late modern world is marked by two broad contradictory tendencies. On the one hand, the drift of globalization is towards homogenization and assimilation. On the other hand, and perhaps in reaction to globalization, is the reassertion of localism – notably in the form of ethnicity, nationalism and religious fundamentalism. Although these tendencies appear to be irreconcilable, he makes a cogent case that cultural identities are emerging that are "in transition", drawing on different traditions and harmonizing old and new without assimilation or total loss of the past. He designates this process as the evolution of "cultures of hybridity" and closely associates the growth in these cultures with the "new diasporas" created by the colonial experience and the ensuing postcolonial migrations.

While the focus on postcolonial diasporas seems especially salient to Hall and to a number of other cultural studies writers, some have sought to extend the notion of diaspora to settings and experiences beyond the strictly postcolonial ones.[1] For example, Rey Chow (1993: 20–1) recalls her childhood experiences in Hong Kong, that "junction between diaspora and homeland", caught between British colonialism and Chinese communism. She expresses indignation that once she had left the colony to work in the USA she found herself trapped in an intellectual culture that demanded that somehow she should be regarded as typical, or "authentic", in short a "native". She resolutely refuses this role (pp. 115–19), although she maintains that the presence of "Third World" intellectuals in the "first world" makes it impossible for Western historians and anthropologists to regard particular cultures as "objects of enquiry within well-defined geographical domains". Nevertheless, she continues, it is not the role of the diasporic intellectual to protest against the intrusion of foreign imperialism on native soil, nor against the continued cultural domination of the homeland by foreign forces in the postcolonial period. Such struggles, Chow indicates, are for the people on the ground. Diasporic intellectuals have to guard themselves against the temptations of exploiting their roles as distant patrons of the homeland culture while simultaneously being privileged "ethnics" and "minorities" in the West.

There is no direct intimation of this, but it is possible that Chow is suggesting a critique of one of the most illustrious of diasporic intellectuals, Edward Said. In his famous book *Orientalism: Western conceptions of the Orient*, Said (1991) had interposed himself between what he called the "guild tradition of Orientalism" and "Third World" realities and perceptions. This posture is mercilessly attacked by Ahmed (1992: 195–6) as pandering to "the most sentimental, the most extreme forms of Third World nationalism". All fault, Ahmed points out, is attributed to the Orientalists, colonialists and imperialists. Implausibly, none is attributed to people in the colonized countries. According to Ahmed, Said's book scored an instant success with the privileged academics from Asia, Africa and the Middle East who had lodged themselves in the humanities and social science faculties of Western universities. They needed a text to prove that they themselves were victims (a bogus claim, says Ahmed), so that they could speak in the name of the oppressed and thereby secure greater legitimacy for their endeavours.

Despite Ahmed's critique of his whole enterprise, Said's own claims are somewhat more credible than those of his epigoni. As a Palestinian *émigré*, he saw himself in a special position to disabuse Westerners of their ridiculous stereotypes of Arabs as "stupid savages" of a "negligible quantity" and with minds that are "depraved, anti-Semitic to the core, violent [and] unbalanced" (1991: 306, 307). He found in exile a cogent means of interrogating such reactionary elements of contemporary Western culture, writing that (Said 1990: 365):

> The exile knows that in a secular and contingent world, homes are always provisional. Borders and barriers which enclose us within the safety of familiar territory can also become prisons, and are often defended beyond reason or necessity. Exiles cross borders, break barriers of thought and experience.

In an engaging but sometimes bewildering display of "me-too-ism", Chambers (1994) acknowledges that he is highly influenced by Hall's and Said's work. However, he maintains that the creation of new identities is a more universal phenomenon than Hall's emphasis on postcolonialism or Said's stress on exile imply. For him (Chambers 1994: 25, 18–19) all identities are formed "on the move", at the unstable point where subjectivity meets the narrative of history. This journey is always "open and incomplete", involving a continual fabulation, invention and construction in which, finally, there is "no fixed identity or final destination". To be lost, to be a stranger in a strange land is typical of the human condition, not just typical of those who suffered the forced migrations of slavery and indentureship. Chambers (p. 27) affirms that:

> The migrant's sense of being rootless, of living between worlds, between a lost past and a non-integrated present, is perhaps the most fitting metaphor of this (post) modern condition. This underlines the theme of diaspora, not only black, also Jewish, Indian, Islamic, Palestinian, and draws us into the processes whereby the previous margins now fold in on the centre. As a further supplement, think of migration, movement and the historical harvest of hybridity that characterize diverse historical novels.

In this genre of analysis, the migrant and the refugee have become the *träger* of the postmodern/latemodern world: a means of globalization from below. What is home? What is exile? Are there any

133

essential elements of a national culture left intact? Do the expressions East and West, North and South still mean anything? Can migrants ever call their places of settlement a home? Is "home" still one's natality or even one's parent's natality? Does one live in a perpetual state of liminality? Can one, to be more flippant, surmount the issue of placement and displacement by devising a new slogan: "It does not matter where you're from, or where you've come to, but where you're at"?[2]

Travelling cultures, travelling nations

The perception that there were seminal changes in cultural interactions arising from migration was first adequately theorized by anthropologists. The subjects of their studies were no longer "there": they had by means of migration escaped the cages of their anthropological zoos. The veteran anthropologist, Clifford Geertz (1986: 118–19), argued that so long as the worlds they were studying really were "there" (as Malinowski found them and as Lévi-Strauss remembered them) the task of fieldwork was a practical problem, not a theoretical one. Though great anthropologists like Malinowski and Lévi-Strauss had very different methods and theories, what they shared was the idea that the "alien" and the "other" were in "a world elsewhere". This world embodied different ways of thinking, reasoning, judging and behaving that were discontinuous with "our own" and acted as alternative "to us".

What migration and the creation of diasporas have done is to move the margins to the centre.[3] The marginal groups are suddenly nearby, present, attendant, co-existent. Geertz warns against the naïve assumption that a reduction in distance automatically means that the gaps between cultures have been overcome. Group identity may remain strong and even strengthen in response to the shrinking of the space between peoples. That space remains and its character has to be explored if we are to understand not only how we are alike and how we may no longer disregard one another, but also how our differences remain profound and sometimes insuperable.

One of the most enterprising and creative scholars exploring this fuzzy frontier between imperfectly conjoined groups is James

Clifford (1992). He fundamentally challenges the anthropological tradition that non-Western people should be nativized and localized. Instead, he concentrates on the ways in which cultures "travel" – a word he prefers to "displacement", "nomadism", "pilgrimage" and "migration" because it conveys a two-way process pregnant with cultural and interactive implications. Flowing both ways into the borderlands of culture are "missionaries, converts, literate or educated informants, mixed bloods, translators, government officers, police, merchants, explorers, prospectors, tourists, travelers, ethnographers, pilgrims, servants, entertainers, migrant laborers, recent immigrants, etc." (p. 101).

Clifford's idea of travelling cultures becomes explicitly linked to diasporas in a subsequent article, where he makes the useful distinction between borderlands and diasporas (Clifford 1994). The first implies a situation of bi-locality where an emerging syncretic culture is temporarily separated by erratically enforced frontier controls, but linked by legal and illegal migration. A good example of a borderland culture is the riverain area of the Rio Grande, the zone supposedly separating Mexico and the USA. But where do El Paso and San Diego end and Cuidad Júarez and Tijuana begin? Although there is a close resemblance between borderlands and diasporas in that they "bleed" into each other, diasporas have some importantly distinct features. They are "caught up with and defined against the nation-state",[4] and are social entities that have different claims from those of indigenous, autochthonous, "tribal" peoples (p. 307).

The cultural forms of diasporas, Clifford (1994) insists, can never be exclusively nationalist. Nation-states are about welding the locals to a single place, gathering peoples and integrating ethnic minorities. Diasporas, by contrast, imply multiple attachments. They accommodate to, but also resist, the norms and claims of nationalists. It is true that some diasporas might contain nationalist groups that seek to create a nation-state (as we have seen in the case of the Khalistanis and Zionists discussed in Chapter 5). However, the most customary diasporic condition does not translate longings, nostalgia and eschatological visions of nationhood into a real nation-state with an army, a police force, a flag and a seat in the United Nations. Diasporas are positioned somewhere between nation-states and "travelling cultures" in that they involve dwelling in a nation-state in a physical sense, but travelling in an astral or spiritual sense that falls outside the nation-state's space/time zone.

The judgement that nation-states and diasporas are foreordained to board historical trains heading towards different destinations is questioned by Dhaliwal (1994a, 1994b). She argues that, while the South Asian diaspora has multiple and shifting relationships with India, these do not automatically challenge the Indian nation. Indeed, she suggests that the diaspora may provide a means of resolving the unconstituted nationhood of India itself – in particular the unresolved difference between Sikh and Hindu. The category "South Asian" (technically Bangladesh, Bhutan, India, the Maldives, Nepal, Pakistan and Sri Lanka) is made an inclusive one, almost inadvertently, through the power of Western liberal-democratic discourses, which require a single, fabricated "culture" for their multicultural ideologies and policies. To be sure, "South Asian" is often in practice reduced to "Indian", which in turn is reduced to a Brahminic elitism. None the less, Indians and South Asians more generally are increasingly understanding themselves as "travelling nations", an understanding generally shared by their countries of origin.

A similar conception is advanced by Basch et al. (1994: 8) who propose that contemporary diasporas are "nations unbound", who "reinscribe" space in a new way. They maintain that:

> both the political leaderships of sending nations and immigrants from these nations are coming to perceive these states as "deterritorialized".[5] In contrast to the past, when nation-states were defined in terms of a people sharing a common culture within a bounded territory, this new conception of nation-state includes as citizens those who live physically dispersed within the boundaries of many other states, but who remain socially, politically, culturally, and often economically part of the nation-state of their ancestors. In the case of the Haitian "tenth department", the Grenadian "constituency" in New York and the Filipino *balikbayan*, transnational ties are taken as evidence that migrants continue to be members of the state from which they originated.

There is an interesting resemblance, as well as contrast, between this idea of "nations unbound" and the colonizing, imperial diasporas considered in earlier chapters of this book. They too were extending their nations by "reinscribing space", but were sufficiently powerful to dominate and subjugate the peoples they met – to the extent that the invaders became the citizenry and the indigenees the subjects. In contemporary unbound nations, an imperial project is an impossible, or at least very remote, outcome. Nations are extended or unconfined from the viewpoint of the sending areas, but they appear as minorities, often quite weak and relatively powerless minorities, in the countries in which they find themselves.

The Caribbean: migration and diaspora

I turn now to my case study, the consideration of whether the Caribbean peoples abroad constitute a "new", "postcolonial", "hybrid" cultural diaspora of the type envisaged by the scholars and novelists discussed above. The first and most evident problem in seeing Caribbean peoples as any kind of diaspora is that they are not native to the area. As is well known, the autochthonous peoples of the Caribbean, the Caribs and Arawaks, failed to survive the glories of Western civilization – nearly all died from conquest, overwork and disease. Virtually everybody in the Caribbean came from somewhere else – the African slaves from West Africa, the white settlers, planters and administrators from Europe, and the indentured workers who arrived after the collapse of slavery from India. This may in and of itself disqualify any consideration given to the idea of a Caribbean diaspora. Settler and immigrant societies are normally conceived of as points of arrival, not departure, sites of a renewed collectivity, not of dissolution, emigration and dispersion.

Secondly, the peoples of the Caribbean may be thought of as parts of other diasporas – notably the African victim diaspora, the Indian labour diaspora and the European imperial diasporas. Again, surely it would be expected that, if they are free to migrate, a significant proportion of any diasporic community should wish to return to their real or putative homeland. Yet, with the partial exception of the Europeans, Caribbean people of Indian and African origin have in recent years been notably disinterested in returning either to India or to Africa.

Despite these considerable conceptual obstacles, Hall (1990: 222–37) none the less is convinced that a distinctive Caribbean diasporic identity can be discerned. Caribbean identity, he argues, cannot be rendered simply as a transposition of an African identity to the New World because the rupture of slavery and the admixture of other peoples built into a Caribbean identity a sense of hybridity, diversity and difference. Hall poses the question, "What makes African-Caribbean people already people of a diaspora?" and answers (p. 235) as follows:

> Diaspora does not refer us to those scattered tribes whose identity can only be secured in relation to some sacred homeland to which they must at all costs return, even if it means pushing other people into the sea. This is the old, the imperializing, the hegemonizing form of "ethnicity". We have seen the fate of the people of Palestine at the hands of this backward conception of diaspora (and the complicity of the West with it). The diaspora experience as I intend it here is defined not by essence or purity, but by the recognition of a necessary heterogeneity and diversity; by a conception of identity which lives with and through, not despite, difference; by hybridity. Diaspora identities are those which are constantly producing and reproducing themselves anew, through transformation and difference.

In this excerpt Hall is essentially concerned with the diasporic identity that Caribbean peoples created within the geographical bounds of the Caribbean itself. A much more challenging field of enquiry is the degree to which they affirmed, reproduced and created a diasporic identity in the places to which they subsequently moved. Before discussing the nature of this Caribbean diaspora abroad, it is necessary to provide a quick brush-stroke picture of their migration history over the last century or so.

I have just mentioned that Indo-Caribbeans did not go back to India, nor Afro-Caribbeans to Africa. Strictly speaking, this was not always true. At the end of the period of indenture about one quarter of the Indo-Caribbeans returned to India. In the African case, the British colonialists recruited a few dozen Afro-Caribbean train drivers for Nigeria, the French appointed an Antillean governor, Felix Eboué, in the Camerouns and a remarkable young psychiatrist, Frantz Fanon, who was later to become one of the most prominent of all Third World intellectuals, was assigned to the colonial medical service in Algeria. Some voluntary migration, including Garveyite and Rastafarian (see below) settlements, also occurred.

However, these were mere drops in the ocean of Caribbean people who decided to migrate to Panama, the USA and Europe. When Ferdinand de Lesseps, the famous Suez Canal maker, floated a new Panama Canal Company to link the Pacific Ocean to the Caribbean Sea, the Bourse went crazy with the prospects of great profits. In fact, the venture proved a long-drawn-out financial failure. The canal and railway works were dogged by mismanagement and the workers suffered greatly from malaria, snakebite, swamp fever, industrial accidents and bad treatment. The hands for this operation were drawn from many countries, but predominantly from Jamaica.

The Afro-Caribbean minority located in the strip of slums surrounding the Panama Canal Company area is descended from these workers. They have remained largely poor and underprivileged in the Panamanian context, with the key positions of authority and influence being occupied by Hispanics. Other small enclaves in Central America are drawn from Caribbean peoples brought there to establish banana plantations, or to undertake public works. Honduras and some small enclaves in Nicaragua and Guatemala (such as the charming Bay Islands) are inhabited by descendants of archipelago Afro-Caribbeans, often still fiercely resisting the abandonment of the English language, which they value as part of their diasporic identity.

Afro-Caribbeans in the USA

The bulk of migrants, however, went to the USA, perhaps one million from the Anglophone Caribbean alone. They went in so many capacities that it would be impossible in this chapter to describe fully the Caribbean social structure in the USA.[6] Temporary contract workers cut cane in Florida, Cuban exiles went to Miami, Haitians often arrived as illegals or boat people; while many middle-class professional people from the Anglophone Caribbean occupied important roles in medicine, in teaching and in retail services. One of the oft remarked on, but imperfectly researched, characteristics of the English-speaking Caribbean peoples in the USA is their extraordinary success and prominence, not only in the wider black community, but in American society more generally. Within some parts of the black community, Caribbean people are sometimes referred to, in a not entirely friendly way, as "Jew-maicans". The Caribbean community monopolizes the laundries, travel agents and hairdressing shops in several New York districts. Moreover, Caribbean people have played a prominent role in political activity – the Garveyite movement, the civil rights struggles and the Black Power Movement being the most notable.

Afro-Caribbeans in the UK

In contrast to the USA, the fortunes of Caribbean migrants in Europe have been less happy. The possible explanations for this relative lack of success are complex: different groups may have gone to Europe, only largely unskilled positions were on offer there, and some migration (notably to the UK and the Netherlands) was "panic" migration – with the networks of friends, relations and openings in business and education not fully prefigured or prepared. A number of scholars, as well as Caribbean migrants themselves, insist that the high levels of racial discrimination and disadvantage they experienced seriously jeopardized their chances of success (Gilroy 1987, Solomos 1989).

The bulk of Caribbean migration to the UK occurred in the 1950s, and came to a rapid halt in the early 1960s with the implementation of the Commonwealth Immigrants Act forbidding further unregulated migration. With the exception of "the rush to beat the ban", the movement of migrants to the UK closely shadowed the ebbs and flows of the job vacancies (Peach 1968). Despite finding unskilled jobs, the early experiences of Caribbean people in the UK were often negative ones. They felt that their wartime loyalty had been unacknowledged and that they were treated as an unwelcome problem rather than as valued citizens of the empire coming to help the motherland. Besides this psychic shock of rejection, at a more practical level occupational mobility was limited, educational successes were meagre and the second generation showed high rates of crime and unemployment.

It is important, however, not be too mired in the negative images that both racists and anti-racists need for their respective political causes. British girls of Afro-Caribbean origin outperform both black and white British boys in school examinations. As in the USA, there is a disproportionately high representation of black athletes and sportspersons in the boxing ring, in track and field events, and in cricket and football.[7] Afro-Caribbeans are also well represented in broadcasting and in literary and artistic pursuits, especially the performing arts. Even though this is a somewhat backhanded compliment, the 1996 *British Crime Survey*, based on a sample of 10,000 people, showed that in the age group 16–29, whereas 43 per cent of whites claimed to have taken drugs, the figure for their Afro-Caribbean peer group was substantially lower, at 34 per cent (*Guardian*, 4 May 1996: 5).

Perhaps a more significant finding is that the latest census, 1991, shows that the level of ghettoization is low and has been falling since 1961. Using a sophisticated index of segregation, Peach (1995) shows that the levels of Caribbean segregation in London are about half those of African Americans in New York. Moreover, only 3 per cent of the Afro-Caribbean population lived in "enumeration districts" (the smallest census unit covering 700 people) in which they formed 30 per cent of the population or more. Taken together, these positive indicators may signify a first stage in a wider and deeper thrust to social mobility – in the third, if not the second, generation.

Caribbean peoples in the Netherlands

The Netherlands received about half as many Caribbean immigrants as the UK – approximately 250,000 compared with Britain's 500,000. The numbers, however, are much more significant when they are considered as a proportion of both the Dutch population and of the Caribbean source populations. Caribbean migrants arrived from all over the Dutch Antilles, but predominantly from the former Dutch colony of Surinam. So large was the departure that the population of Surinam was depleted by about half. In that many people were persuaded to leave because of the prospect of an independence with diminished Dutch support, the Surinamese in the Netherlands can be seen to fit into the category of "panic migrants" mentioned earlier.

The Surinamese in the Netherlands divide, roughly equally, into two ethnic sections – Afro-Surinamese and Indo-Surinamese. The housing situation for many Surinamese is surprisingly favourable – their arrival in Amsterdam conveniently coincided with the abandonment of a "white elephant" set of luxury apartments that the local Dutch did not wish to inhabit. A comparative study of Caribbean peoples in Britain and the Netherlands (Cross and Entzinger 1988) yielded many similarities. In a more recent study, Cross (1995: 72) maintains that exclusion on the grounds of culture, way of life or newness of incorporation is less salient than the class exclusion that arises from the collapse of blue collar industries. In this respect, the cutting of welfare benefits in the UK in response to the ideology of neoliberalism contrasts with the greater endurance of welfare provisions in the Netherlands. The circumstances of Caribbean peoples in the Netherlands may improve relatively given their more benign public provision.

Antilleans in France

Caribbean migration to France arises in an apparently different form from the cases just considered. The major source areas are the DOM (*départements d'outre-mer*) territories of Martinique and Guadeloupe. Because of the juridical status of the DOM as organic parts of France, migration to the continent is officially considered as internal migration – simply as if one French citizen were to move from one *département* to another. The numbers involved are thought to be about 300,000, and the urban centres, particularly Paris, are the main destinations.

Of course it is important not to confuse appearance with substance. Again, we notice a high predominance of unskilled, manual and public sector jobs being held by people from the French Antilles, particularly in the 1970s. However, a significant white collar salariat (for example in the banks and post office) has been recruited by the quasi-official labour agency in the islands. Because certification and formal qualifications are much more important in France than in either the UK or the Netherlands, French Antilleans with the requisite pieces of paper have been able to benefit from the strong meritocratic tradition.

Unlike the British Caribbean population, which has fallen, the French Caribbean population has moved from 165,945 in 1975, to

265,988 in 1982, to 337,006 in 1990 (Condon and Ogden 1996: 38). Although it is difficult to track movements to and from the Caribbean, given that there are no immigration restrictions, Condon and Ogden find that return, circulatory and retirement migration are common, as are family visits and casual tourism. The younger generation of Caribbeans living in France often talk of returning "for their children's sake". They place a high value on what they perceive to be their own culture, shared values and "roots" (p. 46).[8]

At a deeper level, French Antilleans have always shared a Faustian pact with the French state. Should they choose to abandon their Africanness and embrace Mother France, they would become French people, citizens, members of a world culture and civilization. Two possible consequences arise from this pact. The more positive is that the French live up to the revolutionary ideals of liberty, equality and fraternity. The most coherent defence of this position appears in Hintjens's (1995) iconoclastic book, in which she claims that decolonization is possible without formal statehood. She argues that in many cases decolonization can be seen as a form of denial, a shedding of the political and moral responsibilities of the colonial powers, an act of dismissal and disdain. For her, postcolonialism is also a political struggle for equality and recognition. It is even more potent if it can be deterritorialized and taken to the heart of the racist empires. The anti-colonial struggle, in short, is for equality within France.

The more negative outcome, of course, would be if the path of assimilation were to turn out to be an illusion, a trap, ultimately a hoax. This would be the cruellest consequence of all – for the French Antilleans in continental France would become a liminal people, no longer able to express their distinctive ethnic identity or recover a sense of "home". Lodged in a state of limbo or liminality (Turner 1969; Al-Rasheed 1993: 91–2), they would experience a crisis of meaning, where institutions, values and norms dissolve and collapse. Their *communitas* would be reduced to a parody of the old ways and would be incapable of reconstituting itself in the new setting.

Caribbean peoples as a cultural diaspora

Despite the different destinations and experiences of Caribbean peoples abroad, they remain an exemplary case of a cultural diaspora. This arises first from their common history of forcible dispersion through the slave trade – still shared by virtually all people of African descent, despite their subsequent liberation, settlement and citizenship in the various countries of the New World. Partly, this is a matter of visibility. Unlike (say) in the cases of Jews or Armenians, where superficial disappearance is possible in Europe and North America if exogamy occurs, in the case of those of African descent skin colour normally remains a marker for two, three or more generations – despite exogamy. The deployment of skin colour in many societies as a signifier of status, power and opportunity, make it impossible for any people of African descent to avoid racial stigmatization. As one black British writer puts it, "our imaginations are conditioned by an enduring proximity to regimes of racial terror" (Gilroy 1993b: 103).

Although important, being phenotypically African and being conscious of racism are, in themselves, insufficient to assign the label "cultural diaspora" to Afro-Caribbeans. I would suggest that at least four other elements should be present. First, there should be evidence of cultural retention or affirmations of an African identity. Secondly, there should be a literal or symbolic interest in "return". Thirdly, there should be cultural artefacts, products and expressions that show shared concerns and cross-influences between Africa, the Caribbean and the destination countries of Caribbean peoples. Fourthly, and often forgotten by the intensely cerebral versions of diaspora presented by cultural studies theorists, there should be indications that ordinary Caribbean peoples abroad – in their attitudes, migration patterns and social conduct – behave in ways consistent with the idea of a cultural diaspora.

Retention and affirmations of African identity
With respect to the issue of retention, there are clear examples of a return to Africanness in the Maroon (runaway slave) communities of Jamaica and the so-called "Bush Negroes" of Surinam. Other, less dramatic, examples abound. Everything from Brazilian cults, Caribbean savings clubs, folklore, musical rhythms, popular art,

Trinidadian "shouters" and voodoo practices have been minutely recorded by scores of anthropologists (notably Herskovits 1937, 1947, 1961, Herskovits et al. 1947). This evidence of retention must, however, not be narrowly understood as freezing African cultures in aspic. As with other migratory groups, New World Africans took the opportunity to throw off the shackles of their prior social constraints. Thus, the famous founding president of a free Haiti, Toussaint L'Ouverture, was as much Jacobin as African; while, arguably, during the Second World War the French Antilles were more loyal to the idea of the French nation than the metropolis itself. Equally, many Anglophone Caribbeans displayed a remarkable loyalty to Britain in both world wars and showed a fierce adherence to British educational, social and political institutions.[9] Using a reinterpretation of the work of W. E. B. Du Bois, Paul Gilroy (1993a, 1993b) supplies an insightful analysis of how African Americans and Afro-Caribbeans live within a "double consciousness", stemming both from Africa and Europe.

The links between Africa and New World Africans also took the form of literary, ideological and political movements. The African, African-American and Afro-Caribbean intelligentsia has long sought to define some cultural and historical continuities between Africans on the continent and in the diaspora. This movement has flowed in several directions. Kwame Nkrumah, the Ghanaian president, studied in a black university in the USA and articulated the ideas of an African personality and African unity. Léopold Senghor, the president of Senegal, advanced the idea of Négritude. The Trinidadian revolutionary intellectuals George Padmore and C. L. R. James were partly responsible for convening the watershed Manchester Conference of 1945, when the basic lines of struggle for African self-determination were articulated. In the case of the Francophone Caribbean, Aimé Césaire made his spiritual journey to Africa in *Return to my native land* (1956). He and other Caribbean leaders were also an important influence on Négritude and had a continuing dialogue with Africans, and peoples of African descent more generally, in journals such as *Présence Africaine*.

A number of literary figures from Trinidad, whose works are imbricated in the evolution of a Caribbean diasporic consciousness, have been ably analysed by Harney (1996). The creation of a postcolonial identity was the project of novelists Earl Lovelace and

Michael Anthony. The complexities of creating a new nationalism from Indo-, Sino- and Afro-Caribbean elements was addressed by Valerie Belgrave and Willi Chen, while the dilemmas of Caribbean migrants moving to Canada, Britain and the USA were depicted in the writings of Samuel Selvon, Neil Bissoondath and V. S. Naipaul.

Return movements, literal and symbolic

Despite the small number of Afro-Caribbeans who actually returned to Africa, Caribbean visionaries were at the forefront of the Back-to-Africa movements and in the articulation of the idea of a common fate of African people at home and abroad. I have discussed the Garveyite and Ethiopian/Rastafarian movements in Chapter 2. Here I shall simply add some details of how these movements served to link the different points of the cultural diaspora.

The most flamboyant, and immensely popular, of New World return movements was the Universal Negro Improvement Association (UNIA), founded by the Jamaican, Marcus Garvey. Garveyites were particularly strong in the USA, and representatives of small but ill fated colonies were sent to Liberia and elsewhere on the continent. Garvey was born in Jamaica in 1887 and had travelled widely in the West Indies and Central America before starting the UNIA. He drew his inspiration from two main strands – the Maroon revolts, which showed even in the New World, and even after the experience of the Middle Passage and slavery, that blacks could still recover some of their African traditions. Secondly, he was very influenced by the strength of the British imperial idea that people could bluff their way to political dominance by style, appearance and a belief in their own superiority.

He was particularly unimpressed by what he found in the USA. He saw poor blacks beating their heads against "brick wall" situations in which they would never be accepted. This experience provided Garvey with the idea of setting up the Black Star Line, a shipping company owned by blacks with the intention literally of reversing the transatlantic slave trade. Though the line was never a great success, when Kwame Nkrumah came to power in Ghana, he adopted it as the name of Ghana's merchant marine.

Although Garvey had returned to Jamaica, with the exception of one large UNIA rally and a convention in Kingston in 1928, he was largely unsuccessful as a politician. He died in obscurity in London in 1940, but he had succeeded in further promoting the consciousness of Africa that had been well developed in Jamaica since the days of the Maroons. The cultural link with Africa was also enhanced by the deep spirituality that converted Christian Jamaicans acquired. They found in the Bible an identification with the ancient Jews. Like the Jews who were dragged off to Egypt and Babylon to slavery, the Africans had been dragged off to the West Indies as slaves.

This biblical and African consciousness became fused together in November 1930, when a new prince, Ras Tafari, was crowned Emperor of Ethiopia and adopted the name Haile Selassie. Some poor, particularly rural, Jamaicans began to describe themselves as "Ethiopians", or followers of the crowned prince Ras Tafari, namely Rastafarians. The Emperor claimed descent from Solomon and Sheba, which made the Ethiopians a denomination of Christianity that dated back to the very foundations of the religion, and the fact that they had seen off an Italian army in 1898 became their symbol of resistance. An article published in *National Geographic* magazine in January 1931, in which there was a discussion about modern Ethiopia that covered the coronation, was passed from hand to hand. This was no fiction. Here were pictures and an article in a white man's magazine! That the British had taken the coronation seriously enough to send the Duke of Gloucester, the son of King George V, to the event was regarded as further proof. The Jamaican national daily, the *Daily Gleaner* (February 1931), carried this letter.

> The whole Ethiopian race throughout the world, or at least the leaders of thought, should regard with the greatest degree of satisfaction the well considered decision of His Majesty's Government to send a deputation headed by a member of the British Royal Family to represent the great Anglo-Saxon people at the coronation of the only independent state among the millions of Ham's offspring.

The movement itself rapidly spread from its origins in Jamaica, not least because Bob Marley, the celebrated reggae singer, spread the message through the popularity of his music. Yawney (1995) suggests that there may now be more Rastafari living outside Jamaica than on the island, with many activists in the USA, Canada and Britain, as well as Africa itself.[10] Although the movement has often been dismissed as impractical and chiliastic, as Hall (1995: 14) argues, "It was not the literal Africa that people wanted to return to, it was the language, the symbolic language for describing what suffering was like, it was a metaphor for where they were . . . a language with a double register, a literal and a symbolic register."

Shared cultural expressions

The idea that there might be complex connections between Africans at home, in the New World and in Africa has been suggested by black writers and intellectuals for over a century. One poignant exploration of 250 years of the African diaspora is provided by the Caribbean-born writer Caryl Phillips (1993), who chronicles the sense of disconnectedness and homelessness of peoples of African descent abroad and how they sought to reconstitute themselves as acting, thinking, emotionally intact individuals. The title of his novel, *Crossing the river*, evokes the transatlantic slave trade. Phillips (1993: 235–7) hears the drum beating on the far bank of the natal land and sees the "many-tongued chorus of the common memory" in West Indian pubs in England, an addicted mother in Brooklyn, a barefoot boy in São Paulo, the reggae rhythms in the hills and valleys of the Caribbean and the carnivals in Trinidad and Rio. Despite the trauma of the Middle Passage and the human wreckage that resulted, Phillips concludes his novel on an optimistic note. Beloved children arrived on the far bank of the river. They loved and were loved.

Another novelist shows how language and popular expressions are carried by Caribbean migrants to the UK. In this passage the protagonist in Samuel Selvon's (1985) most famous novel, *The lonely Londoners*, significantly and ironically called Moses, tries with his friends to recapture life in Trinidad and adjust to their new life, after ten years, in London:

> [They] coming together for oldtalk, to find out the latest gen, what happening, when is the next fête, Bart asking if anybody seen his girl anywhere, Cap recounting an incident he had with a women by the tube station the night before, Big City want to know why the arse he can't win a

pool, Galahad recounting a clash with the colour problem in a restaurant in Piccadilly. (cited Harney 1996: 103)

While vernacular language crosses the Atlantic in the way demonstrated by Samuel Selvon, a more popular art form is music. Here, in a persuasive essay, Gilroy (1993b: 37) argues that, "The contemporary musical forms of the diaspora work within an aesthetic and political framework that demands that they ceaselessly reconstruct their own histories, folding back on themselves time and again to celebrate and validate the simple, unassailable fact of their survival." The politics of black music are barely beneath the surface in the calypsos of Trinidad, reggae and ska from Jamaica, samba from Brazil, township jazz from South Africa, Highlife from Nigeria and jazz, hip-hop, soul and rap from the USA. In the expressive title of Gilroy's essay, Africans at home and abroad are "one nation under a groove".

The most intellectually ambitious attempt to bring out the crosscurrents of cultural expression in Africa and the diaspora is made by Paul Gilroy (1993a) in *The black Atlantic*. He strongly resists any attempt to hijack the experience of New World Africans to those particular to African Americans, a tendency he found in some of the "Afrocentric" positions of American black intellectuals. Rather, he sees the consciousness of the African diaspora as being formed in a complex cultural and social intermingling between Africa, Europe and the Americas. However, this does not lead to cultural uniformity, but rather to a recognition of "transnational and intercultural multiplicity". Of course, some degree of unity must exist in the Atlantic Africans' diasporic culture for it to be deemed a shared impulse and form of consciousness. This emergent culture is characterized as "the black Atlantic". His influential work (which needs much more exegesis that I have space to give it here) is also a comment on the nature of modernity, on the idea of a nationalism without a nation-state (or a territory), and on the idea of a "double consciousness", prefigured in Hegelian phenomenology and expressed in the New World by the double heritage of Africa and Europe.[11]

Social conduct and popular attitudes

Much of the material on the Caribbean diaspora by writers in the field of cultural studies is both challenging and theoretically sophisticated. But to what extent is a transnational identity a lived experience, demonstrated by migrants' social conduct as well as invented in the minds and emotions of writers, musicians and academics? To this question I do not propose a full reply – for only an extensive research project would yield empirically verifiable answers. However, I thought it might be educative to do what might be called a "reality check" on the broad thesis.

I did this by carefully examining one issue (1–7 May 1996) of the *Weekly Gleaner*, the self-declared "top Caribbean newspaper" published in south London and comprising a digest of Jamaica's *Daily Gleaner*, together with local editorial matter and letters. That a newspaper of this type appears and sells is, in a sense, indication enough of the strength of a transnational Caribbean identity. What I thought particularly illustrative of the continuing relationship between the Caribbean communities in the UK and the Caribbean was a letter to the editor from a Mr R. Francis of south London. He complained about the discourtesy that he had experienced on his last trip to Jamaica in banks, the customs service and government departments. I add the emphasis on the remaining part of his letter:

> I would like to express my view on the way in which *returnees* to Jamaica are treated *back home*. . . . Like other people, I am definitely homesick, I am scared of going back to Jamaica because of the treatment often meted out to returnees and people on holiday. Although *we are away* it should be understood that we have and will always contribute to the finance and development of Jamaica. *It is our country as much as it is those who have never left.*

When one examines the advertisements, the link with "our country" becomes much more concrete. The pages are stuffed with advertisements for shipping lines, airlines, freight handlers, money transfer services ("Send your cash in a flash", says one), plots for sale in Jamaica, architects, removal companies, vacation accommodation and export houses selling tropicalized refrigerators "good with the correct voltage and specification *for your country*". Readers are offered shares on the Jamaican stock exchange and access via a cable company to "Black Variety Television".

Conclusion

Theodor Adorno once remarked that "it is part of morality not to be at home in one's own home" (cited Sanadjian 1996: 5). Certainly this seems to be a recurrent theme in the story of Caribbean peoples abroad. In this chapter I have sought to discover whether the Caribbean peoples constitute a "new", "postcolonial", "hybrid" diaspora of the type envisaged by novelists and scholars of cultural studies. To assess this I had to examine and assess postmodernist and anthropological literature with which I previously had little knowledge and with which, it has to be confessed, I initially had little sympathy.

Somewhat to my surprise, I found the general arguments highly suggestive. They could of course not be conclusive, for the cultural relativism of some anthropologists, together with the resistance to empirical work or to meta-theory on the part of postmodernists, would obviate the possibility of any final argument. However, rather than follow the authors I have cited along an endless roller-coaster of meanings, discourses, representations and narratives, I sought to introduce what I have called "reality markers" to the argument. What was the history of settlement in the Caribbean and migration from the area? What were the fates and fortunes of Caribbean peoples in the different destination areas? Were there systematic differences between those who went to North America, the UK, the Netherlands or France? In fact all sorts of cultural and political compromises with a diasporic identity arose, particularly, I would suggest, among the French Antilleans in metropolitan France. For example, if we take the four criteria I suggested for assessing whether a Caribbean cultural diaspora existed, the level of cultural retention and interest in "return" was lowest among those from the Francophone Caribbean. Not of course that it was absent. For Césaire, as for many in the Anglophone Caribbean, the idea of return was subliminal and symbolic. But there is a significant difference between the two language groups. In the English-speaking Caribbean and in the USA, the idea of return spread beyond the intelligentsia to the masses – through the Garveyite and Rastafarian movements.

In their works previously cited Hall, Gilroy, Harney and others have been able to show that in music, literature, art and language there was considerable cross-pollination of ideas, images and concepts over the waves and the air waves of the black Atlantic. As someone who lived in the Caribbean for two years and maintains ongoing friendships and academic contacts in the area, I recognize many of the nuances proposed by these commentators, who focus on the Caribbean imagination. However, I remain convinced that a more solid and accurate understanding of the nature of the Caribbean cultural diaspora will be possible only by gathering full historical information and sociological data. I cannot provide these here. But I would like to provide something of a preliminary corrective to the "black Atlantic thesis".

I submit, with Craig (1992), that it is not without coincidence that "the enterprise of the Indies" as it was called in Columbus's time, joined the major continents of the globe (Europe, Africa *and* Asia) to the Americas and that with the help of Caribbean labour, the Panama Canal added the Pacific. Thus, whatever the sophistication and complexity of the black Atlantic argument, at root it is a historical simplification, which cannot fully explain the process of indigenization and creolization in the Caribbean, despite the lack of indigenees. Nor can it account for the complexities arising from the large Asian presence in the Caribbean and *its* subsequent diasporization.

The social behaviour of Caribbean people in their places of sojourn and settlement provides telling evidence of the creation of a cultural diaspora, but more sustained empirical work needs to be undertaken on this issue. How, to pick up two of Craig's (1992) examples, did the Caribbean carnival evolve into a circuit, linking the archipelago to the metropolitan cities or New York, Toronto, London and elsewhere? By "how" I mean, who were the principal social actors and social organizations involved? How were the enterprises financed? What was the role of Caribbean governments in cementing these ties? Again, to take another example, the Hindu festival of Phagwa was celebrated by Caribbean people for the first time on the streets of New York in 1991. How was this culture transmitted and borne by migration? How did it become modified? In short, through their roots and branches, or to be precise through their rooting and branching, the people themselves make their diaspora. The frontiers of the region are beyond the Caribbean – not only in the consciousness of Caribbean people to be sure, but also in their social conduct, migration patterns and achievements in their places of settlement and sojourn.

SEVEN

Diasporas in the age of globalization

What is meant here by "globalization", now such a powerful key-word in the social sciences? McGrew (1992) has produced an ambitious synthesis of the main propositions relating to globalization and the construction of a global society. He points to a set of intersecting elements which together signify that a global society is emerging. In particular, he submits:

1. that the claims of the Enlightenment – proposing that human beings are essentially similar and have similar needs and aspirations – have now been embraced by most political leaders and by democratic movements in most countries;
2. that there is worldwide financial, economic, technological and ecological interdependence;
3. that there is a growing perception, aroused and confirmed by the satellite pictures from space, that "planet earth" is a single place;
4. that with the collapse of the Soviet Union the bifurcation of the world no longer exists. The "Third World" has also disappeared as a coherent category. There is, so to speak, only one world;
5. that goods, capital, knowledge, images, communications, crime, culture, pollutants, drugs, fashions and beliefs all readily flow across territorial boundaries; and
6. that we are "on the rocky road" to "the first global civilization" – a discrete world order with shared values, processes and structures.[1]

Despite the surface power and appeal of this argument, we should not be overwhelmed by it. We need to bear in mind at least five major qualifications. First, a number of writers on globalization slip uneasily between description and prediction. Many of the factors mentioned by those who engage in "global babble" are of tendential, not actual, significance.

Secondly, there are some profound disagreements between the statements made by global theorists. For example, the cultural, postmodernist and voluntarist versions of globalization (Featherstone 1994, Robertson 1994) are in marked contrast to the still potent work of Wallerstein (1984), who proposes a leftist, "hard" version of globalization, emphasizing the dominance and fateful impress of the capitalist world economy.

Thirdly, there are two strongly divergent theses about the future of nation-states. The more radical view is that they are in the process of dissolution in the face of global pressures. The more conservative view, which is less well aired but may be correct, is that nation-states are adapting to the new pressures by changing their functions. For example, it can be argued that the nation-state no longer crystallizes and organizes domestic capital, but that it continues to police inward labour flows and seeks to galvanize, although with diminishing capacity, a single identity around a national leadership, common citizenship and social exclusion of outsiders.[2]

Fourthly, a number of the theorists of globalization are remarkably apolitical in describing how globalization occurs. Although a number of the writers concerned announce their left-wing credentials, they implicitly accept the "invisible hand of the (global) market", ignoring the powerful hegemonizing forces at work. As Waters (1996: 3) reminds us, globalization is "a consequence of the expansion of European culture across the planet via settlement, colonization and cultural mimesis". Only the last involves some element of consent.

Finally, there are some clearly observable countertendencies to globalization. Whatever the future of the nation-state, there is no doubt that nationalism as a force and as an ideology is on the increase. National movements organize ethnicities and sub-ethnicities and often seek to find for them an exclusive territorial expression.[3] As with nationalism and ethnicity, so too with religious fundamentalism, racism, sexism and other forms of social exclusion, all of which *also* seem to be on the increase, despite globalization.

Relevant aspects of globalization

Within the rich array of possible understandings of and countertendencies to globalization, I would like to emphasize five aspects that have particular bearing on the study of diasporas. These five elements will form the basis of my subsequent discussion.

- *A world economy* with quicker and denser transactions between its subsectors due to better communications, cheaper transport, a new international division of labour, the activities of transnational corporations and the effects of liberal trade and capital-flow policies;
- *forms of international migration* that emphasize contractual relationships, family visits, intermittent stays abroad and sojourning, as opposed to permanent settlement and the exclusive adoption of the citizenship of a destination country;
- *the development of "global cities"* in response to the intensification of transactions and interactions between the different segments of the world economy and their concentration in certain cities whose significance resides more in their global, rather than in their national, roles;
- *the creation of cosmopolitan and local cultures* promoting or reacting to globalization; and
- *a deterritorialization of social identity* challenging the hegemonizing nation-states' claim to make an exclusive citizenship a defining focus of allegiance and fidelity in favour of overlapping, permeable and multiple forms of identification.

Each of these aspects of globalization has, in different ways, opened up new opportunities for diasporas to emerge, to survive and to thrive. Let me consider them in more detail in turn.

A world economy

It is a commonly expressed belief that markets, technology, capital, trade and migration are remaking the world by sweeping all forms of localism aside. Yet there is a curious fatalism and determinism in such accounts that elides any elaborated consideration of the pertinent institutions and agencies that galvanize this process. This sense of predestination is derived from the almost total hegemony of neoliberal economic thinking in official circles and in the media, which naïvely assume that "the market" is all that is needed to dynamize the global economy. Usually forgotten are the institutional and social mechanisms that manage and structure the market place and the agents who engage in market transactions.

At the peak of the global market are regulatory frameworks like the General Agreement on Tariffs and Trade (now the World Trade Organization) and financial institutions such as the World Bank. Just below are legal-rational entities like transnational corporations (TNCs), which are increasingly escaping their original national origins and functioning as fully global organizations. The economic impact of the TNCs has been extensively documented. For instance, Dicken (1992) argues that much of the world's economic system is dominated by the TNCs in their decisions to invest or not to invest in particular locations. They are responsible for an important chunk of world employment, production and trade. This is particularly true of production and trade, where perhaps between one-fifth and one-quarter of all production is in the hands of the TNCs. Trade is more elusive statistically, but what is clear is that a high proportion of world trade is intra-firm trade, i.e. one bit of the TNC is providing components or expertise to another branch or subsidiary of the same firm. (More than 50 per cent of the total trade of the USA and Japan comprises trade conducted within the TNCs.) Another way of understanding the global economic importance of the TNCs is to take them as equivalent units to countries. Using this measurement, of the 100 most important economic units in the world today, half are nation-states and half are TNCs. As there are about 180 states recognized by the United Nations, this means that 130 of these have smaller economies than the 50 largest TNCs.

The resulting flows of raw materials, components and finished products, technological and organizational expertise, as well as skilled personnel, constitute the basic building blocks of the global economy. There is much less documentation on the extent and impact of personnel moving as a result of TNCs than there is on capital or trade flows, yet the numbers involved are considerable. One good example is the case of the Japanese, who have moved abroad with their expanding companies. In his readable and innovative account, Kotkin (1992) calls the movement a "diaspora by design". He argues (pp. 134–5) that because the Japanese had been frustrated in their plans for conventional colonization, they enlarged their influence in the world economy through other means:

> Among the principal agents for this expansion were the *sogo shosha*, or trading companies. . . . Initially the move abroad was on a small scale and rather poorly co-ordinated. Lacking any foreign markets, the first foreign operations, those of Mitsui, were conducted out of the Japanese embassy in London. . . . By the 1930s nearly a half million Japanese were living temporarily abroad as "birds of passage", including agents for the *zaibatsu* [subsidiaries], independent traders and students. At the top of this worldwide network stood the new breed of college-educated managers . . . who created a large network of related companies, often quite independent, whose products and services they could in turn finance then distribute through their global network.

The most important Japanese colony in Europe is in the UK, where by 1990 Japanese factories, banks, corporate offices and insurance houses had investments totalling $16 billion. These enterprises, Kotkin says (p. 124), employed some 40,000 Japanese nationals. In fact, this figure is a substantial underestimate. By 1996, the official figure was 45,000 and this included only those Japanese who had registered with the embassy in London. The total is likely to be about 90,000. Despite its size, the group has remained largely invisible through the development of its own social institutions. A number of golf clubs, hotels, spas, Japanese schools (there are over 230 worldwide), temples, cinemas, booksellers, restaurants, nightclubs, bars and markets are patronized almost exclusively by overseas Japanese.

Because of the size, and perhaps also the power, of the Japanese community in Britain, intercultural heads have gingerly begun to peek over the parapets. *Sushi* and *karaoke* bars and an immense supermarket in London have begun to attract a British clientele, while the citizens of a depressed area in the North of England have successfully lured Japanese investors with an impressive display of Japanese flower arrangements by women who had learned their craft at evening classes. There has been some movement in the opposite direction too. Unlike in earlier years, the sort of personnel who are sent abroad are no longer only senior established staff, but also younger, more Westernized Japanese who are seen as adaptable and open to new cultural experiences. About two dozen books on social etiquette and other aspects of life in Britain have been published in Tokyo since the late 1980s. In the cultural ranking of desirable Western goods, pork-pie hats have replaced baseball caps and brogues are preferred to sneakers.[4]

However, this massive amount and value of global transactions effected by the transnational corporations and their minions by no means accounts for the full volume of migration or capital movements. One has to move beneath these visible organizations to glean how a significant chunk of the "real" global market works. Traders place orders with cousins, siblings and kin "back home"; nieces and nephews from "the old country" stay with uncles and aunts while acquiring their education or vocational training; loans are advanced and credit is extended to trusted intimates; and jobs and economically advantageous marriages are found for family members.

By being attached to a strong and tightly integrated diaspora, family- and kin-based economic transactions are made easier and safer. Social sanctions provide a cheaper, more effective and more discreet means of collecting bad debts than repossession orders and legal action. And success in business brings not just material rewards, but social approval and prestige, accorded by the valued reference group. Diasporas allow small and family businesses to adjust to a global scale and to assume a more rational, functional, productive and progressive character. A network of mutual trust of global proportions builds up as capital and credit flow freely between family, kin, fellow villagers and even more loosely associated co-ethnic members.

In essence, these flows are similar to the lines of credit that were established by the trade diasporas in, say, early modern Europe or by the Chinese in South East Asia (see Ch. 4). However, electronic banking and communications have vastly speeded up the transactions and their sheer volume and diversity make them difficult to track and police – for example, by the tax authorities of various countries. Although the decision of many governments in the 1980s to lift foreign exchange restrictions is often represented as an expression of newly refurbished neoliberal policy, in truth the cat was already out of the bag. Any country that sought to restrain capital flows could easily be bypassed by traders, fund managers and investors.

I do not dispute the view that many sectors of capital benefited from the deregulation of foreign exchange markets, but argue that diasporic traders and businesspeople were particularly advantaged. On the one hand, they could no longer be accused of "unpatriotic" conduct if they dealt with suppliers abroad or "outsourced" manufacturing contracts to their "home" countries. On the other hand, they were often best placed to reactivate links with countries that, through war or political ideology, had not previously or fully been sucked into international markets. With the collapse of official communism after 1989, groups like the Canadian Ukrainians or American Poles were able to revitalize business links with their countries of origin.

The Vietnamese, Cubans and Chinese abroad are also actively engaged in economic relations with their respective home countries. All three countries have gradually been forced to abandon any attempt at autarky and have joined the global rat race, usually with the mediation of their diasporas. For example, since 1979 China has received $60 billion in foreign investments and about the same in loans, and the overseas Chinese were responsible for a staggering 80 per cent of the total sums involved. In fact 1979 marked the turn of the Chinese towards capitalism, disguised by Deng's claim that all he was doing was decentralizing economic control. Members of the Chinese diaspora took the opportunity to reconnect with their villages and ancestral homes through the influential *guanxi* – elaborated networks of relatives, friends and associates. Legitimate enterprises, the drugs trade and special economic zones – where capitalist relations prevailed – were established on a massive scale. At the disposal of the 55 million overseas Chinese (Hong Kong and Taiwan included) was $450 billion, a sum 25 per cent larger than mainland China's own GNP (Seagrave 1995: 282–5).

International migration

We can recall that the warning to the biblical Jews was that they would be "scattered to all lands" if they disobeyed the Mosaic law. A number of diasporas – the Jewish, Indian, Lebanese and Chinese to name a few – were indeed widely scattered. However, international migration also followed much narrower and more predictable channels – from a colony to a metropole, along language lines or where bilateral migration contracts were signed. Now changes in the technology, ubiquity and awareness of mass transport have uncovered fresh destinations for migrants, so that in addition to the well trodden routes to North America, western Europe and Australia, the oil rich states of the Middle East and the economic hothouses of east Asia have increasingly been brought into the global migration arena. In the age of globalization, unexpected people turn up in the most unexpected places. Their more diverse geographical spread creates a more truly global basis for the evolution of diasporic networks.

These shifting destination patterns have been paralleled by momentous political changes affecting migration at the points of supply. Until 1989, the bipolar world appeared firmly cemented by the political and military duopoly of the USSR and the USA. The cement was unexpectedly friable. Indeed, many people gasped as they saw on their television screens symbolic chunks of the East hammered off the Berlin Wall. The character of international migration has been radically altered as a consequence of the breakup of the familiar international balance of power. As the communist regimes imploded and Western investment and goods poured in, it became impossible to maintain the old restrictions on travel or emigration for work and settlement. An additional axis of migration from relatively poor to rich countries has thus been opened up (East–West as well as South–North migration), giving renewed life to the diasporas of Russians and of east and central Europeans that had evolved over the period between 1870 and 1914.

Regional conflicts have also assumed a new character. Without the Soviet Union to prop up its clients or face down the USA, the social consequences of regional conflicts, including migration, burst more readily through the weaker international constraints of the post-Cold War world. Sudden migration flows have been one of the most prominent manifestations of the conflicts of the post-1989 era. The Gulf crisis, for example, led to the involuntary repatriation of two million Arab and Asian workers and residents; among them were hundreds of thousands of the Palestine diaspora, who were uprooted from the lives they had rebuilt in the Gulf states and forced to seek refuge again in Jordan and elsewhere. The Caribbean showed a similar dynamic. Now that the Soviet Union no longer subsidizes Cuban sugar, Cuba's economy has collapsed and the pressures for emigration to the USA have massively increased. On the nearby island of Haiti, the anti-communist rhetoric of the ruling class was no longer deemed necessary or convincing, so the USA withdrew its support. The consequent flows of migrants and refugees considerably enhanced the numbers of Cuban and Haitians abroad.

Despite the virtually free movement of capital, in the age of globalization no countries welcome mass migration. Even where selective migration is sanctioned, states have officially sought to prevent the settlement of unskilled, elderly or dependent migrants. Unofficially, business migration, some unskilled migration and family reunification have been allowed and even encouraged in most net immigrant countries. Members of a diasporic group have benefited from the wooing of business migrants and the relative laxity in respect of family migration, especially in the USA.[5] Again, despite the rigorous official control of immigration, there has been an extensive and rapid development of a "migration industry" comprising private lawyers, travel agents, recruiters, organizers, fixers and brokers who sustain links with origin and destination countries. Such intermediaries are driven by the cash nexus and make no distinctions, except in terms of price, between refugee and migrant, professional or unskilled, illegal or legal migration. Points of departure and arrival are also linked by friendship, kin and ethnic networks organized by the migrants themselves.

Restrictions on entry for settlement have also given new life to an old diasporic practice – that of "sojourning" (the cyclical pattern of emigration and return) characteristic of the Chinese, but also evident in others like the Mexicans, Dominicans, Puerto Ricans and Italians. As Wang (1992b: 3) points out, many of today's "global" migrants are people of considerable wealth and portable skills – a different group from the unskilled labour migrants of the nineteenth century and the refugees and tightly controlled contract workers of more recent decades:

> new classes of people educated in a whole range of modern skills are now prepared to migrate or re-migrate and respond to the pull of centres of power and wealth and the new opportunities in trade and industry. Even more than the traditional sojourners of Southeast Asia, these people are articulate, politically sensitive and choose their new homes carefully. They study the migrant states, especially their laws on the rights of immigrants and the economic conditions for newcomers. . . . Furthermore, many are masters not only in the handling of official and bureaucratic connection but also in the art of informal linkages.

As I noted in Chapter 4, the Chinese sojourner (*huaqiao*) was regarded with considerable suspicion by nationalists in the emerging post-war states of South East Asia, especially after the governments in Beijing and Tapai sought to command the migrants' ultimate loyalty. Like the Indians in East Africa or the Lebanese in West Africa and the Caribbean, the colonial powers, notably the Dutch in Indonesia and the British in Malaya and Singapore, had "noted the usefulness of the Chinese as local experts and middlemen, more useful than other Asian traders who were not as widespread and who did not have their inter-port networks" (Wang 1992b: 5).

Networks established in colonial times have now been superseded by the emergence of selective migration opportunities in Canada, the United States and Australia. Sojourners to the new destinations are helped by the global communications and transport revolutions, by the need for states to attract foreign investment through the multinationals, by the stronger legal protection accorded to minorities in the receiving countries and by the adaptable tradition of sojourning itself. A diasporic consciousness, with a foot in two or more locations, is highly attuned to contract-driven moves, and to family and clan networking and sojourning as opposed to permanent settlement in a destination country.

Global cities

That power is concentrated is commonplace, but this is not the same thing as knowing *where* power is concentrated. The global shifts in the location of financial services, industrial plant and other constituents of the world economy impose a defining spatial grid on the patterns of global power (Henderson and Castells 1987). The most important nodes in this grid are what have come to be called "world cities" or "global cities" (Friedman 1986, Sassen-Koob 1990). How do global cities arise? The location decisions of TNCs are by no means the only factors involved, yet they are important agents in this process. The placing of their corporate headquarters is of particular salience. Here, high level investment and disinvestment decisions are reached. Which products or markets should the corporation enter or leave? Should an existing part of the operation be expanded? Which companies should be acquired and which should be sold? In performing these strategic tasks, headquarters' staff sift through a large volume of information – which they handle, generate, process and transmit to other parts of the TNC. Advertising and the purchasing of financial, legal and political services further concentrates power in particular cities (Dicken 1992: 196–8).

The TNCs' corporate headquarters tend to be concentrated in a number of key cities strung out across an East–West axis. Before describing the other functions of global cities, let me list those I have in mind in Table 7.1.

The three cities on the top line of Table 7.1 link the principal stock exchanges, insurance houses and banks; those in the other rows are of no particular significance in this respect. However, I do not want to suggest that there is absolute agreement on the nominees. Friedman (1986), for example, produces a slightly different list from that in Table 7.1. Whatever the minor variations involved, there are a number of common features. The core countries and the

Table 7.1 Global cities.

Asia	Western Europe	North America
Tokyo	*London*	*New York*
Osaka	Paris	Atlanta
Seoul	Geneva	Miami
Tapai	Madrid	Mexico DF
Hong Kong	Milan	Los Angeles
Singapore	Zurich	Houston
	Frankfurt	San Francisco
	Brussels	Chicago
	Dusseldorf	Toronto
	Stockholm	Montreal
	Copenhagen	

northern hemisphere are predominant (although we may wish to include Sydney, Johannesburg, São Paulo, Rio de Janeiro and Buenos Aires in a secondary list). Some cities are the homes for TNCs, some are financial centres and some are key national centres of economic activity. Tendentially, however, they bring all these functions together.

Within each column (North American, Asian, Western European) there is a relatively clear subclustering. For example, the North American column contains the core cities of Los Angeles, New York and Chicago, around which the others are arranged; the Asian region involves an axis between Tokyo and Singapore; and the European core is London, Paris and the Rhine valley. Other cities are arranged around these major aggregations of global power in a complex hierarchy. Paralleling the hierarchy of global cities are their specialized functions in the global international division of labour. These functions are not necessarily coincidental with the historical or administrative centrality of the city involved.[6]

Global cities are centres of global transport. A number evolved from their old mercantile functions as natural harbours and ports – Hong Kong, Sydney, Singapore, New York, Paris and London. But air transport has largely superseded this constraint. All global cities are closely connected by air to other global cities. The easiest way to perceive this is to look at an airline map and study the thin filaments that arc across the globe. Suppose you overlay ten such maps of the leading carriers, you would then have an effective map of the global cities. Of course United Airlines would cluster in

Chicago, British Airways in London, and Cathay Pacific in Hong Kong – but the collective effect would be to show intense clumping around certain points. Traffic is extraordinarily dense at some sites. In the case of London, its biggest airport, Heathrow, has an aircraft leaving every 2–3 minutes and a turnstile figure in 1994 of 52 million passengers – about one-third of them using London as the transit and switching point to other destinations.

Global cities are also centres of communications. It is possible to measure this through the density of traffic on the telephone, fax, telex and Internet lines. Again a similar pattern occurs. Since 1980, for example, six-digit telephone numbers in London have grown to seven and then eight digits. The two-digit national code for London (01) changed to two three-digit codes (071 and 081) and in 1995 to two four-digit ones (0171 and 0181); further changes are being mooted as the number and volume of traffic have increased. Being at the hubs of communications flows, global cities are centres of information, news bureaux and agencies, entertainment and cultural products. Television and recording studios are there, as are many of the major book publishers and newspapers.

The net result of these features of global cities is that they become progressively more integrated into other global cities, usually at the expense of their relationship to their hinterland. As transactions and interactions between global cities intensify they lose their major national characteristics and their significance resides more in their global than in their national roles. What effects does this have on the social character and social structure of the global cities themselves? Let me list five, somewhat overlapping, effects:

1. Global cities become international and cosmopolitan, as indicated by all the descriptors that have been used in recent years to describe this condition – "pluralist", "multicultural", "multipolar", "multi-ethnic" and "multilingual". Tastes, consumption patterns and forms of entertainment are drawn more from an emerging global culture than from the national culture. Restaurants, concerts, galleries, museums and theatres change their offerings to appeal to the high income, transit visitors who visit the global cities.

2. Global cities come to share a particular occupational and cultural profile as far as the national population is concerned. They have a high percentage of professionals, business people,

financiers and people working in the global information, media, fashion, computer and news industries. However, the occupational structure is highly dichotomized, and they also contain a large informal sector of low skilled "helots" (Cohen 1987).

3. International migration of a particular kind develops. Briefly, "denizens" (privileged foreigners) appear. These are citizens of other countries who are not necessarily seeking permanent settlement and are normally professionals, managers and entrepreneurs from other countries, usually coming in under the sponsorship of a TNC. At a lower level of skill, entertainers, waiters, prostitutes, maids and chauffeurs service the needs of the rich in personal services and in the hotel, catering and entertainment industries (Sassen-Koob 1990).

4. Global cities also alter the nature of the internal labour market. In general, we see a marked shift from industrial to service and information related employment. Although this is a general trend, it is particularly notable in the global cities. Some sectors of production remain, but they are often related to the garment and fashion industries, which feed off an international clientele. It is no coincidence that Hong Kong, Paris, London, New York and Milan are the key fashion centres with the most prestigious catwalks. The glamorous fashion industry is supported by a very seamy underside of sweatshops, low pay, exploitation (normally of women workers) and the hiring of illegals to reduce costs.

5. The nationalized industries and public services give way to consumer led and insurance supported services. These include private transport, health care, education and housing. In effect, the denizens use employee benefits and insurance policies to "lease" welfare services from the host city – where they are of sufficient quality. Where the public services are so run down that they are not attractive, new commercial services are developed.

By now it should be apparent how the new notions of space and the new connections between global cities advantage diasporas. Members of diasporas are almost by definition more mobile than people who are rooted in national spaces. They are certainly more prone to international mobility and change their places of work and residence more frequently. In previous eras and still in some places, when periods of febrile nation-building take place, their cosmopolitanism was a distinct disadvantage and a source of suspicion. In the age of globalization, their language skills, familiarity with other cultures and contacts in other countries make many members of diasporas highly competitive in the international labour, service and capital markets. In the context of the global cities, this applies irrespective of whether they are competing for professional advantage or in the unskilled labour market – after all, waiters or prostitutes who can address international customers in their own languages are likely to have a distinct edge over their competitors.

Cosmopolitanism and localism

Earlier in this chapter I pointed out that there are some clearly observable counter-tendencies to globalization – nationalism and ethnicity, religious fundamentalism, racism, sexism and other forms of social exclusivism all seem to be on the increase, despite globalization. Thus, a perverse feature of globalization at the cultural level is that it has brought about the fragmentation and multiplication of identities. How do we understand this apparent paradox of particularism in the midst of globalization? In effect, we are witnessing counter-global global movements, movements that draw their inspiration (normally unconsciously) from a felt need to confront and oppose the anonymous, rational, meritocratic, progressive and universal elements of globalization. This requires a return to the local and the familiar. Stuart Hall (1991b: 35–6) is perhaps the most insightful observer of this condition:

The face-to-face communities that are knowable, that are locatable, one can give them a place. One knows what the voices are. One knows what the faces are. The re-creation, the reconstruction of imaginary, knowable places in the face of the global postmodern which has, as it were, destroyed the identities of specific places, absorbed them into this postmodern flux of diversity. So one understands the moment when people reach for those groundings.

A "reach for groundings" can mean a retreat from global realities, an incapacity to respond to the challenges of the ever widening market place and to the new ethical and cultural demands stemming from globalization. To meet both needs, for a meaningful identity and a flexible response to burgeoning opportunities, a double facing type of social organization is highly advantageous. Just such an organization exists in the form of a diaspora.

This is not just a contemporary function of diasporas. They have always been in a better position to act as a bridge between the particular and the universal. Among other arenas, this has allowed them to act as interlocutors in commerce and administration. A few examples must suffice to make this point. According to Armstrong (1976: 396–7), the Spanish Jews were "indispensable for international commerce in the Middle Ages". The Armenians controlled the overland route between the Orient and Europe as late as the nineteenth century. Lebanese Christians developed trade between the various parts of the Ottoman empire. Innovative economic techniques were introduced by diasporic groups – the Chinese introduced tin mines in Malaya and Borneo, while the Huguenots introduced lace-making to Britain and viniculture to South Africa.

Many members of diasporic communities are bi- or multilingual. They can spot "what is missing" in the societies they visit or in which they settle. Often they are better able to discern what their own group shares with other groups and when its cultural norms and social practices threaten majority groups. Such awareness constitutes the major component of what the Jews call *sechal*, without which survival itself might be threatened.[7] It is perhaps because of this need to be sensitive to the currents around them, that, in addition to their achievements in trade and finance, diaspora groups are typically over-represented in the arts, in the cinema and in the media and entertainment industries. Knowledge and awareness have increased to the point of cosmopolitanism or humanism, but at the same time traditional cultural values, which sustain solidarity and have always supported the search for education and enlightenment, have not been threatened. Awareness of their own precarious situation may also propel members of diasporas to advance legal and civic causes and to be active in human rights and social justice issues.

The combination of cosmopolitanism and ethnic collectivism is an important constituent in successful business ventures. Probably the most upbeat analysis along these lines is provided by Kotkin (1992) in a comparative study of why some peoples seem more successful as entrepreneurs than others. In his quest, he provides cases studies of five "global tribes" – the Jews, the British, the Japanese, the Chinese and the Indians.[8] Gone, for Kotkin, are the traumas of exile, the troubled relationship with the host culture and other negative aspects of the classical diasporic tradition. Instead, strong diasporas are the key to determine success in the global economy. As he writes (pp. 255, 258):

> Rather than being a relic of a regressive past, the success of global tribes – from the Jews and British over many centuries to the Chinese, Armenians and Palestinians of today – suggests the critical importance of values, emphasis on the acquisition of knowledge and cosmopolitan perspectives in the emerging world economy. In an ever more transnational and highly competitive world economy, highly dependent on the flow and acquisition of knowledge, societies that nurture the presence of such groups seem most likely to flourish. . . . Commercial opportunism overwhelms the narrower economic nationalism of the past as the cosmopolitan global city-state takes precedence and even supplants the nation.

Naturally not all diasporas have equal success in entrepreneurship. Kotkin (1992) argues that economically successful diasporas are likely to possess three desiderata, namely: (a) a *strong identity*; (b) an *advantageous occupational profile*; and (c) a *passion for knowledge*. Each of these needs some elaboration. Whether a *strong identity* is derived from internal clannishness, external rejection or a combination of the two, a definite ethnic identity engenders a distance from the larger society that can be used for creative and productive purposes. Characteristically, early immigrants came from the same village or region and they may have shared the rigours of a journey.[9] When they arrive they share accommodation and rely on each other for friendship and mutual protection against a threatening world. As an example of the latter, Kwong (1987: 86) avers that as late as the 1980s many apartments in New York's Chinatown had wall-to-wall beds occupied by the tenants in successive shifts. As more people arrived ancillary accommodation would be found, but the core accommodation would become a *fong* (literally a room) where "through games of mah-jong or poker the immigrants made contacts to obtain jobs, found partners for joint ventures, and discussed the pooling or borrowing of funds for new businesses". Above the level of the *fong* would be the village association, often formed by those who shared a similar family name. Migrants from contiguous village associations who spoke a similar dialect might be joined to form a *huiguan*, a district association. And when the going got tough, armed gangs of tongs or triads would be formed to protect property, monopolies or monopsonies.

Rather like a stack of Russian dolls, starting with the smallest and ending up on a considerable scale, members of a diaspora (in this case the Chinese) became locked into one another, reaching down to reaffirm their unshakeable loyalties and reaching up to the market place with the confidence born of their strong sense of identity. Diasporas are thus both inside and outside a particular national society. They are outsiders as well as participants and, as spectators, are able to compare and learn from "how things are done" in other societies as well as in the one in which they find themselves.

Compared with the members of the host society, those who belong to a diaspora characteristically have an *advantageous occupational profile*. They are often more strongly represented in the professions and in self-employment and less vulnerable to adverse shifts in the labour market. The more prosperous members of a diaspora may possess two passports and savings, investments and bank accounts in more than one country. Diasporas thus foster self-help, a family or collective project and a risk-minimalization strategy that transcends national borders.

A *passion for knowledge* is usually reflected in a desire for education or, to be more specific, a passion for certification. Characteristically the choice of qualification coincides with the possibility of migration, forced or self-chosen. Degree certificates, vocational or professional qualifications are the passports of the successful members of a diaspora. Members of a diaspora may choose to work abroad or fear that they may have no other choice. But a passion for knowledge is also adequately or even spectacularly served by intense curiosity. Those with *sechal* or gumption often do not need formal education because they quickly intuit business niches (for example in textiles, communications, or the retail sector) left by other more established groups. Again Kwong (1987: 71–2) provides some useful observations of the Chinese:

> Younger generations of Chinese are achieving upward social mobility through education. They have earned respect for their intellectual achievements, particularly in the difficult subjects of science and technology. There is truth to the belief that Chinese families stress education. ... Good grades in school and entering a first-rate college are praised not only by the family but by relatives and family friends. There is constant pressure and supervision of the young to develop discipline and, most importantly, to internalize their parents' values as their own. As a result, many youths grow up with a high regard for hard work and accomplishment. The Chinese immigrants are not unique in this way. Earlier immigrants, such as the Jews, and more recent groups, such as the Koreans, also value education highly.

What such accounts of ethnic entrepreneurship signify is that economic and cultural analyses are complementary. The crudities of neoliberal economic-speak need to be abolished in favour of a more sophisticated sociological account; the implausible invisible hand of the market replaced by the intimate handshake of ethnic collectivism. As it is with business ventures, so it is with the market place of ideas, the plastic and performing arts, literary endeavours and other forms of cultural production. Diasporas score by being able to interrogate the universal with the particular and by being able to use their cosmopolitanism to press the limits of the local.

Deterritorialized social identities

The final aspect of globalization I want to describe is the deterritorialization of social identities. Perlmutter's (1991) article is probably the most useful starting point in describing this feature. He depicts the world as being organized vertically by nation-states and regions, but horizontally by an overlapping, permeable, multiple system of interaction – communities not of place but of interest, shared opinions and beliefs, tastes, ethnicities and religions (where these are transnational), cuisine, the consumption of medicines (Western and complementary), lifestyles, fashion and music. Unlike those who argue that a single homogenized global culture is emerging, Perlmutter more plausibly suggests rather that multiple cultures are being syncretized in a complex way. The elements of particular cultures can be drawn from a global array, but they will mix and match differently in each setting. If we turn from this general statement to the specific, it is apparent that diasporas are one important form of horizontal social organization. Diasporas may, or may not, arise when mass migration or population displacements occur. Characteristically, a state frontier is breached at these moments. Migration movements are either more or less voluntary. The greater the amount of compulsion involved (as in transatlantic slavery, the recruitment of indentured labour or forced migration arising from civil war), the less likely it is that there will be anticipatory socialization to the new environment and the more likely that over time "literal and symbolic communities" will be created (Khan 1995: 93). The likelihood that such communities will develop is not just a function of the form of migration or the characteristics endogamous to migrants. It also turns on such exogenous variables as the opportunity structure on offer – like the possibilities for educational mobility, the nature of the labour market, the unfilled entrepreneurial niches, the openness of the housing market and the particular phase of the economic cycle. Again, host cultures may be more or less open to newcomers or demand more or less in the way of cultural and social adjustment on the part of the migrants.

Thus it always was. But there are crucial differences between the periods loosely known as "modernity" and "the age of globalization". One of the most important features of modernity was that the leaders of powerful, hegemonizing nation-states sought to make exclusive citizenship *a sine qua non*. The world is simply not like that any more; the scope for multiple affiliations and associations that has been opened up outside and beyond the nation-state has also allowed a diasporic allegiance to become both more open and more acceptable. There is no longer any stability in the points of origin, no finality in the points of destination and no necessary coincidence between social and national identities (*cf.* Khan 1995: 93). What nineteenth-century nationalists wanted was a "space" for each "race", a territorializing of each social identity. What they have got instead is a chain of cosmopolitan cities and an increasing proliferation of subnational and transnational identities than cannot easily be contained in the nation-state system.

Conclusion

It is quite difficult to establish the exact causal connection between globalization and "diasporization" (to coin an ugly word). The relationship recalls Weber's powerful theory linking the emergence of Protestantism and capitalism. He thought there might be an "elective affinity" between the two. A similar thought is found in a popular song that suggests that "love and marriage go together like a horse and carriage". I would hesitate to pronounce on the wisdom of this view, but I like the simile. Globalization and diasporization are separate phenomena with no necessary causal connections, but they "go together" extraordinarily well.

That there is no direct causal link is evident from the fact that the earliest diasporas precede the age of globalization by 2,500 years. Even if we argue that contemporary diasporas are different sorts of social organization from those of the ancient Jews and Greeks, it would be an enormous exaggeration (or indeed completely wrong headed) to suggest that the many changes in technology, economic organization, modes of travel, production, communication, the movement of ideas or the syncretization of cultures that underpin the process of globalization are caused by the existence of diasporas.

However, diasporas are disproportionately advantaged by these changes and are able to exploit them to their own advantage. A world economy is propelled by many social and economic actors, including states, international organizations and transnational corporations. These may be the sinews binding the ends of the earth together, but the flesh and blood are the family, kin, clan and ethnic networks that organize trade and allow the unencumbered flow of economic transactions and family migrants. Again, whereas the location of global economic, political and communication power is now debouching to particular cities, diasporas are often concentrated in such cities and profit from their cosmopolitan character. Deterritorialized, multilingual and capable of bridging the gap between global and local tendencies, diasporas are able to take advantage of the economic and cultural opportunities on offer.

Globalization has enhanced the practical, economic and affective roles of diasporas, showing them to be particularly adaptive forms of social organization. As diasporas become more integrated into the cosmopoli, their power and importance are enhanced. Their relative solidarity and integration are particularly evident in relation to the local populations among whom they live. Of course many powerful and wealthy actors profit from globalization. However, there is often a striking discrepancy between the fate of diasporic communities and the condition of the local working class, where the predominance of unemployment and the temporary and precarious nature of jobs have virtually destroyed any sense of solidarity. This has led to feelings of uncertainty, isolation and often destructive individualism. By contrast, the more mixed profile of diasporas, with many being educated and professionally qualified and others able to engage in *collective* capitalism, has allowed them to avoid the worst impact of global restructuring. By working and living successfully in the most sensitive nodes of the world economy, the global cities, diasporas reinforce, even if they do not exclusively propel, a further stage of globalization.

EIGHT

Conclusion: diasporas, their types and their future

For over 2500 years, one notion of the word "diaspora" has been dominant – one which highlights the catastrophic origin, the forcible dispersal and the estrangement of diasporic peoples in their places of settlement. As I have shown in Chapter 1, this interpretation of "diaspora" may have strong biblical support, but it does not conform to the origins of the concept in the Greek colonizing experience. It is, in any case, too narrow an interpretation of the experience of one of the most commonly recognized diasporas, that of the Jewish people.

In trying to interrogate and transcend the Jewish experience, I considered various theoretical and taxonomic alternatives to give adequate recognition to the more diverse experiences of transnational communities that designated themselves, or were designated by others, as diasporas. For example, I toyed with the idea that one might have "masculine" or "feminine" versions of a diaspora. As Helmrich (1992) had noted, the patriarchal connection to the word is quite strong, the scattering or dissemination of seeds being closely related in Judaeo-Christian and Islamic cosmology to male sperm. A more gender-neutral, or perhaps even feminine, inflection was given by Malkki (1992) who argued that arboreal metaphors – like "roots", "soils" and "family trees" – are intimately related to ideas of kinship and national identity.

Although I ultimately found this gender split to be too limited, as I looked out of my study window I could not help but notice that "roots", "seeds" and "trees" all evoked a horticultural image. In trying to supersede the victim tradition, I had developed at least four other possibilities and interpretations, which I have characterized earlier in this book as trade, labour, imperial and cultural diasporas. Could these types of diasporas be likened to gardening terms? In a somewhat tongue-in-cheek, but I hope none the less illustrative, way I have looked at the implications of this simile in Table 8.1.

Table 8.1 The good gardener's guide to diasporas: "Let five flowers bloom, let five schools of thought contend".

Gardening term	Type of diaspora	Examples in this book
Weeding (1)	Victim/refugee	Jews, Africans, Armenians Others: Irish, Palestinians
Sowing (2)	Imperial/colonial	Ancient Greek, British, Russian Others: Spanish, Portuguese, Dutch
Transplanting (3)	Labour/service	Indentured Indians, Chinese and Japanese, Sikhs, Turks, Italians
Layering (4)	Trade/business/ professional	Venetians, Lebanese, Chinese Others: Today's Indians, Japanese
Cross-pollinating (5)	Cultural/hybrid/ postmodern	Caribbean peoples Others: Today's Chinese, Indians

Notes to the guide: (1) A "weed" is a subjective concept. It is thought either that there are too many of them, or that they are too prominent. They need, some gardeners think, to be uprooted, cast out, destroyed, if possible, by weed killers. The equivalent for diasporas are the practices of expulsion, deportation, genocide and "ethnic cleansing". (2) Increasing plants in a seminal way, from seed. The seed is sown by scattering – the exact original Greek meaning of the word diaspora. (3) Digging up and replanting. This has a high rate of failure, depending on the original condition, the journey and the new site. (On the ships taking "coolies" to the Caribbean 18 per cent died. Another 25 per cent returned to India at the end of their indenture.) (4) Strictly, "layering" is but one method of propagating vegetatively (rather than seminally, as in (2) above). Other possibilities are "dividing", "taking cuttings" and "grafting", all of which have their equivalent sub-categories in the trade/business/professional diasporas. "Layering" is the most common case and comprises taking cuttings without separating them from the parent plant until they are rooted. Establishing trading outposts or branch plants is common among merchants and entrepreneurs. (5) Fruits cannot develop from flowers without adequate pollination. Better crops arise from additional pollinator varieties. Pollen is borne by water and wind. In the case of cultural diasporas it is borne by waves (physical migration) and airwaves (for example, the migration of ideas or music). *Acknowledgement*: My gardening guide was Joy Larkcom et al. (1984).

One of the problems of letting one's imagination roam freely is that others want to join you in your recklessness. What about also seeing *reactions* to the growth of diasporas in terms of a horticultural analogy? For example, *mulching* involves the spreading of safe, neutral material to suppress the growing of weeds (the Protestantization of northern Ireland in the seventeenth century or the Russofication of the Baltic and Caucasian states in Stalin's time provide instances). *Weedkilling* could entail selective, systemic or total strategies, depending on how useful or how detested is the presence of diasporas. Then again, for a "structuralist" reading of diasporas one might contrast the virtues of "wilderness", "foresting" or "cultivation".[1]

However suggestive such analogies are, they should not be understood too obviously. Constructing a taxonomy of diasporas is a highly inexact science, partly because the taxa concerned are overlapping or change over time. For instance, as circumstances altered, one paradigmatic case, the Jews, can have been regarded as a victim, labour, trade *and* cultural diaspora. Despite the weight of previous interpretations, even an imperial phase is evident in the Zionist colonization of Palestine.

So far I have qualified a diaspora with the adjectives of "victim", "labour", "imperial", "trade" and "cultural". I have also proposed, somewhat bizarrely, that diasporas can be compared with gardening. Is there no end to the malleability of our flexible friend? Fearing that the whole intellectual edifice might collapse under the weight it was bearing, I was much consoled by three methodological insights. First, I benefited from an observation made in 1874 by the natural scientist, Jevons, who proclaimed, "A perfect intelligence would not confine itself to one order of thought, but would simultaneously regard a group of objects as classified in all the ways of which they are capable." Secondly, I was influenced by Vygotsky's idea of a "chain complex", a definitive attribute that keeps changing from one link to the next. The variable meaning is carried over from one item to a class of items with no "central significance" or "nucleus". Finally, I was struck by Wittenstein's image of a rope "which does not get its strength from any fibre that runs through it from one end to another, but from the fact that there is a vast number of fibres overlapping" (all cited by Needham 1975: 349–50).

This last metaphor is particularly suggestive in that it provides me with a legitimate mechanism with which to compare systematically how different diasporas conform to the normal, but not invariable, features of most diasporas. The diaspora rope is visible, but old fibres of meaning shrivel, while new strands of meaning are added. Put another way, all the relevant fibres are part of a similar phenomenon, but they are not the same part of that phenomenon.

Comparing diasporas

To compare diasporas, let me, in an abbreviated form, summarize what was set out more elaborately in Chapter 1. Normally, diasporas exhibit several of the following features: (1) dispersal from an original homeland, often traumatically; (2) alternatively, the expansion from a homeland in search of work, in pursuit of trade or to further colonial ambitions; (3) a collective memory and myth about the homeland; (4) an idealization of the supposed ancestral home; (5) a return movement; (6) a strong ethnic group consciousness sustained over a long time; (7) a troubled relationship with host societies; (8) a sense of solidarity with co-ethnic members in other countries; and (9) the possibility of a distinctive creative, enriching life in tolerant host countries. These nine features are analogous to Wittenstein's fibres of meaning. We need now to compare diasporas along the length of each "fibre", bearing in mind that they often entwine with one another to strengthen the "diasporic rope". I shall then, after a detailed comparison of the first two fibres (dispersal and expansion), deal with the remaining seven strands in a more abbreviated way.

Traumatic dispersal

Although many diasporas are seen to be born of flight rather than choice, in practice migration scholars often find it difficult to separate voluntary from involuntary migration.[2] None the less, there are clearly a number of mass displacements that are occasioned by events wholly outside the individual's control – wars, "ethnic cleansing", natural disasters, pogroms, and the like. When we are talking of a trauma afflicting a group collectively, it is perhaps possible to isolate those events in which the suddenness, scale and intensity of exogenous factors unambiguously compel migration or flight.

Being dragged off in manacles (as were the Jews and African captives), or being coerced to leave by force of arms (as were the Armenians), appear to be qualitatively different phenomena from the general pressures of overpopulation, land hunger, poverty or an unsympathetic political regime. Jews were dispersed to such an extent that their diaspora population massively outnumbered the original homeland population, while the number of diaspora Africans amounts to about 40 million people, about one-tenth of the black African population.

On the list of newer claimants to the designation "diaspora", the Palestinians have an unambiguous case of virtually complete population dispersal. In 1947–8 they were violently displaced by the Israeli Zionists who asserted the right – narrowly recognized in a United Nations vote – to a Jewish state. Some 780,000 Arabs were expelled from the territory controlled by the Israeli army, while a further 120,000 Palestinians were later classified as refugees because they had lost their land and livelihoods, although not their homes (Lippman Abu-Lughod 1995: 410).

The cases of the Irish and Lebanese are also dramatic in terms of the numbers of people affected. It is part of Irish folklore, for example, bitterly to recall both the brutality of English occupation and the ordeal of the famine. The Irish lost 25 per cent of their homeland population between 1845 and 1851, the years of the potato famine. Lebanon also experienced very heavy population losses – again about 25 per cent of the population before 1914 and a similar *tranche* consequent on the civil war of the 1970s (Hourani & Shehadi 1992).

The remaining diasporas can be understood as arising from a mixture of underlying causes (such as poverty, insecure land tenure and overpopulation), which are combined with a variety of more immediate precipitating factors that serve to accelerate the basic movement or give to it a particular character and direction. In the case, for example, of Chinese indentured labour, Richardson (1984: 177–9) suggests that migration was caused by a serious disequilibrium between population and land resources in north China, economic dislocation because of Western penetration of the economy, dynastic and social collapse and, in particular areas, the effect of the rebellion and banditry in the countryside. Such complex, multicausal pictures can be replicated for Indian, Italian and other modern diasporic movements.

It should also be remembered that, although migration losses were heavy in absolute terms in the case of some of the new claimants, with hundreds of thousands, even millions, of people leaving, they rarely constituted a serious drain on the capacity for internal reproduction. In the case of the larger population groups (for example, the Chinese and Indians), the proportion of overseas emigrants to the home population was very small.

Expansion through work, trade or empire

The second fibre of the diaspora rope is that of migration for the purposes of work, trade or colonization. Consider the case of the labour diasporas. As I suggested in Chapter 3, few workers – whether they are Indian workers in the plantation colonies or north African construction workers in France – intend to remain as unskilled workers for ever. The issue of whether the many groups that might qualify as labour diasporas attain or remain within that classification turns on a number of variables.

The most important variable is the extent of social mobility in the host society. Many of the European groups that arrived in the USA between 1870 and 1914 comprised manual labourers destined to work in the mass industries of the period. Most were able to escape this status over two or three generations, leaving much of the 3D (dirty, dangerous, difficult) work to new entrants to the USA, to African Americans and to undocumented Mexicans. In short, they lost their status as labour diasporas. On the other hand, labour migrants who circulate or oscillate between their homes and their places of work are also not a labour diaspora, for they are not permanently dispersed. A labour diaspora might, however, arise if an unskilled immigrant group is locked for some time into a subordinate status through lack of opportunity, inappropriate cultural commitments, or prejudice. This is not that common a phenomenon, so insofar as a group returns home (to recommence peasant proprietorship or commence petty entrepreneurship) or, on the other hand, attains middle-class status, a labour diaspora is normally a transitional type. That is not to say of course that there are not a large number of 3D jobs in many societies; it is rather to assert that they are filled by successive cohorts of "new helots" or "new untouchables" from a variety of source countries (Cohen 1987, Harris 1995).

In the case of trade diasporas, these often arose without the approval of the authorities in the home countries. Chinese traders, for example, had to tolerate dismissive official attitudes. In the Confucian system of thought the merchant was at the bottom of a four-tier hierarchy, beneath the literati, the artisan and even the peasant. Wang (1991: 183) points out that this low status was unique to China. Merchants occupied a low status in Hindu culture, but they were never at the bottom of the heap, while in the Christian and Muslim worlds traders often attained positions close to the seats of power.

Despite this disadvantage, the Chinese in South East Asia remain one of the prototypical examples of a trading diaspora. Wang (1991: 4–5) suggests that the long distance trade *within* China provided a model for the overseas Chinese. By retaining their connections or "registration" with their home towns they were able to draw on kin support, inviting kinsfolk to act not only as fellow traders but also as artisans and workers in their various enterprises. More and more agents or young family members were fed into the network to stabilize existing businesses and to start new ventures. They generally remained on the political margins in the countries to which they emigrated. Chinese communities were rarely given the vote and were often regarded as aliens.

Whereas the trade diasporas just discussed were not state directed, but depended rather on the initiative of families and individuals, the modern European explorer-traders – Vasco da Gama, Marco Polo and Christopher Columbus, Bartholomew Diaz and the rest – opened up trade routes on behalf of monarchs. Venture capital and the big European trading companies followed, but found themselves constrained or persuaded that they needed to occupy enclaves (for instance Goa, Shanghai, Hong Kong, Manila and the Cape) to secure their trade routes. As night follows day, the European trade diasporas turned into imperial diasporas. The flag followed trade, with the inevitable outcome of conquest, occupation and the subordination of the indigenous peoples.

In this book I have concentrated particularly on the case of the

British imperial diaspora – one that was by far the most successful – but the Netherlands, Spain, France and Portugal were not far behind. Limping along in the rear were Germany and Italy, both of whom also cherished imperial dreams. These imperial adventures moved from guaranteeing trade flows to using the export or population to establish a hegemony on the ground. The British dominions of Australia, Canada, the USA, New Zealand, South Africa and Rhodesia, all demonstrated the aptness of the designation "dominion".

The European diasporas were "diasporas by design", a model that was to gain new currency in the age of globalization. Rather than following the Europeans into occupation and political domination – the possibility of which was cut off by their defeat in the Second World War – the Japanese used their immense industrial power to extend their power abroad. The personnel who service the banks, insurance companies, import–export houses and transnational corporations are an updated version of the trading and imperial diasporas of old.

Other fibres of the diasporic rope

I have described in some detail the characteristics of the first two fibres that wrap around the diasporic rope. Seven more fibres remain. I am tempted *pari passu* to follow each one along its full length, drawing together salient comparisons as I go. However, this has the serious danger both of being too prolix and of repeating material that has already found expression in earlier chapters. So let me deal with the remaining seven strands in a more abbreviated way.

First, *a collective memory and myth about the homeland*. The idea of a shared origin and birthplace is a common feature of diasporas. The Jews say they are the "chosen people", all descended from Abraham. The Armenians claim they are descended from Haik and that Noah's ark ended up on top of Mount Ararat, where the earth was reborn. The Lebanese proclaim they are Phoenicians. The Indian diaspora – or at least that part of it that is Hindu – looks back to the complex of gods and goddesses (notably Vishnu, Shiva, Shakti) who gave birth to the sacred land of India and the River Ganges. The myth of a common origin acts to "root" a diasporic consciousness and give it legitimacy (Skinner 1993). The more ancient and

184

venerable the myth, the more useful it is as a form of social distancing from other ethnic groups and a means of affecting an air of superiority, even in the teeth of dispossession and discrimination.

Second is *an idealization of the supposed ancestral home.* Needless to say the myths of a common origin are territorialized, while highly romantic fantasies of the "old country" are fabulated and avowed. The "promised land" of the Jews flowed with milk and honey. The aged cedars and scent of mint on Mount Lebanon could be used to brush away the smell of the corpses produced in the recent civil war. The impressive buildings of Zimbabwe stand as a testament to the notion that Africans once had superior civilizations and great empires: a direct refutation of their often low social status in the Americas. The Assyrians in London and Chicago talk of their link to the great civilization in Mesopotamia, while their arch rivals, the Armenians, mount expensive archaeological expeditions to uncover *their* palaces and shrines. It is true that some homelands are more imagined than others, but it is rare that a diaspora does not seek to maintain or restore a homeland to its former glory.

My third fibre is the presence of *a return movement.* The contrast between the current condition of the diaspora and its imagined past is resolved by actual return or help given to return movements by the diaspora. Philhellenism, Zionism, Garveyism, Pan-Africanism, the attempts to create Khalistan and to remake Greater Armenia – all these are represented by the political vanguards of the diasporas as the only certain means to overcome their precarious and isolated existence in exile. Improvement schemes for homelands also were common in other diasporas. Although born in China, Sun Yixian (Sun Yat-sen) developed his political consciousness in Hong Kong and in the Chinese community in Hawaii. His Society for the Revival of China was a crucial instrument in the promotion of a modern Chinese nationalism. His career is interestingly paralleled by that of Giuseppe Mazzini (1805–72); again born in his homeland, but finding an echo for his ideas of Italian unity, republicanism and nationalism in the Italian diaspora.

Fourth is *a strong ethnic group consciousness sustained over a long time.* This historical dimension of diaspora formation was strongly emphasized by Marienstras (1989) who correctly argued that "time has to pass" before we can know that any community that has migrated "is really a diaspora". In other words, one does not immediately announce the formation of a diaspora at the moment of arrival (a tendency that has become quite marked in contemporary use in the USA). A strong attachment to the past, or a block to assimilation in the present and future, must exist in order to permit a diasporic consciousness to emerge or be retained.

A fifth fibre is *a troubled relationship with the host society*. This feature of a diaspora is, unfortunately, all too common and there is barely a group mentioned that did not at some stage experience discrimination in the countries of their migration. The major exceptions to this rule are those diasporas that were, in effect, settler colonies. The British in the Dominions and North America, and the Portuguese in Brazil were able to establish their own hegemony in language, law, property rights and political institutions, thereby forcing the indigenees onto the defensive.

Elsewhere, the rule is pretty unwavering. The Chinese in Malaya, Indians in Fiji, Poles in Germany, Italians in Switzerland, Japanese in Peru, Irish in England, Palestinians in Kuwait, Caribbean peoples in Europe, Sikhs in Britain, Turks and Rom in Germany and Kurds in Turkey have all experienced antagonism and legal or illegal discrimination. A number have become the objects of violent hatred in their countries of settlement. What makes this form of inter-ethnic tension different from the general case is that in some measure these groups can look outside their immediate communities (for comfort, comparison and identification) to co-ethnic communities elsewhere and to the possibility of returning to a real or imagined homeland.

Sixth is *a sense of solidarity with co-ethnic members in other countries*. The sense of unease or difference that diaspora peoples feel in their countries of residence is paralleled by a tendency to identify instead with fellow members of their diaspora in other countries. None the less, there is often a great deal of tension in the relationship between scattered co-ethnic communities. A bond of loyalty to the country of refuge or settlement competes with ethnic solidarity, while there is frequently a considerable reluctance by those who have stepped quite far down the path of assimilation to accept too close a link with a despised or low-status ethnic group abroad, even if it happens to be one's own. It is perhaps predictable that those who have clawed their way to the top should pull up the ladder behind them.

The seventh and final fibre of the diaspora rope is *the possibility of a distinctive creative, enriching life in tolerant host countries*. Even victim diasporas find their experiences in modern nation-states enriching and creative as well as enervating and fearful. The Jews' considerable intellectual and spiritual achievements simply could not have happened in a narrow tribal society like that of ancient Judaea. The Armenians and Irish thrived materially and politically in the "land of opportunity", the USA. The Palestinians are characteristically more prosperous and better educated than the locals in the countries of their exile. Despite their bitter privations, Africans in the diaspora have produced influential musical forms like spirituals, jazz, blues, rock and roll, calypso, samba and reggae, initiated major innovations in the performing arts and generated a rich vein of literature and poetry. (Two Nobel laureates for literature have been awarded to New World writers of African descent in the 1990s).

Cognate phenomena

The fibres in the diaspora rope are all now plaited. However, I am not quite ready to abandon my morphological quest. Where do diasporas end? I do not seek the role of a pope in excommunicating phenomena that I believe are not legitimately part of the "chain complex". Still, lines have to be drawn somewhere, however vaguely. I thought it might be useful to describe three phenomena that are closely related to diasporas, although it seems doubtful that they strictly qualify, even by my loose criteria. I refer to world religions, borderland cultures, and what I shall call "stranded minorities". I shall say something briefly about each in turn.

World religions
Although not fully theorized, the notion of a religious diaspora is alluded to by Smart et al. (1987). The background to their notion is that, with the increased pace of globalization, especially in respect of cheap, long distance travel, even rather poor religious communities can maintain contact with the principal epicentres of their religions: the Jews with Jerusalem and the Wailing Wall, the Catholics with Rome and Lourdes, the Hindus with Varanasi and the Gan-

ges, the Sikhs with Amritsar and the Golden Temple, the Muslims with Mecca and the Kaaba, and so on. Pilgrimage to these sites of religious significance renews both the centre and the periphery – the "fires of passion" often being nurtured by long separation.

Through this renewal, and through proselytizing, certain religions then take on the aspect of "world" or "global" religions. An illustrative case in point is provided by Smart and his colleagues who allude (1987: 290–1) to a newspaper started in the mid-1980s, which styled itself "an international bimonthly newspaper fostering Hindu solidarity among 650 million members of a global religion". Despite some countertendencies towards pluralism and multi-faith protestations, world religions often seem to develop a proclivity towards ecumenism, orthodoxy or fundamentalism. This is evident (and much feared) in Islam, but also arises in religions that have hitherto been interpreted as without a single, narrowly defined set of beliefs and practices. Even Hinduism and Buddhism are moving in an ecumenical direction, the latter under the auspices of the World Federation of Buddhists.

On a much smaller scale, but no less widely dispersed, are groups like the Zoroastrians, followers of one of the oldest religions in the world. Called Parsees in India, the principal country to which they emigrated, their roots go back to ancient Persia. Hinnells (1994: 79) writes:

> As Zoroastrians continue to migrate around the world not only in greater numbers but also and perhaps more significantly, in a greater proportion compared with the population in the "old country", so the threat of dispersal seems to make ever closer the apocalyptic scene of the extinction of the world's oldest prophetic religion.

Yet, as Hinnells explains, there are some Zoroastrians who are more positive about the future. Just as they accept that the move from Persia to India in response to Muslim persecution was a necessary survival strategy, so they think of the dispersal from India to the "new world" (which includes, in this context, Europe) as another stage of "moving on". They are not so much a travelling nation then (see Ch. 6), as a travelling religion. However, this aspect of Zoroastrianism also limits the extent to which we can call

Parsees a diaspora: they do not seek to return to, or to recreate, a homeland.

In general, I would argue that religions can provide additional cement to bind a diasporic consciousness, but they do not constitute diasporas in and of themselves. Hinduism is professed by many in the Indian diaspora; Armenians are often followers of the Catholic Armenian Church or the Armenian Orthodox Church; many Irish and most Italians are Catholics; Judaism and Sikhdom unite many diasporic Jews and Sikhs. Such an overlap between faith and ethnicity is likely to enhance social cohesion. However, even secular members of those communities are part of their respective diasporas, while some diasporas (the Lebanese, Africans and Dutch, for example) have mixed ethnic backgrounds. The myth and idealization of a homeland and a return movement are also conspicuously absent in the case of world religions. Indeed, one might suggest that their programmes are extraterritorial rather than territorial.[3] On the other hand, once we admit the category of a cultural diaspora, as we have in the case of certain Caribbean peoples, we are also opening out the possibility that spiritual affinity may generate a bond analogous to that of a diaspora.[4]

Borderland cultures

In the classic work of Turner (1920) "the frontier" signified free land, an absence of constraint and the possibility of recapturing the innocence of Arcadia, lost in the march of industrial civilization. Such a vision was attractive to many free spirits as they struck out to the American West or further into unexplored territories. For all practical purposes, this process has now ended. As Hennessy (1978: 158) puts it, "In Latin America there is no West, no Frontier, there are only frontiers. Whereas in earlier days the borderlands were inhabited by folk heroes like Kitt Carson, Daniel Boone, Davy Crockett and General Custer, or romantic desperadoes, bandits, runaway slaves and *gauchos*, now the borderlands are peopled by pathetic work seekers". Societies now interpenetrate each other. There are zones that might best be described as "no-group lands", not in the sense of unexplored territory, but in the sense that liminality, syncretism and ambiguity characterize the identities of the people living in the borderlands. As was noted in Chapter 6, Clifford (1994) explicitly distinguishes between borderlands and diasporas. The two-way flows of people, goods, ideas, music and lifestyles erode the sacred spaces carved up by the nation-state. A migratory practice of bi-locality, or the emergence of a syncretic culture, is arrested by border controls, but these become more and more erratically enforced as the extent of interpenetration widens.

The circum-USA provides a variety of good examples of this process. The Rio Grande supposedly separates Mexico and the USA. In the treaty of Guadalupe Hidalgo 1848, Mexico had to cede to the USA over half the territory it had inherited from Spain at the time of its independence in 1821. This included Texas, California, New Mexico, Nevada, Colorado, Utah and part of Wyoming, where many Mexicans lived. Establishing a watertight border was thus, in a sense, doomed from the start. Many people in the south-west now speak Spanish (studying it is required in Californian schools), poor US citizens go south to find cheap booze, sex, drugs and dental treatment, while poor Mexicans cross the border as undocumented workers. Both may eat Tex-Mex food. Let me take a second example. Dominicans coming (principally) to New York have variously been described as (a) *austentes*, the "absent ones", who are nevertheless regarded as an organic part of Dominican society, (b) *residentes*, who may retain some aspects of Hispanic or Latino identity, but are increasingly integrating into US society in terms of citizenship and participation in local politics, and (c) *bi*-nationals, with a foot in each camp – more Dominican when in New York and perhaps more American when in Santo Domingo.[5]

Are Mexicans or Dominicans diasporas? And how about Cubans or Puerto Ricans in the USA, Poles in contemporary Germany, Albanians in Greece or Mozambicans in South Africa? In my judgement, these migrations are examples of borderland cultures rather than diasporas. They represent a failure of the state (sometimes because of incapacity, sometimes through design) effectively to police their boundaries. Societies bleeding into one another create new complex and other intermediate identities, not diasporas.

"Stranded minorities"

A similar phenomenon to a border culture is what may be called a "stranded minority". Such groups often occupy little enclaves that arise through boundary changes. Groups that once were contained within states, or at least definable territories, become separated by war or subsequent peace treaties. There are many examples of this consequence. One arose from the break-up of the Austro-Hungarian empire, when a core majority remained in Hungary but lots of Hungarian minorities were parcelled out to the neighbouring countries. Sometimes a prior state never existed but an ethnic group, like the Kurds, is partitioned into several territories – in this case Iran, Iraq and Turkey and now the Secure Zone, established by the victor powers in the Gulf War.

Numerically, the most important case is that of the Russians, who remained in the successor states of the Soviet Union after its dissolution. Kolstø (1993: 198) explicitly regards this group as a "new Russian diaspora": "For centuries the Russians have moved outwards from the Russian heartland towards the ethnic periphery. With the dissolution of the Union, the Russian population in the outlying regions, as if by magic, has been transformed into a new diaspora, 25 million strong." Of the three cognate phenomena I have considered (world religions, borderland cultures and stranded minorities), this very large group (some 17 per cent of the Russian people) is the most tempting to designate as a diaspora.

But there are real problems in so doing. Clearly, this is not a dispersion in a conventional sense. Most of the migration was voluntary. However, because tsarist and Soviet Russia both had an interest in creating buffer zones in the Baltic states and the Caucasus, there was strong encouragement of the movement by the state. State officials, political officers and educators were sent there, as were numerous divisions of troops. Soon the soldiers spilled outside the barracks and families were established. A minority was born. Although highly significant in most successor countries, this minority was not large enough or powerful enough to "mulch" over the nationalist sentiments that overwhelmed the Soviet Union in 1989. In sum, then, this was a *failed* imperial diaspora, an imperial diaspora in intent if not in result.[6] That it failed does not make it any less dangerous. There are populist leaders in Russia, like Vladimir Zhirinovskii, who threaten that Russian boots will be washed in the Black Sea – a forbidding reminder of Hitler and Sudetenland. Given the proximity of the motherland and its troops, the Baltic and Caucasian states have to move cautiously in asserting their exclusively national rights.

Negative reactions to the growth of diasporas

The sudden proliferation of diasporas and similar phenomena have triggered a considerable degree of apprehension among Western academics and commentators. There has suddenly been a heightened consciousness that diasporas can represent a threat to the nation-state and the liberal-democratic order. A number of these concerns have been articulated by American historians, writers, government officials and opinion-makers – who have been highly critical of any policies to recognize diversity and cultural plurality. Hu-DeHart (1993: 7–8) describes these commentators collectively as "triumphalists". They merit this designation, she maintains, in championing a traditional view of American history that proclaims the triumph of Western civilization and American culture. She quotes George Will (a leading newspaper columnist) to this effect: "America is predominantly a product of the Western tradition and is predominantly good because that tradition is good." Although this position is strongly associated with neo-conservative opinion in the USA, even liberal historians like Arthur Schlesinger Jr (cited in Hu-DeHart 1993: 8) have nailed their colours to the mast of a single national identity:

> The US escaped the divisiveness of a multi-ethnic society by a brilliant solution: the creation of a brand new identity. The point of America was not to preserve old cultures but to forge a new, American culture. "By an admixture with our people", President George Washington told Vice-President John Adams, "immigrants will get assimilated to our customs, measures and laws: in a word soon will become one people".

Unlike in the world of George Washington, however, suddenly language rights, educational provisions and the judicial system have become open to question. As Dickstein (1993: 535), probably more in sadness than in anger, argues:

> Once minority groups had been desperately eager to join the mainstream, to become assimilated. They were looking for simple justice not for ultimate approval. Now, an angry,

even self-destructive separatism, an assertion of group pride at the expense of practical goals, often replaced the old desire for legal equality. Minorities no longer looked to be admitted to the club; instead they insisted on changing the rules.

The debate about the dangers of multiculturalism is paralleled by an even more feverish debate about the dangers that diasporas present in their heedless efforts to have homelands of their own. Where the homeland does not exist, violence, usually terrorism, is common. Illustrative cases are the claims by the IRA (Irish Republican Army) for a united Ireland, Hamas's insistence on a reconstituted Palestine, the formation of militant Sikh groups demanding the Kalsa raj (a Sikh sovereign state) in the wake of the Indian troops' attack on the Golden Temple, and the terrorist section of the PKK (Kurdish Workers' Party) fighting for a sovereign Kurdistan. While such terrorist challenges have by no means totally undermined the power of the nation-states concerned, they have none the less provided formidable security threats.

Nor should we discount these fears as hysterical. On one day alone (30 July 1995), the Associated Press (cited by Riggs 1996) reported three incidents:

- In Frankfurt, activists of the Kurdish Workers' Party firebombed Turkish businesses in Germany for five nights in a row.
- In Paris, Islamic militants from Algeria were suspected of a terrorist bombing of the underground station at St Michel.
- In New York, the militant Palestinian Hamas group demanded the release of one of their leaders, Mousa Abu Marzuk, an immigrant Palestinian who had lived undetected in the USA for the past 14 years.

In a somewhat tenuous link to the Branch Davidian and the Aum Shinrikyo cults, Woollacott (1995), deputy editor of the liberal British daily, the *Guardian*, also expressed his anxieties about the growth of diasporas, in these terms:

> Diasporas have many beneficial effects on both host and migrant communities, but they may also breed pathological attitudes among a small minority. Some may fight their own

wars on foreign soil. Or diaspora communities can provide inadvertent cover, in their separateness from the main society, for terrorists and extremists from inside or outside who want to attack their hosts. .... The global village can be a violent place. Its curse is that new combination of intimacy and aggression, with societies so penetrated by each other physically and culturally that awful damage can be wreaked at close quarters in a way that was not possible in the past.

Although there is an element of melodrama here, there is no gainsaying that metropolitan politics are continually getting sucked into the politics of the homelands. Sikh demands for Khalistan, for example, have resulted in violent protests in Canada, the USA and Britain. Even if we ignore the newspaper headlines, the general point is that many immigrants are no longer individualized or obedient prospective citizens. Instead, they may retain dual citizenship, agitate for special trade deals with their homelands, demand aid in exchange for electoral support and seek to influence social and foreign policy.

Final remarks

Should we be professing sympathy with the contemporary nation-state in the face of the growing number and strength of diasporas? Ever since their state structures first cohered (starting in Europe around the sixteenth century), the leaders of nation-states have sought to have it all their own way. They have coped with ethnic diversity by demanding exclusive citizenship, border control, linguistic conformity and political obedience. Moreover, the nation-state was offered as an object of devotion. Its citizens were enjoined to love their country, to revere its institutions, to salute its flag, to support its sporting teams, and to fight and die for it in war. In the face of powerfully defended nationalist sentiments it has, until recently, been difficult for diasporic groups to express their true attitudes to the nation-states in which they found themselves. I use the expression "found themselves" because many migratory movements (as in transatlantic slavery, the recruitment of indentured labour, or forced migration arising from civil war) involved coercion. There is an inverse relationship between the amount of compulsion involved and the likelihood of anticipatory socialization to the new environment having taken place. In such contexts, ethnic or transnational communities will persist or be re-created. Now, it cannot be denied, many diasporas want to have their cake and eat it. They want not only the security and opportunities available in their countries of settlement, but also a continuing relationship with their country of origin and co-ethnic members in other countries. For such diasporas the nation-state is being used instrumentally, rather than revered affectively.

Unlike adherence to an ethnicity, religion or diaspora, the nation-state is often too large and too amorphous an entity to be the object of intimate affection. One can marry a spouse of one's own kind and feel the warm embrace of kinship; one can kneel in common prayer with one's co-religionists; one can effect easier friendships with those of a common background. Bonds of language, religion, culture and a sense of a common history and perhaps a common fate impregnate a transnational relationship and give to it an affective, intimate quality that formal citizenship or even long settlement frequently lack.

The pessimists claim that certain values and ways of life that are imported are simply incompatible with the way in which Western liberal democracies (in particular) have evolved. To take one important example, the separation of Church and state was resolved through bitter religious wars in Europe and the acceptance of secularism at the time of the founding of the large immigrant-importing states like the USA, Canada and Australia. The difference between the public and private domains is, however, fundamentally challenged by theocratic ideas (not only articulated by Muslims, but notably by them) that deny any domain differences between private worship, the provision of education and the governance of the state.

The optimists aver that liberal democracies can construct "an egalitarian multicultural society" where "it is possible, without threat to the overall unity of the national society, to recognize that minorities have a right to their own language in family and community contexts, the right to practise their own religion, the right to organize domestic and family relations in their own way, and the right to maintain communal customs" (Rex 1995: 30–1). Moreover, diasporas perform a vital social role. They bridge the gap between the individual and society, between the local and the global. The sense of uprootedness, of disconnection, of loss and estrangement, which hitherto was morally appropriated by the traditionally recognized diasporas, may now signify something more general about the human condition. Why not celebrate the creative, enriching side of living in "Babylon", the radiance of difference? As the Nobel prize-winning St Lucian poet, Derek Walcott, once blithely proclaimed, "No nation now but the imagination" (cited in Gilroy 1993b: 120). Others are far less happy about the relative immunity of diasporas from the disciplines and duties of citizenship in a modern nation-state. For them, the nation-state is not only (or at all) an oppressive form of social organization, but also one that protects free expression, political diversity, cultural pluralism and social tolerance. To abandon such features in the face of militant ethnic demands could be a disastrous reverse for the civilizing progress initiated by the Enlightenment. Diasporas themselves articulate their demands in terms of human rights or "group rights". More exactly, the loudest mouths in the diaspora communities articulate these demands, often leaving little room for the dissenter, the individualist and the person who does not wish to affirm any special ethnic identity.

To mediate between these contrasting views is as yet impossible, as the ultimate answer will turn on the capacity of nation-states to manage diversity while permitting free expression and the degree of social cohesion sufficient to ensure legitimacy for the state and its principal institutions. Clearly, however, diasporas have made it impossible to realize the nineteenth-century dream of a place for each "race". What the nationalists wanted was a territorializing of each social identity. What they have got instead (only they do not admit it) is a chain of cosmopolitan cities and an increasing proliferation of diasporic, subnational and ethnic identities that cannot easily be contained in the nation-state system. Will the rash of new diasporas provide an enduring, additional or alternative focus of loyalty and identification to the fealty demanded by the nation-state or traditional religions? Or will they melt away in the face of even more powerful forces like the juggernauts of internationalization and globalization?

Notes

Chapter 1

1. That is, over a wide area, or "to scatter". Helmrich (1992) also notes that the patriarchal connection to the word is quite strong, the scattering or sowing of seeds being closely related in Judaeo-Christian and Islamic cosmology to male sperm. Also see Chapter 8 for a discussion of the masculine and feminine versions of a diaspora.

2. *Marrano*s are "swine". The word derives from the Arabic *moharram* meaning "forbidden". The term is obviously pejorative. The word *conversos* is more polite, but misleading because it has been established that many of the *Marrano*s had little intention of fully converting.

3. This rather sick association of music with misfortune prefigured the even more morbid occasions when Jews had to listen to the strains of Wagner while marching towards the gas ovens in the Nazi concentration camps.

4. Ashkenaz was Noah's great-grandson. According to the Bible, after the flood had subsided "the peoples of the coasts and islands separated into their own countries, each with their own language, family by family, nation by nation" (Genesis 10: 1–5).

5. Koestler (1976: 180–200) has some rather eccentric and some very politically incorrect passages on racial differences, including diagrams of Jewish noses, but it is difficult to refute his main point. On a global scale Jews resemble each other hardly at all, while they resemble their surrounding peoples much more closely. Moreover, phenotypically, Ashkenazim are evidently of a different origin from Sephardim.

6. Some readers might react adversely to my use of the German expression *volkish* to describe the Zionist notion of Jewry. However, as Banton (1994: 341–2) suggests, *Volk* means more than "people". Since the eighteenth century it has implied a group of people with a transcendent "essence".

197

Within this essence, all individual creativity and sense of purpose was to be found. Individuals needed to find unity with other members of the *Volk*. I add that it was proposed by German nationalists and Zionists alike that a *Volk* needed a territory in which to express itself.

7. The revolutionary tradition nurtured in Eastern Europe was often carried abroad by the Jewish emigrants. In the USA, Jews were prominent in the anarchist and labour movements (see Levin 1977). In South Africa, the Communist Party was founded by Jewish emigrants in 1921. Their long struggle finally paid off when, in 1994, the party's most prominent leader, Lithuanian-born Joe Slovo, became minister of housing in the post-apartheid government, just a few months before his death.

8. For example, Daniel Halévy, an eminent French writer thought it essential to escape the confines of a traditional religion: "How happy I am to have left that hell, to have escaped from Judaism." Many other emancipated European Jews shared this sentiment. The German poet Heinrich Heine, who also had Jewish ancestry, was equally blunt. Judaism was not a religion but a misfortune: "Those who would say Judaism is a religion would say that being a hunchback is a religion" (these quotations and next from Lindemann 1993: 62, 15).

9. A reliable account is provided by Marrus (1980).

10. This is not to say that *only* such political leaders could arrive at the same conclusion. In his careful examination of the Jews of France, Germany and Russia, Arnold Ages (1973) ultimately concludes that Jews who sought contentment in these countries were living an impossible dream, one which in the German case was shattered finally by Nazism. He avers (pp. 169–72) that American Jews are also doomed to go through the same cycle of acceptance–integration–superpatriotism–rejection, although this part of his argument is thinly developed.

11. Marienstras (1989: 120) erroneously maintains that there is a rigid distinction by Jewish thinkers between *galut*, implying forced dispersal, and diaspora, implying free and voluntary migration. Would that life were so simple. Although *galut* always implies a negative origin and condition, the word diaspora is used similarly in the Jewish tradition. The word *golah*, although less commonly used now, signifies a more stable community abroad.

12. I have dealt with the ambiguities that Caribbean peoples present under the interrogative title of "A diaspora of a diaspora? The case of the Caribbean", *Social Science Information* 31 (1), 1992, 193–203.

13. The African political scientist, Ali Mazrui (1990: 132) pointed out that the 15 million Jews worldwide (0.2 per cent of the world's population) provided about 25 per cent of Nobel prize winners. Moreover, as George Steiner (the literary critic) noticed in a lecture in Tel Aviv that caused a furore in Israel, the Israelis had made a minimal contribution to the total.

14. Relevant discussion can be found in Cohen (1987: 33–42), Zolberg et al. (1989: 258–82) and Richmond (1994: 47–76).

Chapter 2

1. Indeed the Jewish diaspora was itself initially dispersed to Mediterranean Africa. Oral tradition also has it that the Ethiopian Jews (the term "Falashas" is derogatory) were descendants of a love affair between King Solomon and Queen Sheba. Although this story is somewhat fanciful, part of the Jewish diaspora is undoubtedly African in origin (Friedmann 1994).
2. It is perhaps necessary to mention that I do not use the word "myth" in the popular sense of "an unlikely legend or untruth" but in an anthropological and sociological sense. Myth alludes to collectively generated explanations and understandings that are widely believed and articulated. As Montilus (1993: 159) grandly puts it, myth "is the resurgence of societal thought and consciousness through space and time serving to structure and rebuild experience".
3. It is pertinent to note that in trying to create a "research agenda" for the study of the African diaspora, scholars are increasingly emphasizing "the study of slave rebellions, uprisings, and even possibly revolutionary networks". A major project at Michigan State University stressed "understanding peoples of African descent as subjects of their history and as active participants in their struggle for survival and as active agents for themselves" (Simms Hamilton 1990: 6).
4. This usage is closer to the Greek meaning, which translates as "burnt face" and to the seventeenth-century English understanding, which equated "Ethiopian" with "black".
5. A very detailed description of the military campaign to restore the Emperor is provided in Shirreff (1995).
6. Padmore's break with international communism is explained in his informative *mea culpa* published under the title of *Pan-Africanism or Communism* (1972).
7. It is fairly well known that Elvis Presley "ripped off" black music and exploited his relatively greater acceptability to white audiences by distancing himself from the music's origins. Needless to say, the shrine to the chubby singer at his former residence, Graceland, is not replete with African-American mourners.
8. I do not wish to oppose this statement in a narrow didactic manner, but simply note that we have already come across claims for primacy on behalf of Judaea, Greece, Rome, Islam, Egypt, Mesopotamia (Sumaria and Babylon) as well as Armenia. Such claims have something to do with the idea of the "known world". The list just provided, for example, leaves out some rather significant Asian claimants like China and India, not to mention the Incas and Aztecs. The great world historian, Arnold Toynbee (1934–61), started with a list of 21 civilizations in the first edition of his multi-volume *Study of history*, but by the time the posthumous

one-volume summary of his work was published, he was prepared to admit "up to at least thirty-one, besides a few more that were abortive" (Toynbee 1988: 11). An increased appreciation of the spiritually rich and ecologically friendly ways of life of the native Americans, San, Inuit, Maoris, Aborigines and other indigenous peoples have, in any case, questioned the value of the "great civilizations" approach to history.

9. This is not to deny that there were small bands of Armenian nationalists who wanted to oppose the Ottomans by revolutionary means. However, I do not wish to imply support for the justice commandos of the Armenian genocide or for the Armenian Secret Army for the Liberation of Armenia, which commenced terrorist operations against Turkish targets in the 1970s.

10. The most analytically ambitious comparison is made by Robert Melson (1992) who creates a "scale of genocide" from "massacre or pogrom" to "partial genocide" to "total genocide" to "the Holocaust" or "final solution". According to Melson (p. 29), the difference between the last and the second-last categories is that some members of the victim group may save themselves by abandoning their identity, as apparently happened to some Armenians who embraced Islam. If we need to make this distinction at all I would, with Bauman (1989), focus more on the differential technological capacities and totalitarian characters of the perpetrator states concerned.

11. Hamilian (1981: 155) refutes the claim that Michael Arlen never addressed Armenian themes. He in fact recalls him describing a chance encounter with the Nazi minister of propaganda, Goebbels, whom he observed from the veranda of his hotel in Athens in 1940. He spat on Goebbels's "superb silk hat" as he passed below him and wrote afterwards: "It made me mad. It always makes me mad when people get away with murder and grin happily ever after. I wanted to throw a brick down at him . . . I wanted to knock his hat off. I wanted to forget that I was a naturalized Englishman and become an Armenian again. I wanted to be a Jew and revenge all Jews."

Chapter 3

1. By 1914 nearly one million Italians lived in Argentina while one and a half million lived in the USA, most of them workers. Baily (1995) shows the complexity of the migration process that underlay these figures. Many were content to come on a one-way ticket. Others returned home. And a significant group moved back and forth between Italy and the Americas. The temporary migrants were prepared to stay in the cheapest housing to maximize their savings and remittances. In terms of their occupational profile, data from Argentina can be cited. By 1887, Italians

constituted 32 per cent of the population of Buenos Aires, 53 per cent of the industrial workers and 39 per cent of the workers in commercial enterprises (Baily 1995: 284).

2. Although in fact just such an appellation has been loosely applied *inter alia* to Mexicans, Puerto Ricans, Cubans, Germans and Poles in the USA and to many ethnic groups arriving in Europe or Australasia. I do not accord a "diaspora" designation to such groups, rather I argue that it has to be demonstrated that some of the other general features of a diaspora (as discussed in Chapter 1) have to be shown to be present.

3. Slavery and indenture created new forms of coerced labour, but many workers were unfree before they were transported. Indeed, seen on a global scale, unfree labour was the predominant form of labour control until much later than many might suppose. Even in Europe, Steinfield (cited Brass et al. 1993: 8) suggests that free labour, conceived in the sense of the freedom to choose one's employer, did not become a dominant legal ideal until the late eighteenth century and not the dominant paradigm until the nineteenth.

4. This is the figure for Muslims in Trinidad given by Peach (1994: 43), citing Colin Clarke. The further complications of considering smaller groups – Jains, Parsees, Goans, Ismailis, Baluchis – are not even addressed here. However, it is worth drawing attention to the notable work by Hinnells (1994) on the Zoroastrian/Parsee diaspora. The Parsee diaspora is of notable antiquity and endurance (paralleling the Jews in this respect), beginning in the sixth century BC (see Ch. 8).

5. They were also involved in trying to persuade women, apparently with some success, to return to their conventional roles, to become "pure like Sita".

6. While I am using the British as the exemplary case of an imperial diaspora here, I want to mention two other examples of the phenomenon that preceded and postdated the high point of British expansionism. The first is the case of the ancient Greeks, whose diaspora was more of an imperial than either a labour or victim type. The second possible case is that of the Russians, further discussed in Chapter 8, who were sent as soldiers or arrived as settlers in many of the non-Russian parts of the USSR, especially the Baltic states. Although not normally considered a diaspora, the designation may help to understand the politics of the post-Soviet period. As for the British, the label "diaspora" is unusual, but far from unknown. For example, a conference on the theme of "The Diaspora of the British" was convened at the University of Kent in 1981 and the collection of papers from this conference were subsequently published by London University's Institute of Commonwealth Studies (Anon. 1982).

7. It is perhaps at first surprising that the trade unions supported emigration. However, they had to face up to the redundancies that steam power

would bring and they thought it best to protect the jobs of the members they were likely to retain.

8. More effective were the Empire Settlement Act 1922, where the imperial and dominion governments shared the cost of the transport and care of the children, and the Migration and Settlement Act 1925, which made provision for assisted passages to 450,000 emigrants.

9. English rather than British here, as the sporting traditions of the Celtic fringe diverge radically. The Gaelic Athletic Association, for example, banned all non-indigenous games from 1887. Holt (1990) maintained that sport provided the crucial function of promoting loyalty to the empire by colonial whites (and also by native elites). Cricket, athletics and rugby – the sports of the English public schools – were vigorously promoted in the empire and dominions. (Football was too "working class".) Partly because of the presence of non-British whites, the French Canadians, these sports did not "catch on" in Canada. On the other hand, despite John Buchan's disparaging remark that the Afrikaners of South Africa "were not a sporting race", the Boers took to rugby with such avidity and determination that the mauling scrum became a crucial ritual through which their deep resentment against the British was expressed.

10. The British government has a considerable stake in the success of the post-apartheid settlement as further political destabilization could lead the approximately one million people of British descent (so-called "patrials") to claim their entitlement to settle (or "repatriate") in the United Kingdom.

Chapter 4

1. For China, see also Wang (1991). Curtin (1984: 2) acknowledges his debt to other scholars – in particular, Abner Cohen, Lloyd Fallers and Karl Y. Yambert – in developing his use of the term, but as there are no serious discrepancies between usages, Curtin remains the single most helpful source on trade diasporas. I have diverged from his understanding in that he argues (pp. 230–40) that trade diasporas, strictly speaking, were supplanted between the period 1740 and 1860 by European commercial empires. Certainly, he is right in arguing that trading companies like the English East India Company or the Dutch VOC ushered in a new era where commerce, empire and military conquest went hand-in-hand. However, I would prefer to see these firms as precursors of the transnational corporations, with trade diasporas still continuing, though transmuting and refurbishing themselves as auxiliaries in the colonial era and as ethnic entrepreneurs (see Ch. 7) in the global age.

2. Tinker (1977: 96–137; 1990) uses the two expressions, apparently with-

out a different intent. Although suggestive, his terms are not clearly defined or elaborated. I would prefer to confine the idea of an auxiliary diaspora to an emigrant group, or part of an emigrant group, which more definitely became intermediaries. Thus, I would suggest that whereas Indian traders were the auxiliary part of the South Asian diaspora, Indian plantation workers were not.

3. I exclude the Gurkhas who invariably returned to Nepal. They were none the less invaluable servants of the British Crown, having served in the colonial armies since 1815. Over a quarter of a million served in the two world wars.

4. By the same token, the connection between homeland and diaspora could be revived in response to changes at the political level. After President Nixon recognized the People's Republic in 1972, Chinese-Americans felt free to travel to China without being thought of as "unAmerican". Mainland China also began to encourage tourism, Western investment and an outreach policy to the diaspora (Fitzgerald 1972). As I argue in Chapter 7, in the 1980s and 1990s a modified practice of sojourning has once again become easier as the process of globalization has begun to eat into the capacity of the nation-state to demand exclusive loyalty from its residents.

5. Gangs of Chinese labourers were used on public works in various African countries, but the only significant permanent settlement is in Mauritius. After the disruption caused by the Boer War, 63,000 indentured Chinese were recruited to get the gold mines back into production, but after a political storm in Britain about the use of indentured workers for this purpose, they were repatriated (see Richardson 1984).

6. I speak here of the communities established before the Second World War and the Chinese Revolution. Thereafter, a great number of professionals started migrating, particularly from Hong Kong, Taiwan and China to places like Canada, the USA and Australia. The changed class composition of the Chinese diaspora also allowed a modified version of the sojourner tradition to reassert itself (see Ch. 7).

7. Pan is referring here to the Exclusion Acts directed at the Chinese, the first of which was passed in 1882 in response to prejudice and hysteria about the "Yellow Peril" of truly epic proportions. The attitudes that led up to the 1882 Act are usefully surveyed by Miller (1969).

8. "Lebanon" did not exist as an independent entity until 1946. The Ottoman province of Syria included the *wilayet* of Beirut and the *sanjak* of Lebanon. After the First World War, the French administered the area under a League of Nations mandate, setting up Great Lebanon, a designation that lasted from 1920 to 1946. Its Ottoman history meant that many Lebanese abroad were classified as "Syrians", "Syro-Lebanese", "Ottomans" or "Turks". Their religious differences (Maronite, Greek Orthodox, Greek Catholic, Armenian Orthodox and Muslim), plus the arrival of Middle Eastern Jews and other Middle Eastern Arabs, led to some de-

licious classificatory pickles, particularly in the Americas. I illustrate this with a personal experience. While in the Caribbean, I (of Ashkenazi origins, but born in South Africa) was welcomed and accorded hospitality as a "fellow Syrian", an offer I was only too happy to accept. For the purposes of this chapter I have used the category "Lebanese" as a catch-all, except where it needs more explanation.

9. I was in Nigeria during the Biafra war and in Liberia at the beginning of *its* civil war. Although many international airlines suspended or interrupted their flights to West Africa, MEA, like the famed St Bernard dog coming to the rescue of distressed travellers, could always be trusted to get through to service the Lebanese diaspora (and many others like me). I was sorry to learn that the shelling of the airport in Beirut itself, during the Lebanese civil war in the 1970s and 1980s, temporarily scuppered the airline.

10. Bonacich's equally interesting but more recent work (1988, 1993) lays less emphasis on exploitation by others and more emphasis on self-exploitation. Her sympathetic description of Korean entrepreneurs in the USA points to their health problems, marital breakdowns and long hours of self- and family-exploitation. She is also less inclined to see the external dominant groups as consciously deploying a divide-and-rule strategy to pit ethnic groups against one another. Instead, she argues that ethnic competition is an unintended but, for the ruling groups, welcome consequence of migration and settlement.

Chapter 5

1. In all parts of the empire the British had the unvarying conviction that "northerners" or "hillsmen" made better soldiers than "southerners" or those who lived on the coast. The latter were seen as corrupt and soft, the former as hardened and warlike. The generalization was dubious, but the Sikhs did indeed make remarkable soldiers, partly because of the soldier-saint ideal. The sight of an unyielding turbaned regiment of Sikhs struck fear into Asian, African and European enemies alike. In addition to the Sikhs, the British recruited Gurkhas, Jats, Dogras, Pathans, Rajputs and Garhwalis.

2. The Sepoy Mutiny is also known as the Indian Mutiny and, to Indian nationalists, as the Indian National Rising.

3. For other examples see Zolberg (1983). Of course this does not provide a moral defence of any of these events: it merely shows that each is part of a wider phenomenon.

4. The literature on these themes is so voluminous that I do not pretend to have consulted it all. For those who wish to follow these debates in detail, the following appear to be relevant references: Arendt (1978);

Avineri (1981); Bauer (1980); Endelman (1991); Gilman (1986); Gittler (1981); Heilman (1982); Liebman (1976); Liebman (1979); Liebman and Cohen (1990); Markowitz (1990); Reich (1987) and Vital (1990). I have been forced to rely on the lived reality of these debates among my own friends and family, together with the highly insightful accounts by Goldberg & Krauz (1993) and Gorny (1994).

5. Some of the most important Zionist organizations, most still in existence, are the World Zionist Congress, the Jewish Agency, the Jewish National Fund, the United Jewish Appeal, the Zionist Organization of America and Zionist youth bodies such as *Habonim* (the builders).

6. I was not made of such sturdy stuff and as I grew older in any case had ideological doubts about the whole enterprise.

7. In some Zionist thinking, *golah* (the diaspora) is contrasted to *galut* (the place of exile), but the expressions are also used interchangeably. For Zionists, neither condition is acceptable, but *galut* at least implies that there was no alternative. Zionists also distinguish between *yordim* (the fallen, who have chosen to live outside Israel) and *olim* (the redeemed who have ascended to a full Jewish national identity in the homeland). For more on these distinctions see Shusterman (1993).

8. The *sabras* were named after an indigenous cactus plant, with the implications of virtue, rootedness and authenticity.

Chapter 6

1. One of the difficulties in getting to grips with postcolonial theorists is that they are so maddeningly inconsistent (which perhaps is the point of postmodernism). Some use the term "postcolonial" to signify the situation that followed the end of colonial rule, while others deploy it to allude to the beginning of colonial rule, a hundred years or more earlier. The clumsy word "postcoloniality" has also been deployed to describe a condition of felt inferiority and difference, which is one of the reasons why postcolonial theory has often been rejected by African and Asian intellectuals working in these continents. It is a cogent indictment of the theory that intellectuals in the continents of origin tend rather to favour more humanist and universalist positions (see Hintjens 1995: 165–7).

2. Here I modify the title of one of the chapters in Paul Gilroy's book (1993b: 120). The original read, "It ain't where you're from, it's where you're at".

3. And the centre to the margins, though, given that the centre is often the hegemonic power, it is sometimes able to perpetuate itself through a process of cultural imperialism that may threaten peripheral cultures, but is justified to the dominant groups as "the white man's burden", "civilizing the natives", "converting the heathens", or "economic aid".

4. Strictly, this claim is erroneous because diasporas precede the creation of nation-states by hundreds of years. However, it is right to emphasize, as I also do elsewhere in this book, that the historical trajectories of diasporas and nation-states are often in notable conflict. For a contrary view in the case of India see Dhaliwal (1994a, 1994b).
5. The authors use "immigrants" although this reveals their inadvertent ethnocentric starting point. "Emigrant" would be more accurate.
6. For further information, see DeWind et al. (1979) and Palmer (1990). Foner (1979, 1985) and Sutton and Makiesky (1975) produced pioneering work comparing the fates and fortunes of Afro-Caribbean people in the USA and Britain.
7. I am well aware that stereotyping and channelling may produce successes in these areas and do not, of course, argue that achievement in these fields alone is a remotely adequate measure of social mobility.
8. To be clear here, such is the level of acceptance of French culture that these "roots" are not regarded as being located in Africa, but in Guadeloupe and Martinique.
9. Thus, for example, it presents no paradox to Trinidadians to boast that Prime Minister Eric Williams's famous exposition (1944) of the link between capitalism in Britain and slavery in the West Indies, was presented as a doctorate to the University of Oxford.
10. I do not want to get diverted in my text into a subtheme, but should mention that Yawney's (1995) main thesis is that, with the globalization of Rastafarianism, the conservative dominance of the House of Nyahbinghi in Jamaica is being eroded, particularly in respect of gender relations.
11. In 1995 the first number of a new journal, Social Identities 1 (1), 175–220, provided the ultimate accolade to an academic author – publishing extended reviews by three reviewers of Gilroy's Black Atlantic. This is a useful source from which to begin an appreciation and critique of Gilroy's work. He promises a reply in a forthcoming issue of the journal.

Chapter 7

1. McGrew quotes Perlmutter (1991) in making this argument.
2. As I explain later in this chapter, it may have to reduce its emphasis on social exclusion in order to attract skilled and moneyed members of the global diasporas, who link the national to the world economy.
3. There is no conceptual agreement about using terms such as ethnicity, nationalism, or nation-peoples. A coherent defence of the expression "ethno-nationalism" is provided by Conner (1994).
4. I am grateful to my doctoral student, Masako Ogamato, for information on the Japanese in the UK.

5. One might say that the authorities in countries like the USA, Canada and the UK have been hoist by their own petards. Because it became politically difficult to deny access on racial grounds, family reunification and *jus sanguinis* (the law of blood or descent) have been stressed in recent immigration laws, with a view to strengthening the dominant Anglo-Saxon groups. However, a number of minority groups, especially Asians in recent years, have successfully used the family reunification provisions for immigration purposes.

6. For example, the following are global cities *and* capital cities: London, Paris, Tokyo, Seoul, Geneva, Stockholm, Copenhagen and Mexico DF. However, in Australia the global city is Sydney not Canberra; in South Africa it is Johannesburg not Pretoria; in Canada it is Toronto/Montreal not Ottawa; while in Italy the global city is Milan not Rome. This departure is important because it shows the capacity of global capital to depart from the old political, religious and administrative logic that informed the choice of the capital city and instead effect an intimate tie to the city with the most appropriate features.

7. *Sechal* is Yiddish for intuitive knowledge, being quick witted or streetwise.

8. The idea of "global tribes" does not merit serious dissection because it is not used analytically, but is simply meant as a headline-grabbing device to evoke the powerful sense of ethnic solidarity among the five groups he depicts.

9. "The journey" is a much neglected aspect of migrancy. Reflexive views on the old country, anticipatory socialization, the beginnings of business plans and the bonds of solidarity may all happen on the journey.

Chapter 8

1. I am indebted to my colleague Jim Beckford for these fertile thoughts.

2. Relevant discussion can be found in Cohen (1987: 33-42), Zolberg et al. (1989: 258-82) and Richmond (1994).

3. As noted in Chapter 5, the major exception to this rule is Protestantism, which took a territorial form (for example, the Church of England, the Episcopalians and the Church of Scotland). This is why Protestantism may not qualify as a "world religion".

4. To be clear here, my case for embracing the idea of a Caribbean diaspora does not rest solely on cultural grounds. I also suggested (Ch. 6) that their common history of forcible dispersion through the slave trade is still shared by all people of African descent. Again, the issue of phenotypic difference and consequent racial discrimination is relevant.

5. I am grateful to my old friend, Hoby Spalding, for supplying me with this information on Dominicans in New York.

NOTES

6. A smaller scale version of the phenomenon can be seen in the failure of the English and Scots in Ireland to suppress Irish nationalism, although the imperial diaspora clings on in Northern Ireland.

References

Ages, A. 1973. *The diaspora dimension*. The Hague: Martinus Nijhoff.

Ahmed, A. 1992. *In theory: classes, nations, literatures*. London: Verso.

Al-Rasheed, M. 1993. The meaning of marriage and status in exile: the experience of Iraqi women. *Journal of Refugee Studies* 6(2), 89–103.

Anderson, P. 1992. *English questions*. London: Verso.

Anon. 1982. *The diaspora of the British*. London: Institute of Commonwealth Studies Collected Seminar Papers.

Arendt, H. 1978. *The Jew as pariah: Jewish identity and politics in the modern age*. New York: Grove.

Arlen, M. 1926. *The green hat: a romance for people*. London: W. Collins.

Arlen, M. J. 1976. *Passage to Ararat*. New York: Ballantine.

Armen, G., V-A. Artinean, H. Abdalian (eds) 1987. *Historical atlas of Armenia*. New York: Armenian National Education Committee.

Armstrong, J. A. 1976. Mobilized and proletarian diasporas. *American Political Science Review* 20(2), 393–408.

Avineri, S. 1981. *The making of modern Zionism*. New York: Basic Books.

Azarpay, G. 1968. *Urartian art and artefacts*. Berkeley: University of California Press.

Baily, S. L. 1995. The adjustment of Italian immigrants in Buenos Aires and New York, 1870–1914. In *European migrants: global and local perspectives*, D. Hoerder & L. Page Moch (eds), 282–308. Boston, MA: Northeastern University Press.

Banton, M. 1994. Volk. In *Dictionary of race and ethnic relations*, E. Cashmore (ed.), 341–2. London: Routledge.

Baron, S. W. 1964. *The Russian Jew under tsars and soviets*. New York: Macmillan.

Basch, L., N. Glick Schiller, C. Szanton Blanc 1994. *Nations unbound: transnational projects, postcolonial predicaments, and deterritorialized nation-states*. Basle, Switzerland: Gordon & Breach.

Bauer, Y. 1980. *The Jewish emergence from powerlessness*. London: Macmillan.

Bauman, Z. 1989. *Modernity and the holocaust*. Cambridge: Polity.

Beall, J. 1990. Women under indenture in colonial Natal, 1860–1911. See C. Clarke et al. (1990), 57–74.

Bendix, R. 1973. *Max Weber: an intellectual portrait*. London: Methuen.

Bhabha, H. K. 1994. Frontlines/borderposts. In *Displacements: cultural identities in question*, A. Bammer (ed.), 269–72. Bloomington, IN: Indiana University Press.

Boadi-Siaw, S. Y. 1993. Brazilian returnees of West Africa. See J. E. Harris (1993), 421–37.

Bobb, D. & A. Raina 1985. *The great betrayal: assassination of Indira Gandhi*. Delhi: Vikas.

Bonacich, E. 1973. A theory of middlemen minorities. *American Sociological Review* **38**, 583–94.

— 1988. The costs of immigrant entrepreneurship. In *Immigrant entrepreneurs*, I. Light & E. Bonacich, 425–36. Berkeley: University of California Press.

— 1993. The other side of ethnic entrepreneurship: a dialogue with Waldinger, Aldrich, Ward and associates. *International Migration Review* **27**(3), 685–92.

Boot, A. & M. Thomas 1976. *Jamaica: Babylon on a thin wire*. London: Thames & Hudson.

Boyajian, L. & H. Grigorian 1991. Psychosocial sequelae of the Armenian genocide. See R. G. Hovannisian (1991a), 177–85.

Boyarin, D. 1994. *A radical Jew: Paul and the politics of identity*. Berkeley, Calif.: University of California Press.

Boyarin, D. & J. Boyarin 1993. Diaspora: generation and the ground of Jewish identity. *Critical Enquiry* **19**(4), 693–725.

Boyarin, J. 1992. *Storm from paradise: the politics of Jewish memory*. Minneapolis: University of Minnesota Press.

— 1995. Powers of diaspora. Paper presented to a panel on diaspora at the International Congress of the Historical Sciences, Montreal.

Brass, T. & M. van der Linden 1993. *Free and unfree labour*. Amsterdam: International Institute for Social History.

Castles, S. & G. Kosack 1985. *Immigrant workers and class structure in western Europe*, 2nd edn. Oxford: Oxford University Press.

Césaire, A. 1956. *Return to my native land*. Harmondsworth: Penguin.

Chadney, J. G. 1984. *The Sikhs of Vancouver*. New York: AMS Press.

Chaliand, G. & Y. Ternon 1983. *The Armenians: from genocide to resistance* (translated by Tony Berrett). London: Zed Books.

Chambers, I. 1994. *Migrancy, culture, identity*. London: Routledge.

Chan Kwok Bun & Ong Jin Hui 1995. The many faces of immigration entrpreneurship. See Cohen (1995), 523–31.

Chow, R. 1993. *Writing diaspora: tactics of intervention in contemporary cultural studies*. Bloomington, IN: Indiana University Press.

Clarke, C., C. Peach, S. Vertovec (eds) 1990. *South Asians overseas: migration and ethnicity*. Cambridge: Cambridge University Press.

Clifford, J. 1992. Traveling cultures. In *Cultural studies*, L. Grossberg, C. Nelson, P. A. Treichler with L. Baugham & J. Macgregor (eds), 96–116. New York: Routledge.

— 1994. Diasporas. *Current Anthropology* 9(3), 302–38.

Cohen, R. 1987. *The new helots: migrants in the international division of labour*. Aldershot: Gower.

— 1994. *Frontiers of identity: the British and the rest*. London: Longman.

Cohen, R. (ed.) 1995. *The Cambridge survey of world migration*. Cambridge: Cambridge University Press.

Cohen, S. & L. Taylor 1976. *Escape attempts: the theory and practice of resistance to everyday life*. London: Allen Lane.

Collier, J. L. 1978. *The making of jazz: a comprehensive history*. London: Macmillan.

Condon, S. A. & P. E. Ogden 1996. Questions of emigration, circulation and return: mobility between the French Caribbean and France. *International Journal of Population Geography* 2, 35–50.

Conner, W. 1986. The impact of homelands upon diasporas. In *Modern diasporas in international politics*, G. Sheffer (ed.), 16–45. London: Croom Helm.

— 1994. *Ethnonationalism: the quest for understanding*. Princeton, NJ: Princeton University Press.

Craig, S. 1992. Intertwining roots (review article). *The Journal of Caribbean History* 26(2), 215–27.

Cross, M. 1995. "Race", class formation and political interests: a comparison of Amsterdam and London. In *Racism, ethnicity and politics in contemporary Europe*, A. G. Hargreaves & J. Leaman (eds), 47–78. Aldershot: Edward Elgar.

Cross, M. & H. Entzinger (eds) 1988. *Lost illusions: Caribbean minorities in Britain and the Netherlands*. London: Routledge.

Curtin, P. 1984. *Cross-cultural trade in world history*. Cambridge: Cambridge University Press.

Dabydeen, D. & B. Samaroo (eds) 1987. *India and the Caribbean*. London: Hansib in association with the Centre for Caribbean Studies, University of Warwick and the London Strategic Policy Unit.

Datt, K. 1994. Indo-Fijian concerns. In *Report on consultation on Fiji's constitutional review*. Suva, Fiji: International Alert and the School of Social and Economic Development, University of South Pacific, 89–91.

Dekmejian, R. H. 1991. Determinants of genocide: Armenians and Jews as case studies. See Hovannisian (1991a), 85–96.

DeWind, J., T. Seidl, J. Shenk 1979. Contract labour in US agriculture: the West Indian cane cutters in Florida. In *Peasants and proletarians: the struggles of third world workers*, R. Cohen, P. C. W. Gutkind, P. Brazier (eds), 380–96. London: Hutchinson.

Dhaliwal, A. K. 1994a. Introduction: the traveling nation: India and its diaspora. *Socialist Review* 24(4), 1–11.

— 1994b. Reading diaspora: self-representational practices and the politics of reception. *Socialist Review* **24**(4), 13–43.

Dicken, P. 1992. *Global shift: the internationalization of economic activity*, 2nd edn. London: Paul Chapman.

Dickstein, M. 1993. After the Cold War: culture as politics, politics as culture. *Social Research* **60**(3), 531–44.

Dusenbery, V. A. 1995. A Sikh diaspora. See van der Veer (1995), 17–42.

Encyclopaedia Judaica 1971. [16 volumes, with annual supplements]. Jerusalem: Keter.

Endelman, M. 1991. The legitimization of the diaspora experience in recent Jewish historiography. *Modern Judaism* **11**(2), 195–209.

Epstein, H. 1969. *Jewish labor in USA: an industrial, political and cultural history of the Jewish labor movement*. New York: Ktav.

Esman, M. J. 1994. *Ethnic politics*. Ithaca, NY: Cornell University Press.

Featherstone, M. (ed.) 1994. *Global culture: nationalism, globalization and modernity*. London: Sage.

Fitzgerald, C. P. 1972. *China and the overseas Chinese: a study of Peking's changing policy, 1949–1970*. Cambridge: Cambridge University Press.

Foner, N. 1979. West Indians in New York and London: a comparative analysis. *International Migration Review* **13**(2), 284–97.

— 1985. Race and colour: Jamaican migrants in London and New York. *International Migration Review* **19**(4), 708–27.

Friedman, J. 1986. The world city hypothesis. *Development and Change* **17**(1), 69–83.

Friedmann, D. with U. Santamara 1994. *Les enfants de la reine de Saba: les Juifs d'Éthiopie (Falachas) – histoire, exode, intégration*. Paris: Éditions Métailié.

Fyfe, C. 1962. *A history of Sierra Leone*. London: Oxford University Press.

Gabaccia, D. 1988. *Militants and migrants: rural Sicilians become American workers*. New Brunswick, NJ: Rutgers University Press.

— 1992. Clase y cultura: los migrantes Italianos en los movimientos obreros en el mundo, 1876–1914. *Estudios Migratorios Latinoamericanos* **7**(22), 425–51.

Geertz, C. 1986. The uses of diversity. *Michigan Quarterly Review* **25**(1), 105–23.

Gilman, S. 1986. *Jewish self-hatred: anti-Semitism and the hidden language of the Jews*. Baltimore, MD: Johns Hopkins University Press.

Gilroy, P. 1987. *"There ain't no black in the Union Jack"; the cultural politics of race and nation*. London: Hutchinson.

— 1993a. *The black Atlantic: modernity and double consciousness*. London: Verso.

— 1993b. *Small acts: thoughts on the politics of black cultures*. London: Serpent's Tail.

Gittler, J. B. (ed.) 1981. *Jewish life in the United States: perspectives from the social sciences*. New York: New York University Press.

Glantz, R. 1986. The wandering Jew in America. In *The wandering Jew: essays in the interpretation of a Christian legend*, G. Hasan-Roken & A. Dundes (eds), 105–18. Bloomington, IN: Indiana University Press.

Goitein, S. D. F. 1967–93. *A Mediterranean society: the Jewish communities of the Arab world as portrayed in the documents of the Cairo Geniza* [6 volumes].

Berkeley, CA: University of California Press.

Goldberg, D. J. & J. D. Raynor 1989. *The Jewish people: their history and their religion*. Harmondsworth: Penguin.

Goldberg, D. T. & M. Krausz (eds) 1993. *Jewish identity*. Philadelphia, PA: Temple University Press.

Gorny, Y. 1994. *The state of Israel in Jewish public thought: the quest for collective identity*. London: Macmillan.

Green, N. L. 1995. The modern Jewish diaspora: Eastern European Jews in New York, London and Paris. In *European migrants: global and local perspectives*, D. Hoerder & L. Page Moch (eds), 263–81. Boston, MA: Northeastern University Press.

Grunwald, M. 1936. *History of the Jews in Vienna*. Philadelphia, PA: Jewish Publication Society of America.

Hall, S. 1990. Cultural identity and diaspora. In *Identity: community, culture, difference*, J. Rutherford (ed.), 222–37. London: Lawrence & Wishart.

— 1991a. Ethnicity, identity and difference. *Radical America* 23 (4), 9–20.

— 1991b. The local and the global: globalization and ethnicity. In *Culture, globalization and the world-system: contemporary conditions for the representation of identity*, A. D. King (ed.). London: Macmillan.

— 1992. The question of cultural identity. In *Modernity and its futures*, S. Hall, D. Held & A. McGrew (eds), 273–316. Cambridge: Polity Press in association with the Open University.

— 1995. Negotiating Caribbean identities. *New Left Review* **209** (January–February), 3–14.

Hamilian, L. 1981. The Armenian genocide and the literary imagination. See R. G. Hovannisian (1981), 153–65.

Hammerton, A. J. 1979. *Emigrant gentlewomen: genteel poverty and female emigration, 1830–1914*. London: Croom Helm.

Harney, S. 1996. *Nationalism and identity: culture and the imagination in a Caribbean diaspora*. London: Zed Books.

Harris, J. E. 1971. *The African presence in Asia: consequences of the East African slave trade*. Evanston, IL: Northwestern University Press.

— (ed.) 1993. *Global dimensions of the African diaspora*, 2nd edn. Washington, DC: Howard University Press.

Harris, N. 1995. *The new untouchables: immigration and the new world order*. London: I. B. Tauris.

Hasan-Rokem, G. & A. Dundes (eds) 1986. *The wandering Jew: essays in the interpretation of a Christian legend*. Bloomington, IN: Indiana University Press.

Hashimoto, K. 1992. Lebanese population movements, 1920–1939: towards a study. See A. Hourani & N. Shehadi (1992), 65–108.

Heilman, S. 1982. The sociology of American Jewry: the last ten years. *Annual Review of Sociology* **8**, 135–60.

Helmrich, S. 1992. Kinship, nation and Paul Gilroy's concept of diaspora. *Diaspora* **2**(2), 243–9.

Helweg, A. W. 1979. *Sikhs in England: the development of a migrant community*.

Delhi: Oxford University Press.

Henderson, J. & M. Castells (eds) 1987. *Global restructuring and territorial development*. London: Sage.

Hennessy, A. 1978. *The frontier in Latin American history*. London: Edward Arnold.

Herskovits, M. J. 1937. *Life in a Haitian valley*. New York: Alfred Knopf.

— 1961. *The New World Negro: selected papers in Afro-American studies*. Bloomington, IN: Indiana University Press.

Herskovits, M. J. & F. Herskovits 1947. *Trinidad village*. New York: Alfred Knopf.

Hinnells, J. R. 1994. The modern Zoroastrian diaspora. In *Migration: the Asian experience*, J. M. Brown & R. Foot (eds), 56–82. New York: St Martin's Press in association with St Antony's College, Oxford.

Hintjens, H. M. 1995. *Alternatives to independence: explorations in post-colonial relations*. Aldershot: Dartmouth.

Hitti, P. K. 1974. *History of the Arabs: from the earliest times to the present*. London: Macmillan.

Holt, R. 1990. *Sport and the British: a modern history*. Oxford: Oxford University Press.

Hourani, A. 1983. *Arabic thought in the liberal age, 1798–1939*. Cambridge: Cambridge University Press.

— 1991. *A history of the Arab peoples*. Cambridge, MA: Belknap Press.

— 1992. Introduction. See A. Hourani & N. Shehadi (1992), 3–11.

Hourani, A. & N. Shehadi (eds) 1992. *The Lebanese in the world: a century of emigration*. London: I. B. Tauris for the Centre for Lebanese Studies.

Hovanessian, M. 1992. *Le lien communautaire: trois générations d'Armeniens*. Paris: Armand Colin.

Hovannisian, R. G. (ed.) 1981a. *The Armenian genocide in perspective*. New Brunswick, NJ: Transaction.

— 1981b. The historical dimensions of the Armenian question, 1878–1923. See R. G. Hovannisian (ed.), 19–41.

Hu-DeHart, E. 1993. Rethinking America: the practice and politics of multiculturalism in higher education. In *Beyond a dream deferred: multicultural education and the politics of excellence*, B. W. Thompson & S. Tyagi (eds), 3–17. Minneapolis: University of Minnesota Press.

Hunwick, J. O. 1993. African slaves in the Mediterranean world: a neglected aspect of the African diaspora. See J. E. Harris (1993), 289–324.

Israel, B. J. 1971. *The children of Israel: the Bene Israel of Bombay*. Oxford: Basil Blackwell.

Issawi, C. 1992. The historical background of Lebanese emigration, 1800–1914. See A. Hourani & N. Shehadi (1992), 13–31.

Jacobson, D. 1996. *Rights across borders: immigration and the decline of citizenship*. Baltimore, MD: Johns Hopkins University Press.

Kelly, J. D. 1995. *Bhaki* and postcolonial politics: Hindu missions to Fiji. See P. van der Veer (1995), 43–72.

Kennedy, P. 1988. *African capitalism: the struggle for ascendancy*. Cambridge: Cambridge University Press.

Khan, A. 1995. Homeland, motherland: authenticity, legitimacy and ideologies of place among Muslims in Trinidad. See P. van der Veer (1995), 93–131.

Kinealy, C. 1995. *The great calamity: the Irish famine, 1845–52*. London: Gill & Macmillan.

Kirshenblatt-Gimblett, B. 1994. Spaces of dispersal. *Cultural Anthropology* 9(3), 339–44.

Klich, I. 1992. *Criollos* and Arabic speakers in Argentina: an uneasy *pas de deux*, 1888–1914. See A. Hourani & N. Shehadi (eds), 243–84.

Koestler, A. 1976. *The thirteenth tribe: the Khazar empire and its heritage*. London: Hutchinson.

Kolstø, P. 1993. The new Russian diaspora: minority protection in the Soviet successor states. *Journal of Peace Research* 30(2), 197–217.

Kotkin, J. 1992. *Tribes: how race, religion and identity determine success in the new global economy*. New York: Random House.

Kurkjian, V. M. 1964. *A history of Armenia*. New York: Armenian General Benevolent Union of America.

Kwong, P. 1987. *The new Chinatown*. New York: Hill & Wang.

Lal, V. 1990. The Fiji Indians: marooned at home. See C. Clarke et al. (1990), 113–30.

Lang, D. M. 1978. *Armenia: cradle of civilisation*. London: Allen & Unwin.

Lang, D. M. & C. J. Walker 1987. *The Armenians*, MRG Report no. 32, 5th edn. London: Minority Rights Group.

Larkcom, J., A. Hellyer, P. Dodd 1984. *The Observer good gardening guide*. London: Octopus.

Lemelle, S. J. & R. D. G. Kelly 1994. *Imagining home: class, culture and nationalism in the African diaspora*. London: Verso.

Lemon, A. 1990. The political position of Indians in South Africa. See C. Clarke et al. (1990), 131–63.

Levin, N. 1977. *While Messiah tarried: Jewish socialist movements, 1871–1917*. New York: Schocken.

Lewis, B. 1970. *The Arabs in history*. London: Hutchinson.

Lian, Kwen Fee 1995. Migration and the formation of Malaysia and Singapore. See R. Cohen (ed.), 392–6.

Liebman, A. 1979. *Jews and the left*. New York: Wiley.

Liebman, C. 1976. *The ambivalent American Jew*. Philadelphia, PA: Jewish Publication Society.

Liebman, C. S. & S. M. Cohen 1990. *Two worlds of Judaism: the Israeli and American experiences*. New Haven, CT: Yale University Press.

Lindemann, A. S. 1993. *The Jew accused. Three anti-Semitic affairs: Dreyfus, Beilis, Frank, 1884–1915*. Cambridge: Cambridge University Press.

Lippman Abu-Lughod, J. 1995. The displacement of the Palestinians. See R. Cohen (1995), 410–13.

Maalouf, A. 1984. *The Crusades through Arab eyes*. London: Al Saqi.

McGrew, A. 1992. A global society. See S. Hall et al. (eds), 61–102.

Magubane, B. M. 1987. *The ties that bind: African-American consciousness of Africa*. Trenton, NJ: Africa World Press.

Malkki, L. 1992. National geographic: the rooting of peoples and the territorialization of national identity among scholars and refugees. *Cultural Anthropology* 7, 24–44.

Marienstras, R. 1989. On the notion of diaspora. In *Minority peoples in the age of nation-states*, G. Chaliand (ed.). London: Pluto.

Markowitz, F. 1990. Plaiting the strands of Jewish identity. *Comparative Studies in Society and History*, 32(1), 181–9.

Marriott, Sir J. A. R. 1927. *Empire settlement*. London: Oxford University Press.

Marrus, M. R. 1980. *The politics of assimilation: the French Jewish community at the time of the Dreyfus affair*. Oxford: Clarendon.

— 1981. *Vichy France and the Jews*. New York: Basic Books.

Mazrui, A. A. 1990. *Cultural forces in world politics*. London: James Currey.

Melson, R. 1992. *Revolution and genocide: on the origins of the Armenian genocide and the holocaust*. Chicago: University of Chicago Press.

Miller, S. C. 1969. *The unwelcome immigrant: the American image of the Chinese, 1785–1882*. Berkeley, CA: University of California Press.

Montilus, G. C. 1993. Guinea versus Congo lands: aspects of the collective memory in Haiti. See J. E. Harris (1993), 159–66.

Naff, A. 1992. Lebanese immigration into the United States: 1880 to the present. See A. Hourani & N. Shehadi (1992), 141–65.

Nairn, T. 1977. *The break-up of Britain: crisis and neo-nationalism*. London: Verso.

Needham, R. 1975. Polythetic classification: convergence and consequences. *Man* 10(ns), 349–69.

Nersessian, S. Der 1969. *The Armenians*. London: Thames & Hudson.

Neusner, J. 1985. *Israel in America: a too-comfortable exile?* Boston, MA: Beacon.

Oliver, P. 1970. *Savannah syncopators: African retentions in the blues*. London: Studio Vista.

Ong, Jing Hui 1995. Chinese indentured labour: coolies and colonies. See R. Cohen (1995), 51–6.

Ottley, R. 1948. *Black odyssey: the story of the Negro in America*. New York: Charles Scribner.

Padmore, G. 1972. *Pan-Africanism or communism* (first published 1949). New York: Doubleday.

Palmer, R. W. (ed.) 1990. *In search of a better life: perspectives on migration from the Caribbean*. New York: Praeger.

Pan, L. 1991. *Sons of the yellow emperor: the story of the overseas Chinese*. London: Mandarin.

Parekh, B. 1994. Some reflections on the Hindu diaspora. *New Community* 20(4), 603–20.

Peach, C. 1968. *West Indian migration to Britain: a social geography*. London: Oxford University Press.

— 1994. Three phases of South Asian emigration. In *Migration: the Asian expe-*

rience, J. M. Brown & R. Foot (eds). 38–55. New York: St Martin's Press in association with St Antony's College, Oxford.

— 1995. Trends in levels of Caribbean segregation, Great Britain, 1961–91. Paper presented at a Conference on Comparative History of Migration within the Caribbean and to Europe, Oxford Brookes University, Oxford, 22–4 September.

Perlmutter, H. V. 1991. On the rocky road to the first global civilization. *Human Relations* 44(9), 897–1010.

Phillips, C. 1993. *Crossing the river*. London: Picador.

Post, K. 1978. *Arise ye starvelings: the Jamaican labour rebellion of 1938 and its aftermath*. The Hague: Martinus Nijhoff.

Reich, W. 1987. Israel and the diaspora. *Jewish Social Studies* 49(3–4), 326–32.

Rex, J. 1995. Ethnic identity and the nation state: the political sociology of multi-cultural societies. *Social Identities* 1(1), 21–34.

Richards, E. 1993. How did poor people emigrate from the British Isles to Australia in the nineteenth century? *Journal of British Studies* 32(3), 250–79.

Richardson, P. 1984. Coolies, peasants, and proletarians: the origins of Chinese indentured labour in South Africa, 1904–1907. In *International labour migration: historical perspectives*, S. Marks & P. Richardson (eds), 167–85. London: Maurice Temple Smith for the Institute of Commonwealth Studies.

Richmond, A. H. 1994. *Global apartheid: refugees, racism and the new world order*. Toronto: Oxford University Press.

Riggs, F. W. 1996. Migration and ethnonationalism. Unpublished paper, Ethnicity, Nationalism and Migration panel of the International Studies Association, San Diego.

Robertson, R. 1994. *Globalization: social theory and global culture*. London: Sage.

Robinson, V. 1995. The migration of East African Asians to the UK. See R. Cohen (1995), 331–6.

Rushdie, S. 1991. *Imaginary homelands*. New York: Vikas.

Safran, W. 1991. Diasporas in modern societies: myths of homeland and return. *Diaspora* 1(1), 83–99.

Said, E. 1990. Reflections on exile. In *Out there: marginalization and contemporary cultures*, R. Ferguson et al. (eds), 357–63. Cambridge, MA: MIT Press.

— 1991. *Orientalism: Western conceptions of the Orient*. (first published 1978). Harmondsworth: Penguin.

Sanadjian, M. 1996. An anthology of "the people", place, space and "home": (re)constructing the Lur in south-western Iran. *Social Identities*, 2(1), 5–36.

Saroyan, W. 1962. *Here comes, there goes, you know who: an autobiography*. London: Peter Davis.

Sassen-Koob, S. 1990. *The global city*. Princeton, NJ: Princeton University Press.

Seagrave, S. 1995. *Lords of the rim: the invisible empire of the overseas Chinese*. New York: G. P. Putnam.

Seeley, Sir J. 1895. *The expansion of England*. Cambridge: Cambridge University Press.

Segal, A. 1993. *An atlas of international migration*. London: Hans Zell.

Segal, R. 1995. *The black diaspora*. London: Faber & Faber.

Selvon, S. 1985. *The lonely Londoners*. Harlow: Longman.

Shafir, G. 1989. *Land, labor and the origins of the Israeli–Palestinian conflict, 1882–1914*. Cambridge: Cambridge University Press.

Sharif, R. S. 1983. *Non-Jewish Zionism: its roots in Western history*. London: Zed Books.

Shepperson, G. 1993. African diaspora: concept and context. See J. E. Harris (1993), 41–9.

Shepperson, W. S. 1957. *British emigration to North America: projects and opinions in the early Victorian period*. Oxford: Basil Blackwell.

Shirreff, D. 1995. *Barefeet and bandoliers: Wingate, Sandford, the Patriots and the part they played in the liberation of Ethiopia*. London: Radcliffe.

Shusterman, R. 1993. Next year in Jerusalem: postmodern Jewish identity and the myth of return. See D. T. Goldberg & M. Krausz (1993), 291–308.

Simms Hamilton, R. 1990. *Creating a paradigm and research agenda for comparative studies of the worldwide dispersion of African peoples*. East Lansing, MI: African Diaspora Research Project, Michigan State University.

Singh, G. 1993. Review of Khushwant Singh *A history of the Sikhs. Volume 2, 1839–1988*, 2nd edn. Delhi: Oxford University Press. In *Punjab Research Group: Newsletter of the Association for Punjab Studies in Great Britain* 5 (January), 13.

Singh, K. 1977. *A history of the Sikhs. Volume 2, 1839–1974*, 1st edn. Delhi: Oxford University Press.

— 1991. *A history of the Sikhs. Volume 2, 1839–1988*, 2nd edn. Delhi: Oxford University Press.

— 1992. *My bleeding Punjab*. New Delhi: UBS.

Skinner, E. P. 1993. The dialectic between diasporas and homelands. See J. E. Harris (1993), 11–40.

Smart, N. et al. 1987. The importance of diasporas. In *Gilgul: essays on transformation, revolution and permanence in the history of religions*, S. Shaked, R. Y. Werblovsky, D. D. Shulman, G. A. G. Strounka (eds), 288–95. Leiden: Brill.

Solomos, J. 1989. *Race and racism in contemporary Britain*. London: Macmillan.

Suny, R. G. 1993. *Looking toward Ararat: Armenia in modern history*. Bloomington, IN: Indiana University Press.

Sutton, C. R. & S. R. Makiesky 1975. Migration and West Indian racial and ethnic consciousness. In *Migration and development: implications for ethnic identity and political conflict*, H. I. Safa & B. M. Du Toit (eds), 113–43. The Hague: Mouton.

Tatla, D. S. 1993. *The politics of homeland: a study of ethnic linkages and political mobilisation amongst Sikhs in Britain and North America*. PhD thesis, Centre for Research in Ethnic Relations, University of Warwick.

Thiara, R. 1995. Indian indentured workers in Mauritius, Natal and Fiji. See R. Cohen (1995), 63–8.

Tinker, H. 1974. *A new system of slavery: the export of Indian labour overseas,*

1830–1920. London: Oxford University Press for the Institute of Race Relations.

— 1977. *The Banyan tree: overseas emigrants from India, Pakistan and Bangladesh*. Oxford: Oxford University Press.

— 1990. Indians in Southeast Asia: imperial auxiliaries. See C. Clarke et al. (1990), 39–56.

Tölölyan, K. 1991. Preface. *Diaspora* 1(1), 3–7.

Toynbee, A. J. 1915. *Armenian atrocities: the murder of a nation*. London: Hodder & Stoughton.

Toynbee, A. J. (ed.) 1916. *The treatment of Armenians in the Ottoman empire, 1915–16*. London: HMSO.

Toynbee, A. J. 1934–61. *A study of history*, 12 vols. London: Oxford University Press.

— 1957. *A study of history*. Abridgement of vols 7–10 by D. C. Somervell. London: Oxford University Press under the auspices of the Royal Institute of International Affairs.

Toynbee, A. J. with J. Caplan 1988. *A study of history*. (rev. abridged edn, first published 1972). London: Oxford University Press.

Turner, F. J. 1920. *The frontier in American history*. New York: Holt.

Turner, V. 1969. *The ritual process, structure and anti-structure*. London: Routledge & Kegan Paul.

van der Laan, H. L. 1975. *The Lebanese traders in Sierra Leone*. The Hague: Mouton for the Afrika-Studiecentrum, Leiden.

van der Veer, P. (ed.) 1995. *Nation and migration: the politics of space in the South Asian Diaspora*. Philadelphia, PA: University of Pennsylvania Press.

Vertovec, S. 1995. Indian indentured migration to the Caribbean. See R. Cohen (1995), 57–62.

Visram, R. 1986. *Ayahs, lascars and princes: Indians in Britain, 1700–1947*. London: Pluto.

Vital, D. 1990. *The future of the Jews: a people at the cross-roads?* Cambridge, MA: Harvard University Press.

Waldinger, R. 1996. Review of Seymour Martin Lipset and Earl Raab, *Jews and the new American scene*. Cambridge, MA: Harvard University Press, 1995. *New Community* 22(1), 174–5.

Waldinger, R. & Yenfen Tseng 1992. Divergent diasporas: the Chinese communities of New York and Los Angeles compared. Unpublished paper, Department of Sociology, University of California, Los Angeles, CA.

Walker, C. J. 1980. *Armenia: survival of a nation*. London: Croom Helm.

Wallerstein, I. 1984. *The politics of the world economy*. Cambridge: Cambridge University Press.

Wang, Gungwu 1991. *China and the Chinese overseas*. Singapore: Times Academic Press.

— 1992a. *Community and nation: China, Southeast Asia and Australia*. St Leonards, Australia: Allen & Unwin for the Asian Studies Association of Australia.

— 1992b. Sojourning: the Chinese experience in Southeast Asia. Jennifer Cushman Memorial Lecture, mimeo.

Waters, M. 1996. *Globalization*. London: Routledge.

Weiner, M. 1986. Labour migrations and incipient diasporas. In *Modern diasporas in international politics*, Gabriel Sheffer (ed.), 47–74. London: Croom Helm.

Williams, E. 1964. *Capitalism and slavery*, (first published 1944). London: André Deutsch.

Wilson, F. M. 1959. *They came as strangers: the story of refugees to Great Britain*. London: Hamish Hamilton.

Woolfson, M. 1980. *Prophets in Babylon: Jews in the Arab world*. London: Faber & Faber.

Woollacott, M. 1995. Living in the age of terror. *Guardian* 22 August.

Wright, R. 1944. *American hunger*. New York: Harper & Row.

Yawney, C. D. 1995. The globalization of Rastafari: methodological and conceptual issues. Paper presented at the annual meeting of the Society for Caribbean Studies (UK), London.

Zborowski, M. & E. Herzon 1952. *Life is with people: the culture of the Shtetl*. New York: Schocken.

Zolberg, A. 1983. The formation of new states as a refugee generating process. *Annals of the American Academy of Political and Social Science* **467**, 24–38.

Zolberg, A., A. Suhrke, S. Aguayo 1989. *Escape from violence: conflict and the refugee crisis in the developing world*. New York: Oxford University Press.

220

Index

abolitionists, slavery 36–7
Abraham (Bibl.) 11, 123
achievements
  African diaspora 42, 141, 153
  Indian diaspora 80
  Jewish diaspora 5–6, 21, 24
  Lebanese diaspora 98
Adorno, T. 151
African diaspora 27, 31–2, 40–2, 54–
  5, 137, 148–9
  origins 33–9
Afro-Caribbeans 139–41, 144–5
Ages, A. 3, 6, 8
Ahmed, A. 132
Al-Rasheed, M. 143
American colonies, loss of 74
Amritsar massacre 111, 115
Amsterdam, 17th century Jewry 9–10
Anderson, P. 77
Anglo-Boer War 75
anthropology 151
anti-Semitism 19–20
Anti-Slavery Society 35
Arabs, Western stereotypes 132–3
Ararat 43, 55
Argentina, Middle East settlers 96
Arlen, M. J., Jnr 49–50
Arlen, M., Snr 50
Armen, G. 44, 48
Armenia 43–4, 54

Armenian diaspora 2, 27, 31–5, 46–55
  creation of 42–6
Armstrong, J. A. 58, 170
artistic attainments, diaspora groups
  170
Ashkenazim 15–20, 32
assassination, Indira Gandhi 113
assimilationists 122–3
Australia, settlement of 71
auxiliary diasporas 84–5, 103
Azarpay, G. 55

Babylon
  Jewish achievements 5–6, 21, 24
  Jewish exile 3–6
Babylonian Talmud 5
Baily, S. L. 57
Baron, S. W. 17
Basch, L. 136
Beall, J. 63
Ben Gurion, David 119
Bendix, R. 101–2
Berger, Elmer 121
Bhabha, H. K. 129
Bible, King James version 10
black athletes 141
Black Power Movement 140
Boadi-Siaw, S. Y. 37
Bobb, D. 113
Bolívar, Simón 67

Bonacich, E. 103
Boot, A. 38–9
borderland cultures 135, 189–90
Boston Tea Party 74
Boyajian, L. 49, 51
Boyarin, D. 123
Boyarin, J. 3, 123
British imperial diaspora 76, 78, 80–1, 102, 171, 184
British rule, Punjab 108

Calouste Gulbenkian Foundation 51
capitalism
    affinities with Protestantism 101–2, 175
    world economy 156
Caribbean cultural diaspora 127–8, 137–53
Castells, M. 165
Castles, S. 57
catastrophic origins, diasporas 1–2, 27–8
Catholicism 8–9, 125–6
Césaire, Aimé 42, 145, 151
Chaliand, G. 45–6
Chambers, I. 133
Chan Kwok Bun 101
Chinatowns 91–3, 172
Chinese diaspora 85–94, 161–2, 171, 183
Chinese revolutions 89
Chow, R. 131–2
Christianity, Armenia 6–10, 43–4, 147
Christians, in Muslim communities 11–14
civil rights, US 140
clan solidarity, Chinese 86
classical world, trade diasporas 83–4
Clifford, J. 2, 13, 135, 189
Cohen, R. 57, 77, 106, 129, 168, 183
Cohen, S. 79
collective memory 184
Collier, J. L. 42
colonial diasporas 178–9
Commonwealth 76, 77
Commonwealth Immigrants Act, UK 140

communications, global cities 167
Communism, fall of 162
Condon, S. A. 143
Conner, W. 105
coolie trade, Chinese diaspora 91
Corn Laws, repeal of 70
cosmopolitanism 130–1, 157, 169–73
Craig, S. 152
Cross, M. 142
Crusaders 8, 11
Cuba 163
cultural achievements
    African diaspora 42
    Afro-Caribbean 141
    Jewish diaspora 5–6, 21, 24
cultural diasporas 127–53, 178–9
culture
    Afro-Caribbean 148–9, 151, 152–3
    Jewish flowering of 5–6
    Lebanese 99–100
cultures, multiple 174
Curtin, P. 83–4
Cyrus, King of Persia 5

Dabydeen, D. 61–2
Damascus Affair, the 18–19, 25
Datt, K. 65
decolonization, Malaya 90
Dekmejian, R. H. 32–3
Deuteromony 1
Dhaliwal, A. K. 136
Diaspora 127
diaspora groups, sensitivity 170
diasporas
    changing character of 131
    Clifford 135–6
    contemporary 168–70
    dangers of 193–4
    definitions of 2, 21–7, 180
    globalization advantages 175–6
    types of 178
Dicken, P. 158, 165
Dickstein, M. 192
discrimination, host societies 186
Dole, Senator Robert 51
dominion diaspora 74–6
Dreyfus Affair, the 19

DuBois, W. E. B. 41, 145
Dundes, A. 7
Dusenbery, V. A. 113

elitism, imperial diaspora 77–8
emigrations 57, 59
  British 67–73
  Irish 67, 69–70
  Italian 57, 59
  juveniles 41–2
  Lebanese 94–8
  women 72
England, 17th century Jewry 10
English Book of Common Prayer 1
Enlightenment, the 155
entrepreneurship, "global tribes" 171–2
Entzinger, H. 142
Epstein, H. 58
Esman, M. J. 57
Ethiopia
  African "homeland" 37–40, 43, 55
  Rastafarianism 147
ethnic collectivism 171
ethnic group consciousness 185
European diasporas 137, 184
European Economic Community 76–7
European Union 76
exogamous marriage, Jews 122
Ezra 5, 21

Fanon, F. 139
fatwa, Rushdie 130
Featherstone, M. 156
Fiji, Indian diaspora 65, 79
foreign exchange markets, deregulation 161
France
  Armenian diaspora 51–2
  Caribbean immigrants 142–3, 151
  Jewish population 18–20
French Antilles 142–3
Friedman, J. 165
fundamentalists, Jewish 5
Fyfe, C. 37

Gabaccia, D. 57, 59

gallantry awards, Sikhs 111
Gandhi, Indira 113
Gandhi, Mahatma 65
Garvey, M. 40–1, 146–7
Garveyite movement 40, 140, 146, 152
Geertz, C. 134
gender imbalance, Indian diaspora 63
genocide, Armenian 44–5, 51
Germany 105–6, 118
Gilroy, P. 140, 144, 145, 149, 152, 196
Glanz, R. 7
global cities 157, 165–9
globalization 131, 155–76
Goitein, S. D. F. 12–13
Goldberg, D. J. 3–4, 12
Golden Temple, attack on 113, 114–15, 193
Gorny, Y. 118, 121
Greek diaspora (800–600BC) 2
Greeks, classical 83
Green, N. L. 58
Grigorian, H. 51
group identity 134
Grunwald, M. 24
Guide to the perplexed (Maimonides) 13
Gulbenkian Foundation *see* Calouste Gulbenkian Foundation
Gulf crisis 163, 191
Guru Nanak, Sikh religion 107
gypsies, "pariah people" 101

Haile Selassie 39, 147
Haiti 163
Hall, S. 52, 131, 133, 138, 148, 152, 169
Hammerton, A. J. 72
Harney, S. 145, 149, 152
Harris, J. E. 35
Harris, N. 183
Hasan-Rokem, G. 7
Hashimoto, K. 95, 98
Helmrich, S. 177
Helweg, A. W. 107
Henderson, J. 165

Hennessy, A. 189
Herskovits, M. J. 145
Herzl, T. 8
Hindu diaspora 62–4, 79
Hinnells, J. R. 188
Hintjens, H. M. 143
Hitti, P. K. 12
Hokkien merchants, Chinese trade
 diaspora 85–6, 102
Holocaust 20, 32, 118
 Armenian parallels 46
Holy Land, the 13
homeland 58, 104, 105–6
 African 36–9
 British 78, 106
 Chinese 87, 89
 dangers of concept 193
 diaspora relationship to 125
 idealization of 185
 identity with nation 127
 Jewish 13, 16, 19, 115–25
 Lebanese 98–9
 myth 184
 Sikh 110–13, 115
Homer 83
Hong Kong 92–3, 131–2, 162, 185
horticultural analogy, diasporas 178–
9
host society, troubled relationships
 with 186
Hourani, A. 14, 96, 98, 99, 181
Hovanessian, M. 51
Hovannisian, R. G. 45
hsiang (home), Chinese diaspora 87,
 89
Hu-DeHart, E. 192
hua-chiiao, Chinese diaspora 87–8
human rights 170
Hunwick, J. O. 34
hybridity 130–1, 133, 138

identity
 building blocks of 129
 Caribbean 138, 144–5, 150–1
 Jewish 122–4
 social 129, 157, 173–5
Iliad (Homer) 83

immigrant groups, commercial
 success 101
immigration
 Australia 74
 Caribbean 141–3, 151
imperial diasporas 57, 66–72, 74, 77–
8, 137, 178–9
indentured labour
 Chinese 91, 181
 Indian 57, 59–62
Indian labour diaspora 57, 59–66,
 79–80, 137, 171
indigenous populations, settlers'
 effect on 74
intolerance, Christian 9
IRA (Irish Republican Army) 193
Irish diaspora 27–8, 31, 35, 55, 67,
 69–70, 181
Irish famine 67, 69–70, 181
Islam, Jewish diaspora 10–15
Israel, state of 8–9, 15, 17, 115–25,
 181
Israel, B. J. 24
Issawi, C. 95

Jacobson, D. 125
James, C. L. R. 41, 145
Japan 159–60, 171
Jerusalem, destruction of 3
Jesus Christ 7, 8, 9
Jevons, W. S. 179
Jewish diaspora
 Christianity 6–10
 enduring sense of unease 20
 entrepreneurship 171
 experience of 177
 foundation of state of Israel 115–
 25
 homecoming of 28
 Islam 10–15
 parallels with African 31–2, 35
 Sikh comparisons 114
 tradition 1–6, 21–5
 Zionism 17
Jews
 in Muslim communities 11–14
 origins of 15–16, 21

"pariah people" 101
Judaism
  evolution of 5
  universal principles 121–3
juvenile emigration, from Britain 71–2

Kelly, J. D. 64
Kennedy, P. 102
Khalistan 106, 107, 112, 125–6
Khan, A. 80, 174–5
Khazar Jews 15–16
Kinealy, C. 28
Kirschenblatt-Gimblett, B. 3
Klich, I. 96
knowledge, passion for 172–3
Koestler, A. 15
Kolsto, P. 191
Kosack, G. 57
Kotkin, J. 102, 159, 171
Kurdish Workers' Party 193
Kurkjian, V. M. 43
Kwong, P. 92, 171–3

labour diasporas 29, 57–66, 178–9, 182
Lal, V. 216
Lang, D. M. 43–4, 45, 48, 53, 55
Latin America 67
Law of Return 117, 124–5
Lebanese trade diaspora 83, 94–101, 181
Lebanon 100–1
Lemelle, S. J. 37
Lemon, A. 79
Lewis, B. 11
Lian, Kwen Fee 90
Lindemann, A. S. 16–18
Lipman Abu Laghod, J. 181
local cultures, creation of 157
localism 131, 169–73

McGrew, A. 155
Magubane, B. M. 38, 39, 41
Maimonides, Moses 12–13
Malaya, decolonization 90
Malkki, L. 177

Malouf, David 99–100
Manchester Conference (1945) 42, 145
Marienstras, R. 24, 185
Marley, Bob 42, 147
Marriott, Sir J. A. R. 69–71, 73, 74
Marrus, M. R. 19
Marxism, social identity 129
massacres, Armenian 44–5, 51
Mau Mau, Kenya 75
Maurice, Emperor of Byzantium 44
Melson, R. 45
Menshevik revolution 47
Middle East, Jewry 15
middleman minorities, diasporas 103
migration 134
  Caribbean peoples 138–43, 151
  international 157, 162–5
migrations, French Antilles 142–3
"mobilized diaspora" 58
Montilus, G. C. 36
Moses (Bibl.) 11
Mount Ararat 43
Muhammad 11, 130
multiculturalism 192–3
Muslims
  Indian diaspora 62
  Jewish diaspora 10–15

Naff, A. 95
NAFTA see North American Free Trade Agreement
Naipaul, V. S. 80, 146
Nairn, T. 126
nation state 126
  Clifford 135–6
  diasporic groups 194–5
  dual loyalties 119
  formation of 117
  future of 156
  Israel 121
  Sikh claims for 115
  superior validity assumption 103
  threats to 192
nationalism 125
  Chinese 88
  Sikh 111–14

Nazis 19–20, 33
Nebuchadnezzar, King of Babylon 3
Needham, R. 179
Négritude 145
Nersessian, S. 55
Netherlands, Caribbean immigrants 141
Neusner, J. 25
New World Africans 145
New World return movement 146, 149
Nobel Prize 196
  African descent laureates 187
  Jewish laureates 25
North America, British emigration 68, 73
North American Free Trade Agreement (NAFTA) 76

Odyssey (Homer) 83
Ogden, P. E. 143
Oliver, P. 42
Ong Jing Hui 91, 101
Orientalism 132
Orientalism: Western conceptions of the Orient (Said) 132
Ottley, R. 41
Ottoman empire 13–14, 33, 45, 94, 95–6

Pact of Omar 11–12
Padmore, G. 41–2, 145
Palestine 5, 14, 117
Palestinian diaspora 28, 31, 55, 100, 144, 163, 181
Palestinians 117, 138
Pan, L. 86–7, 92
Parekh, B. 61–4
"pariah people" 101, 103
Pascal, Blaise 7
Passage to Ararat (Arlen, Jnr) 49–50
Peach, C. 140–1
performing arts, Afro-Caribbeans 141
Perlmutter, H. V. 173–4
persecution, of Jews 8–9
Phillips, C. 148

Phoenicians, trade diasporas 83
pogroms, Russia 16–17, 20
Post, K. 38
post-Zionism 123–5, 126
postcolonial diasporas 131, 137–53
postmodernism 127–8
  literature 151
  views of diaspora 129–34
  Zionism 124
Présence africaine (Césaire) 42
production, TNCs 158
"proletarian diaspora" 58
Protestantism
  affinities with capitalism 101–2, 175
  attitude to Jews 9
  rise of 126
proto-Zionists, state of Israel 120
Punjab state 108, 112
Puritans, England 9–10
purity, preoccupation with 130

racism 109–11, 140–1, 144, 157
Raffles, Sir Stamford 86, 91
Raina, A. 113
Ramayana 62–4, 79
Ranjit Singh 107–9
Rastafarian movement 38–9, 42, 146, 147–8, 152
Raynor, J. D. 3–5, 12, 213
religions
  Sikh 107
  world 187–9
religious fundamentalism 130–1, 157
religious reform groups, Jewish 121–2
repatriations, abolitionist 36–7
return movements 146–8, 185
Return to my native land (Césaire) 42
Rex, J. 196
Rhodes scholarship programme 76
Richards, E. 71
Richardson, P. 181
Robertson, R. 156
Robinson, V. 66
Rushdie, S. 130
Russia, Jewish population 16–17, 25

Russians, new diaspora 191

sabras, state of Israel 124
Safran, W. 21–3
Said, E. 10, 132–3
Samaroo, B. 61, 211
Sanadjian, M. 151
Saroyan, William 49
Sassen-Koob, S. 165, 168
The satanic verses (Rushdie) 130
sechel 170
Seeley, J. 69
Segal, R. 33–4, 42
self-determination, African 42
Selvon, S. 148–9
Sephardim 15, 21, 24
Shafir, G. 116
Sharif, R. S. 117
Shehadi, N. 96, 181
Shepperson, G. 32, 35
Shepperson, W. S. 68, 69–71, 73
Shusterman, R. 124
Sikh diaspora 105–15
Sikhs 62, 84
Singapore 86, 90–1
Singh, G. 115
Singh, K. 108–9
Skinner, E. P. 184
slavery 33–5, 59, 144
Smart, N. 187
social identity 157, 173–5
social justice 170
social mobility, Afro-Caribbeans 141
sojourning 85, 87, 90, 164–5
Solomos, J. 140
Southey, Robert 69
Soviet Armenia 47, 52–4, 55
Spain, Sephardim 15, 21, 24
Spanish Inquisition 9, 11
statehood, anachronism of 125
stranded minorities 190–1
Sun Yat-sen 89, 185
Suny, R. G. 48, 55
Surinamese, Netherlands 142

Taiwan 92–3, 162
Talmud, Babylonian 5

Tatla, D. S. 110, 112, 113, 114
Taylor, L. 79
Temple
    destruction of 3, 6, 35
    rebuilding of 4–5
Ternon, Y. 45–6
terrorism 114, 193
Thiara, R. 65, 219
Third World 132
Thomas, M. 38–9
Tinker, H. 61, 84, 219–20
TNCs *see* transnational corporations
Torah 5
Toynbee, A. J. 45, 102–3
trade, TNCs 158
trade diasporas 57, 66, 83–104, 178–9, 183
trade routes, European explorers 183
tradition 21–5, 103
transnational corporations (TNCs) 158–60, 165, 168
traumatic dispersal 180–1
travelling cultures/nations 134–7
Turks, Armenian genocide 44–5, 51
Turner, F. J. 189
Turner, V. 143
Tzarist Russia, Jewish subjects 16–18, 20

Ulysses (Joyce) 31
United Kingdom (UK)
    Afro-Caribbeans 140–1
    Japanese workers 159–60
United States (US)
    Afro-Caribbeans 139–40
    Chinese settlers 92–3
    Jewish population 32, 122–3
    Lebanese settlers 95, 99–100
    single national identity 192
Universal Negro Improvement Association (UNIA) 146

van der Laan, H. L. 97
Vatican, state of Israel 8–9
Venice, sixteenth century 84
Vertovec, S. 128
Vichy France, Nazis 19–20

INDEX

victim diasporas 2, 6, 25–8, 31–55,
137, 178–9
Visram, R. 109–10

Walcott, D. 196
Waldinger, R. 122–3
Walker, C. J. 45, 47, 48, 53
Wallerstein, I. 156
"wandering Jew" myth 6–8
Wang, Gungwu 85–9, 164, 183
Waters, M. 156
Weber, Max 101, 175
Weekly Gleaner 150
Weiner, M. 58
Weitzmann, Chaim 17
Williams, E. 68
Wilson, F. M. 10
Wodehouse, P. G. 78
women
emigration from Britain 72
Indian diaspora 63
Woolfson, M. 14

Woollacott, M. 193
World Bank 158
world economy 156, 157–62
World Trade Organization 158
Wright, R. 40

Yawney, C. D. 147–8
Yordim 124
Young Turks 33
youth movements, Zionist 119–20

Zborowski, M. 24
zealots, state of Israel 120–1
Zedikiah 3
Zionism 16–17, 20
Herzl 19
Muslims 11
Palestinians 179, 181
state of Israel 107, 115–20
territorialism 21
Zoastrianism 188–9